NIGHT VOYAGER

NIGHT VOYAGER

A Reading of Céline

by

Philip H. Solomon

SUMMA PUBLICATIONS, INC.
Birmingham, Alabama
1988

ISBN 0-917786-66-1
Library of Congress Catalog Number 88-62811

Printed in the United States of America

For

Risa, Elycia, and Cynthia

Contents

Preface

"May he be transformed, finally, by eternity into himself." So wrote the French poet Stéphane Mallarmé in "The Tomb of Edgar Poe," conveying the hope that Poe, to whom the symbolist movement in France was so heavily indebted, would one day be freed from the accusation that his art was a by-product of his overindulgence in alcohol and drugs. Posterity would thus, according to Mallarmé, restore to Poe his artistic consciousness and the responsibility for his creativity. One of Céline's admirers might have expressed analogous sentiments regarding Céline's *œuvre* upon learning of the author's death in July 1961. That "poet" might have invoked posterity to remove the various charges made against Céline during his lifetime—anti-Semite, Nazi collaborator, traitor, misanthrope, subversive, to name but a few—so that his future readers and critics could properly appreciate his writings. So long as Céline was alive, one could hardly hope for a dispassionate view of the artist, given his penchant for presenting himself as others thought he was. Believing that it was useless to try to change peoples' minds about his "political" activities, Céline during the last years of his life (following his return to France in 1951 after imprisonment and exile in Denmark as a Nazi sympathizer) would often play to his public image.

Although no one has written a "Tomb for Louis-Ferdinand Céline," posterity has indeed begun the task of rehabilitation. As the horrors of the Nazi period have receded into the past, as our sense of outrage against those who abetted, even indirectly, the extermination of millions has diminished, and as the studies of Céline's fiction have multiplied, a dichotomy has been established between Céline the novelist (and playwright) and Céline the anti-Semitic pamphleteer and writer of articles in the collaborationist press. Despite Ferdinand's protests of innocence in the later novels (beginning with *Féerie* I), there is a decided tendency to view this second Céline as an embarrassing aberration—the better to dismiss him after the usual pieties have been uttered. Although copies of the pamphlets (they are book-length volumes) can be located quite easily in libraries and in rare book shops, they have not been reprinted since the war. Reissuing the pamphlets would no doubt encourage critics to give them the sustained analysis they merit individually, collectively, and with respect to the place they occupy in Céline's *œuvre*. No study to date, including François Gibault's monumental three-volume biography of Céline, adequately explores, I believe, the question of Céline's anti-Semitism. Such an examination is, of course, beyond the scope of this present volume.

Céline left behind a considerable literary production: theatre, ballets, novels. Fragments such as *Casse-pipe* and the *Carnets du cuirassier Destouches* (Destouches is Céline's family name—he took as his *nom de plume* the name of his maternal grandmother when he wrote *Voyage au bout de la nuit*) are pieces of longer works that circumstances forced Céline to abandon. The pillaging of Céline's Montmartre apartment, following his flight to Denmark in July 1944, apparently led to the destruction of several manuscripts. Some of Céline's youthful works have been published post-humously.[1] However, Céline's reputation and interest as a writer rest upon an essential corpus of one play and nine novels. It is these works that will be the subject of this study.

Céline's writings lend themselves, of course, to a variety of critical perspectives and methods. My approach to Céline will be essentially thematic in nature, as a means of exploring his particularly disturbing but ultimately elucidating vision of the human condition. Examining the works in their chronological order, I will analyze their major themes, as they are constituted by specific patterns of imagery, with particular emphasis on the nature of Céline's landscapes—the mental space where the fictionmaking process is self-consciously engendered, and various external spaces that assume a metaphorical function according to the ways in which they are perceived, occupied, or traversed by the protagonist and/or narrator.

Using a term coined by Serge Doubrovsky, Philippe Lejeune in his most recent study of autobiography, *Je est un autre,* proposed that Céline's novels be placed in a new, to-be-defined category, that of *autofiction*. By referring to this theoretical classification, Lejeune means to indicate that Céline's novels should indeed be considered as fiction—rather than some form of romanticized autobiography—but that nonetheless one needs to take into account not only the presence of numerous elements from Céline's life, more or less transposed, but also such matters as the relationship between narrator and protagonist and the quality of the narrator and/or protagonist as witness to certain events.[2] A definition of *autofiction* as it applies to Céline's novels will no doubt be one of the subjects that Lejeune will be examining in future publications. For the purposes of this present study, I have provided a brief biographical introduction as a means of furnishing the reader with important reference points in Céline's life that are relevant to his fiction. These facts will, I hope, present the reader not only with biographical material that is intrinsically and historically interesting but will also subsequently afford some insight into the sort of creative tension that shapes the passage from biography to fiction.

Another of Céline's works that might be placed in the category of *autofiction* is his *Entretiens avec le professeur Y,* published in 1955. Playing on (and with) a traditional format, Céline invents an interviewer, and a hostile one at that, as a foil for himself as author so that he can more forcefully extol his stylistic innnovations. Although most of the material in *Entretiens* can be found in previous writings, this particular volume draws together various scattered pronouncements and background materials so as to offer a more substantial and more sharply focused examination of Céline's writing than had hitherto been available. In particular, he will focus upon his concept of writing as a "métro émotif" [emotional underground]. My study of *Entretiens* will hopefully elucidate Céline's perceptions of his own writing and, in so doing, permit the reader to judge whether Céline's theory is consonant with his praxis.

There is little point in reiterating the obvious problems posed by the translation of fiction in general and, as the reader will perceive, by the translation of Céline's prose in particular. I have quoted the original French text and followed it by an English translation within brackets. For the sake of consistency, and remaining as close to the French as possible, I have made my own translations. With the exception of *L'Eglise* and the second volume of *Guignol's Band,* all of Céline's major literary works are readily available in English.

Acknowledgments

I am grateful to the Trustees of Southern Methodist University and to the Dean of Dedman College for their support of this publication in the form of research leave and financial assistance.

Sections of chapters 2, 3 have previously appeared in, respectively, *Yale French Studies,* "The View from a Rump: America as Journey and Landscape of Desire in Céline's *Voyage au bout de la nuit* (No. 57); "Céline's *Death on the Installment Plan:* The Intoxications of Delirium" (No. 50). A portion of chapter 5, "Louis-Ferdinand Céline's *Normance:* The Weight of Guilt," was published in Eugene J. Crook, ed., *Fearful Symmetry: Doubles and Doubling in Literature and Film* (Tallahassee: University Presses of Florida, 1981). I wish to thank *Yale French Studies* and the University Presses of Florida for their permission to reprint this material.

I would like to thank as well Sue Sturgeon of SMU for her help in typing the manuscript and Lynn Carter of Summa Publications for editing it. I am indebted to Professor Germaine Brée, in whose employ I first became aware of Céline's writings, for her encouragement in my pursuit of this project. Last, but by no means least, I owe more than I can express to my wife Risa for her patience and understanding.

—*P. H. S.*

Editions

Footnote numbers within parentheses in my text will refer to the following editions of Céline's works.

Entretiens avec le professeur Y. Paris: Gallimard, 1955.

L'Eglise. Paris: Gallimard, 1952.

Voyage au bout de la nuit, Mort à crédit. Paris: Gallimard, Bibliothèque de la Pléiade, 1962.

Guignol's Band. Paris: Gallimard, 1962.

Guignol's Band II: Le Pont de Londres. Paris: Gallimard, 1964.

Féerie pour une autre fois. Paris: Gallimard, 1952.

Féerie pour une autre fois II: Normance. Paris: Gallimard, 1954.

Romans II: D'un château l'autre, Nord, Rigodon, ed. Henri Godard. Paris: Gallimard, Bibliothèque de la Pléiade, 1974.

The *Cahiers de l'Herne* will be abbreviated as *CH,* 3 (1963) and *CH,* 5 (1965).

Biographical Introduction

LOUIS-FERDINAND DESTOUCHES was born on May 27, 1894. His parents, Ferdinand Destouches and Marguerite Louise Céline Guillou, were then residing in the Parisian suburb of Courbevoie, near Neuilly. His father, an educated man, held a modest position with an insurance company; his mother at the time was the proprietor of a lingerie shop. After the failure of her business, the family moved to the Passage Choiseul, in Paris, not far from the Avenue de l'Opéra. The Passage was (and still is) a pedestrian walkway lined with shops and protected by a thick glass "awning" that ran along the first-floor level. Above the ground-level shops were the living quarters of the store owners and their families, occupying the two floors above. Céline's mother ran a shop in the Passage that specialized in the sale and repair of old lace but sold an occasional piece of antique furniture as well. Céline's family life—he was an only child—was relatively tranquil, fairly secure financially, and resolutely middle class in outlook and values. The family resided over the shop for three years, 1904-07, and then took an apartment outside the Passage. One salient aspect of Céline's family life, particularly in the light of later developments, was his father's frequent railing against the Jews, supported, according to François Gibault, by comments on the writings of the notorious anti-Semite Edouard Drumont. The latter's two-volume opus, *La France juive* (published in 1886), was vastly popular and had become one of the basic texts of European anti-Semitism. Drumont was also the author of numerous anti-Semitic pamphlets and the editor of an anti-Jewish newspaper, *La Libre Parole*. We can assume as well that the Dreyfus affair, which began in the year of Céline's birth and was not concluded (with the rehabilitation of Dreyfus) until 1906, did not pass unnoticed in the Destouches household. The petty bourgeoisie, largely anti-Semitic and politically conservative, was strongly anti-Dreyfusard.[1]

In 1907, his obligatory schooling completed and a career in commerce envisaged for him by his parents, Céline was sent to Germany and, the following year, to England, in order to acquire foreign languages. Although Céline was in later life to deprecate languages other than French as barbaric, he was an excellent linguist and would achieve a good command of both English and German. In 1912, Céline volunteered to join the army, hoping to put his compulsory military service behind him so that he would be free to look for employment. When war broke out, he had reached the rank of Maréchal des Logis, the equivalent of Master Sergeant. In October of that year, Céline, serving as a messenger, was shot in the right arm. The wound entailed serious muscle and nerve damage as well as a bone fracture, and Céline would have only limited use of the limb for the rest of his life. Céline successfully completed his mission, despite his injury, and was cited in the order of the day, made the subject of an article in a national magazine, and was awarded a medal for his heroism. He also claimed to have been trepanned for a head injury suffered during the same heroic exploit. Indeed, friends would testify that they had felt the steel plate in his skull. Céline himself had written a document in 1946 in which he accurately (he was, after all, a doctor) described the true nature of his war injuries. He notes that in a separate incident he had been thrown against a tree when a mortar shell exploded nearby, sustaining ear and head damage. He states that the wound resulted in insomnia and a frequent buzzing noise in his ear.[2] In addition to his physical disabilities, Céline's combat experience left him with a profound loathing for war.

Demobilized as a result of his injuries, Céline was assigned to the French Consulate in London. He was married there in 1916, but the marriage was annulled, owing to procedural irregularities and perhaps in part to parental pressure. That same year, Céline took a job in the Cameroons with a French trading company. Although the position was a promising one, Africa did not agree with Céline. After becoming ill with dysentery and malaria, he was compelled, less than a year later, to return to France. Despite the problems with his health, Céline profited from his sojourn in Africa to begin writing. His first literary works date from this period—two poems and a short story entitled *Des Vagues*.[3]

Back in Paris in April 1917, Céline tried his hand at various jobs. His most significant position was as an errand boy for a magazine for inventors called *l'Eureka,* owned and directed by Raoul Marquis (pseudonym of Henri de Graffigny), an eccentric and a prolific writer of self-study manuals on a variety of subjects ranging from bicycle maintenance to stargazing. Céline's interest in medicine lead to a job with the Rockefeller Foundation, traveling through the French countryside lecturing on tuberculosis and its dangers. During a stopover in the city of Rennes he was introduced to Edith Follet, the daughter of a prominent local physician. They were married in August 1917, and Céline, having decided to become a doctor, would finish his medical studies some six years later. Completion of a medical degree also required the writing of a dissertation. Céline wrote his (published in 1937) on the career of the Hungarian physician Ignaz-Philipp Semmelweis (1818-65), the discoverer of the need for asepsis in attending women in childbirth so that doctors would not spread puerperal fever to their patients. Driven to the point of madness by the refusal of his colleagues to accept his theories, Semmelweis himself died of an infection contracted in the operating room.

In 1920, Céline became the father of a daughter, named Colette. He was in the enviable position of looking forward to becoming a wealthy and respected physician in Rennes. Céline had "made it" but had also perceived that he would not fit into the mold of the comfortable bourgeois existence that awaited him. By 1924, when Céline took a medical position with the League of Nations, his marriage to Edith had begun to disintegrate. They were divorced two years later. Céline's new post permitted him to indulge his penchant for travel, notably a trip to America in 1925. He remained with the League for three years. His position with the League became terminal after he showed his superior, a Polish Jew named Ludwig Rajchman, a manuscript of a play he had written, *L'Eglise*, in which there is a vicious anti-Semitic caricature of the League's officials. One of the characters in the play, Yudenzweck (German for 'the purpose of the Jew'), is obviously patterned on Rajchman. Although Céline would subsequently admit that he had little talent as a playwright, his interest in writing for the theatre was considerable at this point in his life. A second play entitled *Progrès*, which remained unpublished until 1978, dates from this period. The play, a curious mixture of drama and ballet, reveals Céline's interest in both the theatre and the dance. Céline will write several ballets, none of which will ever be produced.[4] It was about this time, 1926-27, that he met the American dancer Elizabeth Craig, the first of several dancers who would share Céline's life, and the woman to whom Céline would later dedicate *Voyage au bout de la nuit*. Their tumultuous relationship lasted until 1933, when Elizabeth returned definitively to America.

In 1928, Céline established an office in Clichy. Although there is general agreement among those who knew him as a doctor that Céline was a devoted and competent physician, he was never able to develop a successful practice. Perhaps his lack of (financial) success was the result of his reluctance to collect his fees. Finding himself without sufficient funds to continue in private practice, Céline accepted a position at a nearby clinic and also worked in a commercial laboratory. Both the clinic and the laboratory were directed by Jews. They had no other choice but to dismiss Céline when his first anti-Semitic pamphlet, *Bagatelles pour un massacre,* appeared in December 1937.

The publication of Céline's first novel, *Voyage au bout de la nuit,* in 1932 had radically altered his mode of existence. Years later he would contend that his political difficulties arose from the fame and notoriety engendered by the novel. Begun in 1928 or 1929, *Voyage* was written mostly at night after the author had finished his medical tasks.[5] Published by the fledgling firm of Denoël and Steele after having been turned down by the prestigious Gallimard publishing house, the novel was greeted with great critical acclaim and was considered for the Prix Goncourt. Céline moved to Montmartre, where he would reside until his flight to Denmark in 1944. He was proud of being a Montmartrois and partook of the varied artistic life of the area.

Voyage brought Céline considerable fame and a measure of financial success. An inveterate traveler, Céline made a number of journeys during the period immediately following the appearance of his novel. Among these trips were several he made to Denmark, to see the dancer Marie Jensen and, with her help, to secret away (in gold) some of the monies from his royalties. Céline no doubt suspected that one day he would need such a haven. Capitalizing on the success of *Voyage,* Céline published *L'Eglise* in 1933. In 1936, Céline brought out a second novel, which he had begun to write four years earlier, *Mort à crédit.* The novel received mixed reviews from the critics, a number of whom were disturbed by its obscene language. It was in *Mort à crédit* that Céline first began to use ellipsis points systematically. This stylistic trait, which Céline would later designate as the "ties" of his "métro emotif," gives Céline's writing its particular pulsating rhythm. Dislocated phrases, the connective tissue between them having been replaced by ellipsis points, are meant to bombard the reader with almost explosive verbal energy.

Céline published a film script in 1936 entitled *Secrets dans l'île,* a bizarre tale of murder and sorcery whose protagonist is Erika, an American film star. As was the case with his ballets, *Secrets* was never produced. Céline had previously gone to Hollywood to investigate the possibility of filming *Voyage* but was equally unsuccessful. Céline made a trip to the Soviet Union in 1936. *Voyage* had been translated into Russian by the poet and novelist Louis Aragon and his Russian-born wife Elsa Triolet and had been received enthusiastically by the Russians. Since his royalties from the Russian edition could only be spent in the Soviet Union, Céline elected to visit the country. He was well treated but nonetheless published in 1937 *Mea culpa,* a denunciation of Russian communism for its lies about the nature of the human condition and its materialism. *Mea Culpa* also contains attacks upon the Jews who, according to Céline, are the founders and manipulators of the communist system.[6] Indeed, 1937 will mark another turning point in Céline's career. He will take a step backward, as it were, with the publication of his dissertation on Semmelweis but also a step forward in a new direction with the appearance of the first of three anti-Semitic "pamphlets" (the term refers to the partisan nature of the arguments contained therein, not to the brevity of the works; they are all book-length), *Bagatelles pour un massacre. L'Ecole des cadavres* and *Les Beaux Draps,* the other two pamphlets, will appear in 1938 and 1941 respectively.

Céline, of course, did not suddenly become an anti-Semite. Although we may never be able to discuss the precise motivation for his attitude, his father's influence notwithstanding, all three pamphlets reveal a thorough familiarity with the same tenets of racist anti-Semitism that had served so well as a platform for the Nazi party. There was abundant and easily obtained literature on the subject, of which Céline availed himself. We know that in 1937 and 1938 Céline used the facilities of the Parisian Centre de Documentation et Propagande, a repository of anti-Semitic documents.[7] He and many other members of the so-called Intellectual Right looked forward to the German conquest of France as a means of revitalizing a country they considered to be morally, spiritually, and socially corrupt, and whose decline, they claimed, had been brought about by the Jews. France and Germany working together would, they believed, dominate a Europe that was *Judenrein,* 'cleansed of Jews,' as Hitler had promised.[8] Well acquainted with events in Germany, Céline could not have failed to be aware that by 1937 anti-Semitic rhetoric was being translated into imprisonment, torture, and death.

Céline's pamphlets speak for themselves. Although they deal with such diverse subjects as alcoholism, education, minimum wage, and modern materialism, it is their anti-Semitism that unifies them and constitutes their principal concern—and the obvious justification for the condemnation of their author, as one can judge from the following examples.

> Les Juifs, hybrides afro-asiatiques, quart, demi nègres et proches orientaux, fornicateurs déchaînés, n'ont rien à faire dans ce pays. Ils doivent foutre le camp. Ce sont nos parasites inassimilables, ruineux, désastreux, à tous les égards, biologiquement, moralement, socialement suçons pourrisseurs.   (*L'Ecole des cadavres*, p. 215)

> [The Jews, Afro-Asiatic hybrids, a quarter, half negroes and middle-easterners, unbridled fornicators, have no purpose in this country. They must get the hell out. They're unassimilatable parasites, ruinous, disastrous, in every respect, biologically, morally, socially, corrupting leeches.]

> Les Juifs, stériles, fats, ravageurs, monstrueusement mégalomaniaques, pourceaux, achèvent à présent, en pleine forme, sous le même étendard, leur conquête du monde, l'écrasement monstrueux, l'avilissement, annihilement systématique et total, de nos plus naturelles émotions, de tous nos arts essentiels, instinctifs, musique, peinture, poésie, théâtre... "Remplacer l'émotion aryenne par le tam-tam nègre".
> (*Bagatelles pour un massacre*, p. 170)

> [The Jews, sterile, conceited, despoilers, monstrously megalomaniac, swine, are now completing, in excellent form, under the same banner, their conquest of the world, the monstrous crushing, the abasement, the systematic and total annihilation of our most natural emotions, of all our most essential and instinctive arts, music, painting, poetry, theatre . . . 'To replace Aryan emotion by the negro tom-tom.']

> Le Standard en toutes choses, c'est la panacée du Juif. Plus aucune révolte à redouter des individus pré-robotiques, que nous sommes, nos meubles, romans, films, voitures, langage, l'immense majorité des populations modernes sont déjà standardisés. La civilisation moderne c'est la standardisation totale, âmes et corps sous le Juif. Les idoles "standard", nées de la publicité juive, ne peuvent jamais être redoutables pour le pouvoir juif. Jamais idoles, à vrai dire, ne furent aussi fragiles,

aussi friables, plus facilement et définitivement oubliables, dans un instant de défaveur. L'adulation des foules est au commandement du Juif.

(Bagatelles pour un massacre, p. 185)

[The Standard in all things, that's the panacea of the Jew. No longer
any revolt to fear from the pre-robotic individuals that we are, our
furniture, novels, films, cars, language, the immense majority of
modern populations are already standardized. Modern civilization is
total standardization, body and soul, under the Jew. The 'standard'
idols, born from Jewish advertising, can never be dangerous for Jewish
power. Never were idols, if you want to know the truth, as fragile, as
crumbly, more easily and definitively forgettable, in a moment of
disfavor. The adulation of the crowds is at the command of the Jew.]

Les Democraties veulent la guerre. Les Democraties auront la guerre
finalement. Democraties = Masses aryennes domestiquées, rançonnées,
vinaigrées, divisées, muflisées, ahuries, par les Juifs au saccage. . . .
Perclues, affolées par la propagande infernale youtre: Radio, Ciné,
Presse . . . conjuration juive, satrapie juive, tyrannie gangrenante juive.

(L'Ecole des cadavres, p. 25)

[The Democracies want war. The Democracies will finally have war.
The Democracies = the Aryan masses, domesticated, ransomed, seasoned
with vinegar, divided, scoundrelized, crazed by the Jews for pillage. . . .
Paralyzed, driven mad by infernal kike propaganda: Radio, Movies,
Press . . . Jewish scheming, Jewish satrapy, gangrening Jewish
tyranny.]

A qui je vous le demande un petit peu a profité le Front Populaire?
Aux Juifs strictement et aux maçons, (juifs synthétiques).

. . . .
. . . les acheteurs de biens, d'hypothèques (tous juifs), les marchands
de canons, d'avions, (tous juifs ou enjuivés essentiellement), nos deux
cents familles juives, nos deux mille familles juives internationales,
nos grands Molochs affameurs, affairistes, mobilisateurs, nos
Rothschilds, nos Lazares, nos Cohens, nos Sterns. . . .

(L'Ecole des cadavres, p. 139)

[Who benefited, if I may inquire, from the Popular Front? Strictly the
Jews and the Free Masons (synthetic Jews).

. . . .

. . . the buyers of properties, of mortgages, the merchants of cannons, of planes (all Jews, or essentially judeofied), our two hundred Jewish families, our two thousand international Jewish families, our great Molochs, starvers, corrupt politicians, mobilizers, our Rothschilds, our Lazares, our Cohens, our Sterns. . . .]

. . . les Soviets n'ont été conçus, engendrés, maintenus, propagés, que pour la progression glorieuse de la plus grande juiverie, en exécution du plan de guerre talmudique mondial dressé, modernisé, par le général Marx. (Même guerre judaïque en Espagne, en Chine.)

(*L'Eglise des cadavres*, p. 185)

[. . . the Soviets have been conceived, engendered, maintained, propagated only for the glorious progression of greater Jewry, as the implementation of the world-wide Talmudic war plan, drawn up and modernized by General Marx. (Same Judaic war in Spain, in China.)]

Communisme? A ma manière? . . . Pas de charrue avant le bœuf! Virez le juif d'abord! Il a tous les leviers en mains, et tout l'or et toute l'élite! Si vous en tâtez il vous coiffe! c'est reglé dans l'heure! Tous les cadres sont prêts, les affiches, il étouffe, il accapare tout. Vous respirez plus. Simulateur, fainéant, sadique, bouzilleur, queutard, negroïde, il sera inapte à rien construire. (*Les Beaux Draps*, p. 195)

[Communism? In my own way? . . . But no cart before the horse! Throw out the Jew first! He has all the controls in hand, and all the gold and all the elite! If you put him to the test, he'll have you in his power! it'll be over in an hour! All the cadres are ready, the notices, he smothers, he grabs hold of everything. You can't breathe any more. Simulator, do-nothing, sadist, bungler, hot-pants, negroid, he will be unfit to construct anything.]

Je me sens très ami d'Hitler, très ami de tous les Allemands, je trouve que ce sont des frères, qu'ils ont bien raison d'être racistes. Ça me ferait énormément de peine si jamais ils étaient battus. Je trouve que nos vrais ennemis c'est les Juifs et les francs-maçons.

(*L'Ecole des cadavres*, p. 198)

[I feel very friendly toward Hitler, toward all the Germans, I am discovering that they're my brothers, that they're right to be racists. I would

be very hurt if they were ever beaten. I find that our true enemies are
the Jews and the Freemasons.]

C'est la présence des Allemands qu'est insupportable. Ils sont bien
polis, bien convenables. Ils se tiennent comme des boys-scouts.
Pourtant on peut pas les piffer. . . Pourquoi je vous demande? Ils ont
humilié personne. . . Ils ont repoussé l'armée française qui ne demandait
qu'à foutre le camp. Ah! si c'était une armée juive, alors comment
qu'on l'adulerait!
Supposez une armée youpine, qui vienne mettons d'un peu plus
loin. . . Y aurait rien de trop splendide pour elle! . . . C'est ça qui
manque au Français la férule du Juif. . . .   (*Les Beaux Draps,* p. 41)

[It's the presence of the Germans that's unbearable. They're quite
polite, quite proper. They behave like boy scouts. Nevertheless, we
can't stand them. . . Why, I ask you? They've humiliated no one. . .
They repelled a French army that wanted only to take it on the lam.
Ah! if it had been a Jewish army, then how it would have been adored!
Let us suppose a kike army, coming, let's assume, from a bit farther
away. There would be nothing too splendid for it! . . . What the
Frenchman misses is the rule of the Jew. . . .]

Céline's signature appears some thirty-two times in various pro-
Nazi journals and newspapers during the Occupation. Most of these pieces
are brief letters, expressing the author's views on various political and
social themes, including, of course, anti-Semitism and the need for Franco-
German cooperation in the New Order of Europe. Céline would later claim
that these brief articles were not his and that his name was attached to them
for reasons of publicity. Despite his professed pacifism, Céline volunteered
shortly after the outbreak of the war to serve as a navy doctor aboard an
armed transport ship, the *Chella*. Two incidents ended his brief stint in the
navy. The first was the collision of the *Chella* with an English patrol boat,
which was lost with all hands as a result of the accident. After temporary
repairs, the *Chella* was torpedoed by a German submarine while returning
to its home port of Marseilles.

In October 1940, Céline returned to Montmartre and moved into an
apartment opposite the once famous nightclub, celebrated in the drawings of
Toulouse-Lautrec, the Moulin de la Galette. During the course of the
Occupation Céline became aware that one of the apartments on the floor
below him was being used to shelter Resistance fighters. He kept the secret

and was even called in at one point to administer to a member of the
Resistance who had been tortured by the Gestapo. The following year, he
published a third pamphlet, *Les Beaux Draps*. He joined a group of French
doctors in 1942 to tour several hospitals in Berlin. A reprinting of *L'Ecole
des cadavres,* originally published in 1938, came out in 1943. That same
year, Céline married Lucette Almanzor, a dancer whom he had first met in
1935 and with whom he had lived for several years. In 1944 Céline
published the first volume of *Guignol's Band.* The second volume would
not be discovered until after the author's death. It was published in 1964 as
Le Pont de Londres, the title given to it by its editor Robert Poulet.

Although his writings in the collaborationist press and his pamphlets were obviously ideological in nature, Céline remained essentially
uninvolved in the politics of the Occupation. As for the Vichy government
under Pétain, Céline did not share the national reverence for the Maréchal
and went so far as to denounce in his newspaper pieces its hypocrisy and
general ineptitude. Although he continued to support the Nazi cause, long
after German losses on the battlefield had begun, Céline became convinced
that the New Order, such as Hitler was seeking to implement it, would not
conquer the world.[9] With the Allied landing in Normandy, it became
apparent to Céline that he was in imminent danger of execution by the
Resistance as a German collaborator. They had already sent him miniature
coffins, symbolizing his having been marked for death. The BBC in its
broadcasts to France had also denounced him as a traitor. Céline decided
that his best course of action was to flee Paris and seek refuge in Copenhagen. He had money hidden there and believed he could live among the
Danes in relative security until he could return safely to France. Separating
Paris and Copenhagen was a hostile territory that had to be crossed, where
survival would be more a matter of luck than planning. Céline, his wife
Lucette, along with their cat Bébert, left Paris by train in July 1944. The
principal stops on their journey were to be Baden-Baden, Berlin, Kränzlin,
and Sigmaringen.

Despite the reverses of the German army and the war raging close
by, Baden-Baden still functioned as a grand resort. Its sumptuous accom-
modations occupied principally by wealthy industrialists, its restaurants and
casinos filled with elegant people, Baden-Baden presented a kind of illusion, from which Céline would briefly profit. At Baden-Baden, Céline was
joined by his friend Robert Le Vigan, a well-known film actor and, during
the Occupation, a pro-Nazi broadcaster for Radio-Paris. Le Vigan would

subsequently accompany Céline for most of his voyage through Germany. With the help of his friend Karl Epting, transferred back to Berlin after having served as director of the German Institute in Paris, Céline was able to leave Baden-Baden for the German capital. He arrived there in August. It was too dangerous to stay in Berlin for any length of time, given the constant bombardment to which the city was being subjected. Céline made contact with a German doctor, a certain Hauboldt, whom he had met before the war and who had become a high official in the Health Ministry. Hauboldt obtained for Céline a permit to practice medicine in Germany and found lodging for him and his companions on an estate in Kränzlin, some fifty kilometers northwest of Berlin; part of this estate was being used to house offices of the Health Ministry.

The Schertz family, owners of the estate, were not very friendly to Céline and his party, but were by no means the vicious and perverted individuals that Céline would later portray in *Nord*. He was forced to change several of the names used in the original edition of *Nord* when a lawsuit was filed against him for defamation of character. During the course of his stay in Kränzlin, Céline was able to travel to the not-too-distant ports of Rostock and Warnemünde, where he thought he might find a ship that would take him to Denmark clandestinely. However, military surveillance of the area was very strict, and he realized that escape in this manner would be impossible. Having no desire to remain on the Schertz estate and unable to reach Denmark by sea, Céline took the opportunity of being assigned to Sigmaringen, in southwestern Germany. In September 1944, the Germans had resettled many of the Vichy government officials in Sigmaringen, including Pétain himself. The most important officials were lodged in the immense Hohenzollern castle that dominates the town. Those who were less fortunate, including large numbers of political refugees, collaborators who were, for the most part, being left defenseless in the wake of the retreat of the German armies, were placed wherever space could be found. Conditions of overcrowding, poor nutrition, and stress, coupled with a lack of medical supplies, made the refugee population very susceptible to disease. Poorly housed (a hotel room served as bedroom and office) and poorly fed himself, Céline conscientiously served the medical needs of the French community, often purchasing drugs for his patients out of his own funds.

In March 1945, Céline was able to leave Sigmaringen, having obtained permission from the German authorities to travel to Copenhagen by train. The journey took five days, given the irregularities of rail schedules, with the final stage of crossing the Danish border having been made in a Swedish Red Cross train. Céline and Lucette found a comfortable hotel in Copenhagen and announced their presence to the Danish authorities in order to obtain a residence permit. Eight months after his arrival, the French Embassy discovered that Céline was in Copenhagen and immediately requested that the Danish police take him into custody while his extradition to France was being prepared. Although Céline would treat the Danish authorities unkindly, complaining about their callousness and indifference, it is obvious, as Helga Pedersen indicates in her book, *Le Danemark a-t-il sauvé Céline?*, that Céline's life was spared only because the Danes were scrupulous about determining whether Céline was subject to extradition as a traitor or should be given the privilege of political asylum.[10] The longer Céline waited for the Danes to make up their minds, the less chance he had of being extradited to France, where he would no doubt be swiftly executed in the settling of accounts that followed the Liberation. When Céline eventually returned to France, voluntarily, in July 1951, there was no longer the same climate of retribution. Moreover, the legal delays had permitted influential friends to rally to his cause.

Before being able to return to France, Céline would spend five years in Denmark. Following his arrest he spent eleven months in the prison infirmary so that he could be treated for a variety of ailments, among them rheumatism and pellagra. After his release form incarceration, Céline spent two months in Soundby hospital for further treatment. After promising not to attempt to leave Denmark, Céline was permitted to reside in Copenhagen and, subsequently, on the property of his devoted Danish attorney, Thorvald Mikkelsen. Several friends and supporters made the "pilgrimage" to Klarskovgaard. The "Céline affair" remained a subject of controversy in both the French and Danish presses.

On November 6, 1946, Céline drafted a document in response to the accusation that he was guilty, under Article 75 of the French Penal Code, of betraying his country by supporting the Nazi cause, notably through his anti-Semitic writings. Entitled "Réponse aux accusations formulées contre moi par la justice française au titre de trahison et reproduites par la police judiciaire danoise au cours de mes interrogatoires, pendant mon incarcération 1945-1946 à Copenhague" ["Response to the accusations formulated against me by French law on the grounds of treason, and reproduced by the Danish investigatory police in the course of my interrogations, during my incarceration 1945-1946 in Copenhagen"]. In this statement, which was to be the basis of his legal defense, Céline, as we might expect, vigorously protested his innocence. The scope of this biographical introduction does not permit a detailed examination of all the charges made against Céline and his subsequent reply to them. Since Céline's anti-Semitism is the major issue at stake, one might note his reply to the accusation that he had since the time of the Occupation encouraged anti-Semitic persecutions. In his "Réponse" Céline unequivocally states:

> Je ne me souviens pas d'avoir écrit une seule ligne antisémite depuis 1937. Je n'ai d'ailleurs jamais à aucun moment, dans une seule ligne de mes livres, poussé à la persécution antisémite. J'ai protesté contre l'action de certains clans sémites qui nous poussaient à la guerre. *C'est bien différent* [italics in the original].[11]

> [I do not recall having written a single anti-Semitic line since 1937. Moreover, I have never at any moment, in a single line in my books, incited anti-Semitic persecution. I protested against the action of certain Semitic clans who were pushing us into war. *That is very different.*]

The first part of Céline's statement is blatantly false given the publication date of *Les Beaux Draps* (1941), unless Céline means to assert that the nature of his attacks against the Jews, begun before the Occupation, remained unchanged once the Germans had taken control of France. As for the second part of his statement, Céline never identifies the "clans" in question, and his remarks and the tone in which they are expressed plainly call for the persecution of all Jews. To argue that the pamphlets are something other than a deliberate and carefully composed corpus of anti-Semitic propaganda intended to incite hatred and violence against the Jewish community is to ignore the text of the pamphlets and the historical, social, and political context in which they were written. Céline's anti-Semitic views were a matter of personal conviction. He was certainly not, as Sartre wrote in his *Réflexions sur la question juive* (1946)—translated as *Portrait of the Antisemite*—in the employ of the Nazis. Sartre's accusation elicited an acerbic reply from Céline, published in 1948 as *A l'agité du bocal,* a title, as one discovers after having read the text, that is meant to evoke the image of an angry fly (Sartre) trapped in a bottle.

On February 21, 1950, the French Court pronounced its verdict. Céline was guilty as charged. He was condemned to a year in prison and a fine of 50,000 francs. He was also declared to be in a state of national disgrace, with half his holdings, present and future, to be confiscated by the Government. The sentence was a relatively light one, given the seriousness of the crimes for which Céline was declared guilty. Less than a year later, Céline received a pardon as a wounded war veteran. He was now free to return to France, which he did in July 1951, in the company of Lucette, Bébert, and several of the animals he had acquired during his stay in Denmark. While in Denmark, Céline had finished the second volume of *Guignol's Band* and had worked on both volumes of *Féerie pour une autre fois*. Back in France, Céline signed a publishing contract with Gallimard, which included reprinting the works—but not the pamphlets—initially published by Denoël and Steele. Céline acquired a house in the Parisian suburb of Meudon. He was reinstated as a doctor and practiced medicine on an occasional basis. Although he is sometimes referred to as the "Hermit of Meudon," Céline was by no means a complete recluse. A small but steady stream of friends and admirers sought him out and, given his notoriety, he was frequently approached by the media for interviews.

Whatever else he did, Céline devoted himself to his writing. The two volumes of *Féerie pour une autre fois* appeared in 1952 and 1954, respectively. *Entretiens avec le professeur Y* also appeared in 1954. Céline would devote his remaining years to the writing of the wartime trilogy. *D'un château l'autre* was published in 1957, *Nord* in 1960. On July, 1961, Céline, having just put the final touches to the manuscript of the third volume of the trilogy, *Rigodon,* died of a stroke.[12]

Some Comments on Céline's Style:
Entretiens avec le Professeur Y

IN HIS *DEGRÉ ZÉRO DE LA LITTÉRATURE,* Roland Barthes remarks that all written literature "makes manifest" ["affiche"] its identity as literature. That is to say that style—or writing [*écriture*], to use the more inclusive term—is necessarily ideological in nature.[1] Style reflects, by affirmation or negation, the socio-historical circumstances within which a given work of literature was produced. Barthes focuses on those conventions by which literature is recognizable as such. In the French context, one can refer to "Classical Literature" and, presupposing a certain level of education, be quite certain that the (French) reader can readily enumerate its essential characteristics.

Classical Literature, according to Barthes, arose within the aristocracy of the seventeenth century and eventually became the property of the bourgeoisie, when the latter in the course of the nineteenth century became the dominant class of French society. The signs by which such literature identifies itself are, among others, the elaboration of an omniscient narrator, the use of the *passé simple* (a preterit not employed, except for very rare instances, in the spoken language). For Barthes, a crucial confluence of tendencies can be discerned in France around 1850, when major changes in French society call into question the "universality" of bourgeois ideology and with it Classical Literature. The resultant plurality of ideologies, Barthes argues, leads to a plurality of writings, each reflecting in its own way a departure from, or support of, those conventions by which literature has hitherto been recognized.[2] However, any writer who seeks to escape the bounds of convention remains, Barthes notes, in a paradoxical, or even contradictory, situation, for the writer must continue to work with—or against—those literary and linguistic forms imposed by history.[3] As for Céline, whom Barthes mentions on several occasions in *Degré zéro,* his sense of his own style is, as we shall shortly see, self-consciously ideological.

Céline refers to himself as a "styliste" and even a "maniaque du style" [obsessed with style].4 Putting a certain distance between himself and such writers as Sartre and Malraux, Céline rejects any notion of literature as a vehicle for ideas or philosophy. He notes, in a reference to one of Cézanne's still lifes, that what is important is not that there may be an apple in a given painting but how that apple is painted.5

Céline condemns Classical French Literature for, among other reasons, its lack of emotional intensity. For Céline it constitutes for its writers as well as for its readers an arid, intellectual exercise. It fails, he believes, to shock, enrage, and, ultimately, captivate the reader and thus does not afford its audience a more profound insight into the reality of the human condition. Céline claims that he is the "dernier musicien du roman" [the last musician of the novel] because he is the inventor of a unique style, his "style émotif parlé" [emotional, spoken style].6

Before I examine in much closer detail what the above-noted style consists of, it would be useful to explore the ideological context in which Céline places it. For Céline, the French middle class, traditionally the class to which most French novelists and their readers belong, has become emotionally bankrupt. In his pamphlets Céline places the blame for this condition upon Jewish influence. The Jew, he remarks in *Bagatelles pour un massacre,* "ne redoute en ce monde que l'authentique émotion spontanée" [fears in this world only authentic, spontaneous emotion] (p.183). Jewish influence upon French Letters begins, he tells us, in the elite high schools. There, the children of the upper middle-class become manipulators of second-hand emotions, "read" rather than "felt." The two writers he holds most responsible for shaping conventional French literary style, which he terms the "fier classique corset tout bardé de formules, d'emprunts, de références" [proud classical corset, thoroughly larded with formulas, borrowings, references] (p. 167), are Montaigne and Proust, both of whom were half-Jewish (on their maternal side). Montaigne, Céline notes, writes "en juif" [in the Jewish style] and thus his works become "du Pre-Proust" [pre-Proust] (p. 217). As for Proust himself, whom he never wearies of criticizing, Céline accuses him of writing in a convoluted, "Talmudic style," of creating a "Semitic poetry" whose superficial brilliance has been lavishly praised by undiscerning critics.7

In order to recover the spontaneous emotion that writers like Proust and Montaigne, and, more recently, Gide, Claudel, and Mauriac, have supposedly refined out of French Letters, Céline turns to the resources of the spoken language. However, he is not so naive as to believe that a simple transcription of conversational French will achieve the results he seeks. He rejects this sort of "stenography," as he calls it, for the illusion of spoken language—his "impressionism":

> Le truc consiste à imprimer au langage parlé une certaine déformation de telle sorte qu'une fois écrit, à la lecture, IL SEMBLE au lecteur qu'on lui parle à l'oreille—Mais le langage parlé réel sténographie ne donne pas du tout en réalité cette impression. . . . Cette distortion est en vérité un petit tour de force harmonique. Ainsi le bâton qu'on plonge dans l'eau n'aura l'air droit en l'eau qu'à condition que vous le cassiez avant de l'enfoncer dans l'eau—mais pas trop casser—juste ce qu'il faut. . . . [8]

> [The trick consists of imposing upon spoken language a certain deformation, in such a way that once written, upon reading it, IT SEEMS to the reader that one is speaking in his ear—but real spoken language transcribed does not really give that impression at all. . . . This distortion is in truth a minor feat of harmonics. Hence the stick that you plunge into the water does not seem to be straight in the water unless you break it before inserting it into the water—but not breaking it too much—just what is necessary. . . .]

One salient feature of spoken language with which Céline is most frequently associated is the use of slang—*argot* in French. "C'est la haine qui fait l'argot" [It's hatred that makes slang], Céline writes, and then adds, in a more general sense, that "l'argot est fait pour exprimer les sentiments vrais de la misère" [slang is made to express the true feelings of misery]. Yet Céline is aware that slang is ephemeral—"ne peut pas vivre" [cannot live];[9] a predominance of slang would quickly date a novel and render it increasingly difficult to comprehend as time passed. Hence, although the use of *argot,* as with spoken language in general, can help to restore to writing some of the emotion Céline felt had been drained from French literature and is also the expression of an oppressed social order as opposed to the speech of the middle class, it can "spice" a novel but never become its principal ingredient.

In 1955 Céline published a curious volume, whose cover bears the following information: *Entretiens avec le professeur Y* par Louis-Ferdinand Céline [*Conversations with Professor Y* (the letter is called *i grec* in French) by Louis-Ferdinand Céline]. One would expect the title to be *Conversations with Louis-Ferdinand Céline* and the author to be a relatively unknown person, who has been afforded the honor of interviewing an illustrious writer. Given the actual title of the work, we can anticipate that Céline's interviewer will be fictitious and the traditional relationship between interviewer and interviewee will be radically modified. Indeed, Céline's interviewer, the so-called Professor Y, will function in many of the same ways as the narratees one finds in Céline's novels—hostile readers, invented by the narrator, who serve as foils for the latter so that the author can build into his novels, particularly those of the period following his condemnation as a Nazi collaborator, his own defense. One should note that Céline has supposedly consented to be interviewed upon the recommendation of Jean Paulhan, one of the directors of Gallimard, Céline's publisher. Paulhan, we are told, believes that the publicity generated by the appearance of the interview will stimulate the sales of Céline's novels.

Céline portrays himself in *Entretiens* as *sui generis,* unique as a writer but also unique as a personality. Given his reputation as a subversive writer and a traitor to his country—in short, a thoroughly disreputable person—Céline is "forced" to select an interviewer who will reflect his subject's public image, someone who is "tout à fait hostile . . . sournois et méfiant" [completely hostile . . . sneaky and distrustful] (p. 14). Not wishing to soil his own reputation, the interviewer refuses to speak with Céline in the latter's residence in Meudon or in his own home but opts to conduct the interview in a public square in Paris. Moreover, the Professor in not even a Professor but an army colonel named Réséda. Céline will direct the interview, and the colonel, who suffers from prostate troubles, will spend a good deal of time at a nearby public urinal. Finally, drunk, loaded down with flowers for his boss, Gaston Gallimard, he will be directed by Céline to the offices of the Gallimard publishing house and left asleep in a courtyard.

Despite the unorthodox nature of the interview—or perhaps because of it—Céline will elaborate on several aspects of his concept of writing. One of those aspects is the subjectivity of Céline's novels, as opposed to the relative objectivity of Zola's naturalist novels. In *Entretiens* Céline claims that his writing is truly lyrical in that he exposes a self that is both himself and detached from himself. Rather than embellish that "I" so as to make it more attractive to the reader, or even leave it simply "naked," Céline claims that his strategy is to blacken that self, to present it "à la merde" [its shitty sides] (p. 67) so that it becomes an expressive device, one calculated to shock the reader, and thus a more effective focus for the misery and evil that the I, serving as exemplary victim, attracts to itself.

Céline's lyricism—such as he defines it—can be subsumed by those broader stylistic concerns that he refers to as his "métro émotif" [emotional underground] (p. 102). That Céline should use the metaphor of the *métro*—the 'underground' as the British aptly call it (and in this context a better translation than the American 'subway')—is, of course, no happenstance. The *métro* plays an important role in several of his novels (*Voyage au bout de la nuit, Guignol's Band I, Nord*). Beyond these explicit references, there is the constant image of Ferdinand as an underground man, a marginal creature, and then, later, a criminal fleeing to Denmark to escape the retribution of the Resistance. The trains that he will take in his flight across war-ravaged France and Germany might be considered undergrounds in that Ferdinand and others like him no longer have a place on the surface, in the light of day, but must, with the collapse of the New Order, hide from public scrutiny until it is once more safe to emerge. The terminus of Ferdinand's underground journey will be the subterranean prison of Vestre Faengsel in Copenhagen. Lastly, if one compares the underground—the train, the tunnels, the passageways—to the viscera, as Jean-Pierre Richard has noted, then one can think of Céline's characters as travelling through the bowels of human existence, a peristaltic journey by means of which the narrator discovers the ugliness of the human condition.[10] Céline's concept of the lyrical "I" as made "shitty" is consonant with this association between the *métro* and the intestines.

As for the term "émotif," it recalls Céline's frequent lament, as I have already noted, that modern French literature has become a dull unimaginative pensum, shaped by, appealing to, and ultimately sustaining a comfortable bourgeois audience. Céline's vision of modern European society is that of stultified masses of consumers, rendered passive by the cinema, television, and advertising, and addicted to an overindulgence in food and alcohol. For Céline, who compares himself to the seventeenth-century moralist Blaise Pascal—"je suis un type dans le genre de Pascal" [I'm a guy like Pascal] (p. 98)—the frenzied materialism and hypnotizing entertainment of the modern European constitute a Pascalian "divertissement," a

"distraction" by virtue of which one avoids confronting the true nature of
the human condition. By means of his "métro émotif" Céline intends to
shatter the deceptive surface of such an existence, an existence supported by
traditional realistic writing, so as both to express and expose its specious
nature. "Et toute la surface avec moi! . . . embarquée! amalgamée dans le
métro! tous les ingrédients de la Surface! toutes les distractions de la Surface! de vive force! je lui laisse rien à la Surface! . . . je lui rafle tout! . . ."
[And the entire surface with me! . . . taken aboard! amalgamated into the
underground! all the ingredients of the Surface! all the distractions of the
Surface! by sheer force! I leave nothing on the Surface! . . . I make a
clean sweep of it! . . .] (p. 103).

There are two other elements that constitute an integral part of
Céline's "métro émotif." One of these is the rails along which the train
rides. Céline refers to the rails as "profilés" [shaped] (p. 102). The shape
in question is intended to be the opposite of the straight, parallel rails that
Céline uses as an image of the elegant periodicity of classical French
writing, a middle-class refinement that produces "phrases bien filées" [well-
spun sentences] (p. 103). The repetition of *filé(e)s* reinforces the opposition Céline is making. One can assume from Céline's novels, since
Entretiens does not usually delineate specific stylistic devices, that a general
procedure for dismantling that classical style and, perforce, the ideology it
conveys, will be the recourse to a variety of semantic, syntactical, and
grammatical dislocations. Another dislocation that Céline emphasizes in
Entretiens, will be the frequent use of ellipsis points, a practice begun in
Mort à crédit. They are supposed to serve as the ties upon which the rails of
his "métro" are laid. "Mes trois points sont . . . indispensables à mon
métro" [My three periods are indispensable for my underground] (p. 115).
Céline's intention is to use the ellipsis points in place of the connective
material that links the principal elements of the sentence so that the reader is
attacked, as it were, with pulsating bursts of verbal energy.

Céline, as has already been indicated, categorized his writing as a
form of verbal "impressionisme" (p. 122). Although Céline does mention
artists such as Van Gogh and Debussy, usually associated with nineteenth-
century impressionism in art and music respectively, it is not so much a
particular style that he has in mind as the concept that artists working in the
medium of language have no less a right to deform reality—and thus rebel
against the conventions of realism—than do painters or musicians. He
reiterates a familiar argument—that literature has not undergone the same

kinds of revolutions that have so radically changed other arts. Literature, he laments, remains the "serve du journal quotidien" [the serf of the daily newspaper] (p. 115). His own writing, he implies, should be considered revolutionary.[11]

One could, of course, simply dismiss *Entretiens* as a self-serving polemic by an author unable—or unwilling—to bear the scrutiny of a "real," objective interviewer. One could just as easily assume that Céline's claims to stylistic innovation should be taken at face value and, armed with that conviction, find the evidence to support those claims. Will the reader discover in Céline's novels that heightened perception of reality that will resonate within him to create the emotional effect that the author sought— "dans l'intimité de ses nerfs! en plein dans son système nerveux! dans sa propre tête" [in the recesses of his nerves! right in the middle of his nervous system! within his own head] (p. 122)? Let the reader then deposit his token (or ticket) and judge for himself as he rides Céline's "métro." The journey, whatever its trajectory, is certain not to lull him to sleep.

1
Setting the Stage: *L'Eglise*

L'EGLISE IS CÉLINE'S FIRST MAJOR CREATIVE WORK. Although published in 1933, one year after the celebrated appearance of *Voyage au bout de la nuit, L'Eglise* was written during the period 1925-27 and terminated shortly before Céline began to write *Voyage*. The author himself has, on several occasions, manifested his dissatisfaction both with writing for the theatre and with this play in particular. "Je n'ai pas le don du théâtre"; "je ne sens pas théâtre" [I have no talent for the theatre; I don't feel the theatre] he wrote to Milton Hindus.[1] And in a letter to Edith Follet he referred to *L'Eglise* as "le prototype de la pièce ratée" [the prototype of the failed play].[2]

Although Céline did not wish to have the play performed, it has nonetheless been brought to the stage twice: in Lyon, in 1936, by a company called Le Chantier, under the direction of Charles Gervais, and in Paris in 1973 by a company also named Le Chantier, directed by Louis Joxe. Reviewing the 1973 production in *La Quinzaine littéraire,* Gilles Sandier took due note of the anti-Semitism expressed in Act III and dismissed the play overall as lifeless: "Stage tricks, naturalism, and melodrama, silhouettes more than characters, there are only the trappings, never any life, never the opacity of reality."[3] The reader will no doubt find some truth in Sandier's criticism, though it is undeniably too harsh. *L'Eglise* is certainly not without interest in its own right, but its principal appeal lies in the various ways in which it anticipates *Voyage au bout de la nuit*. My analysis of the play will attempt to take both perspectives into account.

The first three acts of *L'Eglise* take place respectively in Africa, America, and Geveva; and the last two in a suburb of Paris. These geographical divisions mark the journey of the protagonist Ferdinand Bardamu (*barda,* a 'back pack' of the sort worn by soldiers in World War I; *mu,* past

participle of the verb *mouvoir,* 'to move') in space and time as he is transformed from an itinerant medical officer working for the League of Nations
into the doctor of the poor in the *zone* of Paris (the squalid settlements just
beyond the old fortifications). Africa, America, and the Paris *zone* constitute as well landscapes that symbolize contrasting modes of being. But
before examining these landscapes it is important that we turn our attention
to Act III, the Geneva episode, for it occupies an exceptional place in the
structure of the play.

As the third of five acts, the Geneva episode is situated in the middle
of the play. Corresponding to its centrality, it functions as the point of
transition between Bardamu as voyager and Bardamu as doctor. Of course,
Bardamu does not cease being a doctor in the first two acts; nonetheless, he
does not assume his full role as a doctor until he is "fixed" in Blabigny-sur-
Seine (Blabigny suggests blaba). The transformation in question takes
place in Geneva: the capital of a country known for its neutrality; a landscape that is never particularized as are the others; and, above all, the
headquarters for an international organization in which converge all the
continents Bardamu has visited. Hence Geneva, especially as the seat of the
League of Nations, constitutes a non-place, a utopia whose pretentions
Céline will thoroughly deflate. Céline's satire of the League portrays it as
paralyzed by innumerable interlocking committees, endless debates, and
mountains of multilingual reports. He will ridicule the League's attempts to
regulate the course of nations and, ultimately, change the nature of individuals. Its goals, Céline would have us believe, are simply beyond human
capacity. Moreover, its premise, the possibility of collective action to solve
the world's problems, is an illusion. Yudenzweck's denunciation of Bardamu as an "individualiste" (p. 173) is, in effect, an affirmation of the limits
within which Barbamu will operate in his solitary struggle against disease
and misery.

Radical contrasts in dramatic technique between Act III and the rest
of the play also reveal the special function of the Geneva episode. Like the
comic interludes in the religious theatre of the Middle Ages, Act III is a
farce, a humorous "stuffing" (the word *farce* is derived from the Old French
farcir 'to stuff') inserted into a generally "serious" play. True to the nature
of farce, we find in the third act an emphasis upon stereotyped characters,
physical action, improbable situations, verbal incongruities, in addition to
the caricature of a particular institution. Thus, for example, various characters parade across the stage dressed in fanciful garments that suggest a

masquerade. One of the many military men serving as delegates (thus calling into question their devotion to peace) is "vêtu en magyar de fantaisie, hongrois, du genre le plus guerrier, large sabre pendant et bringuebalant, éperons infinis" [dressed as an imaginary Magyar, Hungarian, of the most pronounced warrior type, with a broad saber hanging and bouncing, huge spurs] (pp. 128-29); another is "habillé dans le genre Bonaparte à Brienne [site of Napoleon's victory over the Prussians and Russians under Blücher, 29 January 1814] mais vieux, très vieux, et son habit trahit une certaine détresse pécuniaire. Il tire un petit canon modèle" [dressed in the style of Napoleon at Brienne, but old, very old, and his dress betrays a certain financial distress. He is pulling a toy cannon] (p.136). At one point, replying to a delegate's request for copies of his report, several aids drag a number of carts across the stage "absolument bondés, et au-delà, de papier en liasses" [absolutely packed and overflowing with bundles of paper] (p. 129). These voluminous documents engendered by just one report, like some of the growing or proliferating objects in Ionesco's plays, are the material equivalent of the League's endless, vacuous discussions. Céline's representation of these debates depicts their comical inanity and absurdity. For the most part, the spectator is given only bits and pieces of these arguments, as a sort of noise coming from offstage. Occasionally, larger fragments are presented as illustrative, for example:

> Au nom de mon gouvernement, je suis chargé, messieurs, de demander à notre Commission qu'elle intervienne d'une manière aussi formelle que judicieuse, que diplomatique, dans les différends qui divisent en ce moment la troisième Commission d'experts de la quatrième sous-commission du Comité permanent pour l'étude des cerfs-volants au point de vue de la défense des sémaphores en cas de mobilisation. Je vous ferai l'histoire de ce litige . . . (p. 130)

> [In the name of my government I am charged, gentlemen, with asking our Commission to intervene in a manner that is both categorical and judicious, as well as diplomatic, in the dispute that is dividing at this time the third Commission of experts of the forth subcommission of the permanent Committee for the study of kites from the point of view of the defence of semaphore signals in the event of mobilization. I will give you the history of this litigation . . .]

This sort of involuted verbiage constitutes the linguistic aspect of the specious utopia that is the League of Nations. It is a form of self-delusion, one that will be qualified as delirium in Céline's works, where it may be shattered with catastrophic results. Although Céline could not have known at the time of the play's writing what would transpire in Europe with the coming to power of Hitler, his readers in 1933 and *a fortiori* the audience (albeit minuscule) that viewed the play's production in 1936 could not have been totally unaware of another kind of delirium that had already been unleashed—the madness of History itself that would soon expose the inefficacy of the League of Nations and bring about its demise.

As I have indicated in my preliminary biographical sketch of Céline, a thorough study of Céline's anti-Semitism has yet to be written. One cannot, however, discuss the third act of *L'Eglise* without confronting its treatment of the Jews.[4] Most critics have dismissed the portrait of Yudenzweck and his coreligionists as harmlessly caricatural and thus in keeping with the tone and substance of Act III.[5] Should Céline be accused of hating the Dutch, for example, when he names a delegate from the Netherlands "le Président van den Prick" and describes him as the "genre gros Hollandais officiel" [typical fat official Dutchman] (p. 124)?

That the Jews should constitute a nationality unto themselves—or be condemned to do so—is, of course, a tenet of modern anti-Semitism. As for their dress and physical characteristics, long black caftan, thick glasses, severely hooked nose, Céline endows the Jews in Act III with a repulsiveness that not only surpasses in degree the "accidental" characteristics of the other nationalities he depicts but is drawn from an established iconography that associates these same characteristics with the diabolical. Consonant with these attributes is the placing of Jews in the important directorial posts of the League. The Director of the "Compromise Service," and Bardamu's superior, is named Yudenzweck. His name—'for the purpose of the Jews'—indicates that, as a special brotherhood, the Jews had acquired these positions for the purpose of manipulating the organization for their own power and profit.

Throughout the twenties and thirties the French anti-Semitic Right, and particularly the Action Française, would attack the League as the instrument of the sort of Jewish conspiracy to dominate the world portrayed in the counterfeit but widely circulated "document" *The Protocols of the Elders of Zion*.[6] Roger Lambelin, associated with the Action Française and responsible for one of the French translations of the *Protocols,* gave vent in

his *Le Règne d'Israël chez les Anglo-Saxons* to both the anti-Semitism and
the anglophobia of the French Right in denouncing the League of Nations:
"Because [it] constituted a supergovernment of the world's peoples, responsible for controlling nations, it was to the advantage of the Jews to rule over
it as masters. The Anglo-Saxons seconded their ambitions and opened wide
for them the doors of the international house."[7] Céline himself would
express similar sentiments in his anti-Semitic pamphlet *Bagatelles pour un
massacre:* "Je regrette pas mon temps de Genève. J'ai vu travailler les
grands Juifs dans les coulisses de l'univers, préparer leurs fricots . . . Ils y
viennent tous tôt ou tard. C'est un endroit de leurs dévotions" [I don't
regret my time in Geneva. I saw the great Jews at work in the wings of the
universe, preparing their private deals. Sooner or later they all come there.
It's one of the places where they worship] (p. 98).

Although Céline in *L'Eglise* does not go so far as to portray
Yudenzweck and his assistants as money-mad international gangsters, he
leaves little doubt that the conspiracy denoted in Yudenzweck's name is
being actively pursued. He has them deem as "unfortunate" (p. 152) a possible peace treaty between la République des Blagamores de Sicilies and the
Clovaques de la Boucle de Brame because, Céline suggests, Yudenzweck,
backed by his fellow Jews, has been profiting from the war by lending
money to both sides. A dialogue between Yudenzweck and Mosaïc, one of
his assistants, which ensues after Mosaïc expresses concern at the unfavorable attention that might be attracted by the number of Jews in the League,
presents the assumed cunning behind Jewish power:

> Mosaïc: Ne crains-tu pas, Alexandre, qu'on finisse par nous redouter?
> Toi, par exemple, tu fais tant de choses, tu fais les emprunts . . .
> tu fais les communiqués . . .
> [Aren't you afraid, Alexandre, that they will wind up fearing us?
> You, for example, you do so many things, you make loans . . .
> you issue communiques . . .]

> Yudenzweck: Mais personne ne connaît mon nom, Mosaïc, à deux kilomètres
> d'ici. On m'ignore, je t'assure . . .
> [But no one knows my name, Mosaic, two kilometers from here.
> They know nothing of me, I assure you . . .]

> Mosaïc: Oui, oui, mais les Jésuites non plus, personne ne les connais-
> sait, Alexandre, et vois comment ils ont fini.

> [Yes, yes, but nor were the Jesuits, no one was aware of them, Alexandre, and see how they ended up.]
>
> Yudenzweck: Les Jésuites n'avaient pas assez d'argent.
> [The Jesuits didn't have enough money.]
>
> (p.150)

Yet Yudenzweck treats Bardamu quite generously, going so far as to offer him another mission, albeit in Japan, despite the unfavorable reports that he has received about him and despite his condemnation of Bardamu's individualism: "Il parlait la langue de l'individu, moi je ne parle que le langage collectif" [He spoke the language of the individual, as for me I speak only the language of collectivity] (p. 163). The pertinence of this remark with respect to Bardamu raises some doubt as to the collectivity to which Yudenzweck adheres. If we are to assume that Bardamu, unlike the reader, is unaware of Yudenzweck's Jewish allegiance, then the irony of the remark would not seem consonant with the astuteness of the observation. On the other hand, are we to assume that Yudenzweck's "collectivity" indicates that, despite everything, Yudenzweck believes in the work the League is attempting to accomplish? Céline's satire of the League, as opposed to the evolution of Bardamu as an "individual," indicates that Yudenzweck's comment is to be read without irony.[8] Céline's logic condemns the League both for its Jewishness and for its altruistic view of people in general.

In conclusion we may say that although in *L'Eglise* we are far from the vituperative anti-Semitism of the French Right and of Céline's pamphlets, the portrait of the Jews in Act III as ugly, rapacious, and deceitful, as seeking to infiltrate international organizations in order to gain power and wealth, exploits a number of anti-Semitic clichés whose hostility cannot be adequately attenuated by the permissive context of farce, Yudenzweck's treatment of Bardamu, or cynicism toward the premises of the League of Nations. These same clichés, given legal force, were shortly to enter into a justification for mass murder.

The first act of *L'Eglise* takes place in Central Africa, in the city of Cancanville (*cancan*, 'malicious gossip'), capital of the French colony of Bragamance (*braguette*, 'fly' [of a pair of pants]), where Bardamu in his capacity as a doctor-investigator for the Commission on Epidemics of the League of Nations has been sent to determine the cause of death of a certain American epidemologist by the name of Gaige. He quickly discovers that

Gaige has died from the pneumonic form of the Bubonic Plague. He is also able to ascertain that the colony's medical officer, a doctor Varenne, who died during an inspection tour and was buried in the bush, also succumbed to the same malady.

The appearance of the Plague in the colony is consonant with the sort of African landscape Céline describes. It is an archaic, primitive landscape in which nature flourishes in rampant abandon, a hothouse that encourages the growth of "astounding vegetation" (p. 14), and an equally astounding proliferation of animal and, especially, insect life. It also favors persistence of diseases that have long been eradicated in more temperate climates. In these conditions the activity of the European colonizers is marginal, like the roads built by Pistil, the assistant to the chief administrator of the colony, roads that go nowhere, are almost never used, and are quickly reclaimed by the jungle. Pistil, cynical and alcoholic, summarizes the nature of existence in Bragamance and in the African colonies in general: ". . . c'est fait pour les singes pendant la journée et les chacals pendant la nuit. Il n'y a qu'un bon moment, c'est le crépuscule, eh bien! c'est l'heure des moustiques" [it's made for monkeys during the day and for jackals during the night. There's only one good moment, that's dusk, very well! that's the time for the mosquitoes] (p. 55).

Although Céline does not elaborate in *L'Eglise,* as he will in *Voyage,* on what he terms the "biological confession"—the acceleration of the disintegration of the body that takes place in the African climate—he nonetheless presents the Europeans as being progressively enfeebled by the oppressive weather. Pistil wagers that Larjunet, Varenne's replacement, will last, along with his wife, no longer than six months. As for himself, he has found his consolation in alcohol. If there is any pleasure in his existence, it is ice—to suck on, to put into drinks, to rub on his face. He eagerly awaits the arrival of the river boat, the colony's principal link with the outside world, for it brings a new provision of ice. Ice here has a symbolic function that transcends its property as a cooling substance. It is a perishable commodity, the supply of which must constantly be renewed, and offers only a momentary respite from the heat. It is thus an image of the ephemerality of European existence in the colonies; it quickly dissolves as do the minds and bodies of the Europeans deteriorating in the heat and humidity.

Bardamu arrives in the colony intent upon doing his job and subsequently returning to Geneva to file his report, after a brief stopover in

New York to attend a medical convention. We are given very little information about his background, but he is presented as someone who, though relatively young, thirty-three, has no illusions about the realities of existence. He is weary and wary of the authorities and the labels by which those in power organize the people around them.

When he sides with Pistil in the latter's condemnation of life in the colonies, he is upbraided by the officious chief administrator Tandernot and called an "anarchist" (p. 31). He is willing to accept this epithet but notes that poverty tends to level such distinctions and render them meaningless for those who are inextricably trapped in the dirty business of life: "Les vrais anarchistes, ce sont des gens riches. . . . Pour bouffer, faut tous faire des petits trucs, et anarchistes ou non, ce sont presque les mêmes" [True anarchists, they're the rich people. . . . In order to eat everyone's got to do the little jobs and, anarchists or not, they're about the same] (p. 31).

Bardamu's fidelity to the tasks, however mean, that constitute his existence is put to the test with the arrival of Clapot (*clapoter,* 'to lap,' as waves lap against an object), the chief medical officer of the colony. Clapot makes Bardamu aware of the repercussions of the report he will make in Geneva—the quarantining of the colony. Such a measure would be, he informs Bardamu, inimical to the economic welfare of the colony, and he subsequently asks that the report be falsified to indicate that Gaige died of yellow fever and Varenne of measles. When Bardamu refuses to accede to Clapot's request, the latter asks him if he is a "compatriot" (p. 61). Clapot's appeal is plainly to Bardamu's pride as a Frenchman. Bardamu's reply is to portray himself as bereft of any national identity and thus of the shared values that Clapot supposes he possesses. "Est-ce que c'est ma faute?" [Is it my fault?] (p. 61), he asks, indicating that his nationality is only accidental. One cannot help but think here of Bardamu's fall from com/patriotism in *Voyage,* where his initial patriotic zeal in joining the army is rapidly transformed into a loathing for a country that asks its young men, essentially the poor, to transform themselves into cannon fodder.

The second act of *L'Eglise* takes place in New York, given as the typical American city, and, in particular, within the theatrical milieu as represented by the Quick Theatre on Broadway. Bardamu has gone to the Quick Theatre to inform Elisabeth Gaige, a dancer, of her husband's decease. A mixture of French and Americans make up the motley group, associated directly or indirectly with the theatre, that Bardamu will meet during the course of his visit. Céline's depiction of the Quick Theatre is meant to be both stereotypical—for a French audience at least—and, indeed, in many ways caricatural. Accordingly, Bardamu encounters a curious mixture of eccentricity, egotism, criminality, liberated sexual mores, and naiveté. For example, Vera Stern, a dancer and the director of the Theatre, has been involved in activities dealing with violations of the Prohibition Laws and with the smuggling of marijuana (or hashish) and will ask Bardamu to marry her—he will agree—so she can accompany him to France as his wife and escape from the American police. Elisabeth Gaige has been married four times—her husband's death having saved her from yet another divorce proceeding. Although married, she has maintained several liaisons with both men and women. Raspoutine, a member of a Russian dance troop called Caviar's Folly arrives on the scene to direct Elizabeth in an "electric dance," a domain in which he is accorded a certain expertise given that he is the inventor of vibrators that are designed to be inserted into the armrests of theatre seats so that a sympathetic resonance can be created between spectator and performer.

Although circumstances have brought Bardamu to the Quick Theatre, he is no stranger to the theatrical milieu. In what is perhaps a reference to Céline's expressed dissatisfaction with *L'Eglise* and with his ability to write for the theatre in general, Bardamu tells Flora Bonjour, one of the French girls at the theatre (her improbable name suggests an ingenue, but she is one of Elisabeth's lovers as well as an organizer of sexual orgies): ". . . j'aurais aimé à faire du théâtre, à en écrire plutôt" [I would have liked to have done some theatre, to have preferably written for it] (p. 86). Bardamu then describes his failure when he and a friend attempted to establish a theatre on the outskirts of Paris in an abandoned factory. The project died for lack of capital but a first play, upon which Bardamu apparently collaborated, was deemed "promising" (p. 87).

Curiously, Bardamu never is forceable enough to intrude upon Elisabeth's dancing and tell her of her husband's death. He is content to spend his time chatting with those around him, though he is a great admirer of American women, with whom he became acquainted through Hollywood movies, and particularly of those who have the long muscular legs of a dancer.

Before Vera Stern proposes marriage, Flora offers herself to Bardamu, hoping he will take her back with him to France as a nurse. Flora also appeals to Bardamu's com/patriotism by telling him that she is a good cook. Her assumption is that as a Frenchman Bardamu will be swayed by the prospect of the *haute cuisine* Flora will prepare for him. His response is analogous to the one he gave Clapot. He informs her that as the son of a small time pharmacist in the suburbs of Paris, he grew accustomed to foul tasting food since his meals were prepared by his father's laboratory assistant, who imparted to his cooking the odor and taste of whatever chemicals he had just been mixing. Bardamu continued the practice when he prepared his own food as a medical student, with the odors of dissection passing from his hands into his sandwich. Once again Bardamu is arguing that poverty erases those differences that constitute a national personality. Just as he told Tandernot that in order to be a true anarchist one had to be rich, he informs Flora that one needs to be wealthy in order to be a true Frenchman.

Bardamu's repudiation of his born status as a Frenchman is consonant with his rejection of official truths in general. Once again, Gaige's death is the occasion for Bardamu to rebel against authority and its manipulation of the "facts." When questioned about the cause of Gaige's death by a member of the foundation for which Gaige worked, a man named Darling, who has also come to the Quick Theatre to inform Elisabeth of her husband's demise, Bardamu confesses that, contrary to sound medical practice, he never performed an autopsy on Gaige's body. He justifies his action—or lack thereof—on the grounds that whatever his findings might have been, they would have been disputed by the special interest groups involved:

> Pour la recherche de la vérité . . . il y a une tradition internationale des plus sévères d'ailleurs; mais c'est sur la vérité même qu'on n'est jamais d'accord. Elle a un mètre vingt-cinq en Bragamance, un mètre soixante-quinze à New York; elle aura peut-être deux mètres à Genève et ça a l'air tout de même d'être du même mètre dont on s'est servi. (p. 105)

> [As regards the search for the truth . . . there is an international tradition, one of the most rigorous, I might add; but it is on the truth itself that they're never in agreement. It measures a yard and a quarter in Bragamance, a yard and three quarters in New York; it will perhaps measure two yards in Geneva and yet they all seem to be using the same yardstick.]

Amid this welter of truths, Bardamu opts to fall back upon his own subjective experience, not only his own diagnosis of the cause of death but also the circumstances of the event—the sounds of mosquitoes in the hot night, the abundant vegetation, the rantings of the officials. There are obvious dangers in this affective, individual approach to reality, dangers already manifest in *L'Eglise* and which, amplified at times to the point of hallucination, will play a major role in shaping the existence of Céline's narrative and dramatic personae and, one might add, of Céline himself. One danger would be the emergence of a persecution complex stemming from the perception that others, particularly collectivities of various sorts (the State, other writers, the Jews), are conspiring to silence the bearer of an intuitive, personal truth. A second danger would be the tendency to ignore rational evidence that would call subjective truth into question and perhaps, even retrospectively, demonstrate its inadequacy or error. The most salient manifestation of these two closely related attitudes will, of course, be the ravings (coherent ravings) of the anti-Semitic pamphleteer and the project of self-justification and self-exoneration that will shape the later fiction.

Contrasted with Africa, America (as typified by New York) represents the modern, man-made landscape. Bardamu perceives the New York landscape as a place of intimidating verticality. That dimension is opposed to the horizontality of the European city by means of a series of metaphors whose common term is the image of the acquiescent woman:

Flora: Ici il n'y a que les femmes qui valent la peine d'être regardées. Ils devraient en faire des jardins publics, parce que leurs villes ce qu'elles peuvent être vilaines. (p. 89)
[Here it's only the women that are worth looking at. They should make them into public gardens because their cities can really be ugly.]

Bardamu: Chez nous, les villes, c'est couché, hein, et elles attendent le voyageur, tandis qu'ici elles sont toutes droites, debout, ça vous la coupe. (p. 90)
[At home our cities lie down, don't they, and they await the voyager, whereas here they are erect, standing, it takes your breath away.]

In this context one can interpret "ça vous la coupe" (literally, 'it cuts yours off') as an image of castration. The masculine, phallic image of conquest—making a new and better life for oneself—has been transferred from Bardamu to the landscape in his perception of his own impotence with regard to the possibility of his practicing medicine in America: "Oh! New

York, vous savez, ça demande vraiment d'être Américain. Je voudrais bien. Il faudrait que je repasse tous mes examens; j'arriverais pas, je suis déjà trop vieux" [Oh! New York, you know, you've really got to be an American. I'd like to. I'd have to retake all my examinations; I wouldn't make it, I'm already too old] (p. 226). Bardamu must settle for a vicarious triumph—Vera Stern, who offers herself to him for the ulterior motives I have already noted. Her initial verticality gives way to the horizontal acquiescence associated with the European city, but her transformation is perhaps as derisory a conquest for the Bardamu of *L'Eglise* as will be the conquest of Molly, the prostitute with the heart of gold, for the Bardamu of *Voyage*.

Wherever his voyages may take him, Céline's hero eventually falls back upon the practice of medicine in Paris or its environs, where he functions not only as a doctor to the poor but also shares the poverty of his patients. Although in *L'Eglise* the poverty and decay of Blabigny are not described in detail, the medical problems that arise from these conditions, and which Bardamu must confront as he makes his rounds, are the classic ones inherent to such an environment: alcoholism, venereal disease, pregnancy, and its complications. Neither "primitive" like Africa nor "modern" like New York, the *zone,* where Acts IV and V take place, is the measure of the real, a landscape with which Bardamu is intimately familiar and where he can function on a person-to-person basis with little interference from the authorities.

If we are to believe Bardamu, his practice of medicine, however selfless it may appear with respect to the time spent with his patients and the fees they are able, or often unable, to pay, does not stem from entirely altruistic motives. On the contrary, it provides a framework for playing out his adversary relationship with his fellow human beings: sickness, according to Bardamu, has its positive aspect in that it neutralizes their inherent aggressiveness and meanness:

> J'aime mieux les rapports avec ceux qui sont malades. Ceux qui sont bien portants sont si méchants, si bêtes; ils veulent avoir l'air si malins, aussitôt qu'ils tiennent debout, que tout rapport avec eux est presque aussitôt malheureux! Quand ils sont couchés et qu'ils souffrent, ils vous foutent la paix. (p. 172)

> [I prefer to have relationships with people who are sick. Those who are healthy are so mean, so stupid; they want to appear so cunning, as soon as they are on their feet, that any relationship with them is almost

immediately unhappy! When they're in bed and suffering, they leave
you in peace.]

If one were to extend Bardamu's argument to Bardamu himself, one would
be forced to conclude that the doctor, as a healthy man, would be guilty of
the same predispositions as the rest of mankind. His patients should therefore fear him as he fears them. At the same time, one might inquire, why
cure sickness if it will result in the renewal of the patient's capacity for evil?
As for the first of these apparent inconsistencies, implicit in Bardamu's
view of humankind, and indeed at its very source, is that he himself has, by
virtue of his personality and his profession, acquired a lucidity, and thus a
self-control, that so many others do not possess. As for the second, it
would seem that Bardamu is more sensitive to suffering than his cynical
outlook could permit him to express directly. In addition, Bardamu's activities as a doctor afford him a means of action on an individual scale which,
even if limited in its efficacity, is, Céline would have us believe, more
significant than the collective absurdities of the League of Nations.

Although Bardamu, unlike later heroes, does not assume the dual
function of doctor-author, he has, as I have already noted, written for the
theatre. However, he terms writing "disgusting" and the activity itself a
"secretion" (p. 112). This last designation, a medical term with negative
connotations, reminds us that Bardamu has chosen medicine over art and
also suggests that writing is a symptom of illness. This opposition between
doctor and author will be somewhat modified in later works, with the
introduction of the theme of the obligation to write (for the protagonist as
doctor-novelist) and the convergence between the protagonist and Céline
himself. Céline would maintain both that medicine was his true vocation
and that writing was a sort of illness in that it was a manifestation of the
artist's dissatisfaction with reality and his desire to transform it verbally
through the creation of fictions.

There is one aesthetic activity that already in *L'Eglise* occupies the
privileged role it will assume throughout Céline's works—the dance. To
use the concepts Nietzsche formulated so brilliantly in *The Birth of
Tragedy,* a text with which Céline was probably familiar, the dance serves
as a synthesis of the Apollonian elements of plasticity and perfection of
form and the Dionysian element of overflowing life. In the words of Erica
Ostrovsky, the dance for Céline "can be considered the movement of
life . . . transferred into art."[9] For Céline, the dancer—the living creature—

is inseparable from the dance, the art. She must be a beautiful woman with long muscular legs. Her dancing body by virtue of its elasticity courts but does not succumb to the flaccidity that is a sign of the inevitable decay to which the flesh is heir; and the dance itself, as structure, gives form to movement that is otherwise directionless and disorganized. Bardamu has, of course, been living with the dancer Vera Stern. She announces her return to the Quick Theatre (her troubles with the police are apparently over), for she can no longer tolerate the tedium of existence in the *zone,* despite her professed love for Bardamu. Her imminent departure prepares the arrival of another dancer, Elisabeth Gaige, who is performing in Paris and has come to Blabigny to pay a visit to Bardamu. We can anticipate that Elisabeth will replace Vera in Bardamu's life.[10]

But before discussing that visit and the dance Elisabeth will perform, we need to examine the respective roles played by two other characters in *L'Eglise* who will, by virtue of their defective bodies, also anticipate Elisabeth's appearance. The first of these is a character with whom we are already familiar from Bardamu's African adventure—Pistil, Tandernot's administrative assistant and the colony's road builder. A cynical observer of colonial politics, as I have already noted, Pistil has profited from a convalescence in Europe, after an attack of fever, to leave the colonial service. He has used the money from his pension to buy a bistro in Blabigny, a locale that Bardamu, unable to find space in the area, uses as an informal office and message center. Pistil—whose name evokes a flower—has "blossomed" since the first act and will continue to do so as we pass from Act IV to Act V: his alcoholism, which will ultimately force him to give up the bistro, since he will be unable to drink with his customers, has produced cirrhosis, which is accompanied by the bloating of his body. Although he lets Bardamu transform his bistro into a clinic, he stays to help with the patients and thus finds himself frequently taking a social drink with them. In short, Pistil is dying, and his bloated body is a manifest sign of the deterioration of his health, and of the decay of human flesh in general. Given the state of Pistil's body, his remarks on female beauty and on the dance, taken from Bardamu, reinforce the latter's views on the subject while investing them with a compelling cogency: "Ah! la danse, mon ami! . . . Les femmes qui ne font pas de danse . . . ça n'existe pas; c'est bon pour les couturières et les photographes mais pas pour un anatomiste" [Ah! the dance my friend! Women who don't dance . . . they're not real; they're

okay for dressmakers and photographers but not for a student of anatomy]
(p. 238).

The second character in question is Janine, a teenager who has fallen
in love with Bardamu. But her body has been rendered defective by the
ravages of polio and although Bardamu has arranged physical therapy
sessions for her, he informs her that he can never return her affection
because he can love only beautiful women, and particularly dancers. His
appreciation for female beauty is, in part, a result of his admiration for
anatomical perfection but, more important, it is a manifestation of his
philosophia mortis. Beauty, he believes, can be defined as such only by its
perishability: "La beauté au moins, on sait que ça meurt, et comme ça on
sait que ça existe" [Beauty, at least, you know it dies, and so you know it
exists] (p. 253). Beauty therefore conveys in the most striking manner the
absolute and indisputable truth about life—death. Thus, Bardamu argues,
his relationships with beautiful women offer him an insight into the nature
of existence that less fortunate creatures, like Janine, are unable to provide.
Vera Stern tells Bardamu as she is readying to leave—"tant que vous vivrez,
vous irez entre les jambes des femmes [i.e., beautiful women] demander le
secret du monde" [as long as you live, you will seek the secret of life
between the legs of women] (p. 223).

When Pistil perceives Elisabeth he is enthralled by her beauty.
Upon learning she is a dancer, he desires to have her perform for him, even
if it costs him his life. He begins to drink, hoping that his intoxication will
permit him to "see" her dance. He is ready to sacrifice himself in order to
bring forth his vision of the goddess-dancer. At this point, the stage grows
dark, suggesting a dreamlike atmosphere. But, in response to Pistil's
desires, it is the real Elisabeth who disrobes and begins to dance. And as
she dances the clinic fills with spellbound onlookers, the people of the
quartier served by Doctor Bardamu. Thus the clinic, a place of disease and
misery, becomes a temple in which the magical, transforming power of the
dance is embodied, in which one can witness the triumph, however
provisional, of beauty and form. Even Janine's attempt to shoot Bardamu
in a fit of frustration and jealousy fails to disturb this extraordinary moment.
Janine is quickly calmed and becomes one of the awe-struck spectators.

Although the play ends with the transformation of the clinic into a
temple, an opposing spatial metaphor, previously enunciated, conveys a
countervailing vision and the sense of the play's title. Describing the nature
of the human condition to Janine, Bardamu states: "C'est un bagne! Faut

pas essayer d'habiller les murs en église . . . il y a des chaînes partout"
[It's a penitentiary! You mustn't try to dress up its walls like those of a
church . . . there are chains everywhere] (p. 253).[11] Uncompromising
lucidity does not permit self-delusion. The realities of existence, such as
Céline perceives them, are inescapable—death, of course, but also exploitation, disease, despair, cruelty. We have seen, nonetheless, that there are
positive elements in this otherwise bleak vision of humanity—the sisyphean
efforts of the individual who chooses to alleviate pain and suffering,
whatever his motives; beauty, however perishable; and the transformation
of reality into aesthetically satisfying form that art alone is able to achieve.

2
The Journey Begins:
Voyage au bout de la nuit

"ON EST PUCEAU DE L'HORREUR comme on est de la volupté"
[One is a virgin with regard to Horror as one is with regard to sexual
pleasure] (p. 17), confesses Bardamu, the protagonist of *Voyage au bout
de la nuit. Voyage* traces, among other things, Bardamu's progressive loss
of virginity in the sense of his inexorable initiation into the horrors of
existence. Unlike his predecessor in *L'Eglise,* this Bardamu will undergo,
within the framework of the text, a long, painful process of education that
will transform him from a naive young man into a disillusioned doctor, one
who has traveled too far and seen too much, one who approaches in
wisdom his older and wiser incarnation, the narrator of the voyage. Each of
the four principal landscapes of the novel—wartime Europe (Paris and the
fields of Flanders), Central Africa, America (New York and Detroit), the
Parisian *zone* —will embody a particular stage of that initiation, a particular
modality of existence, a particular loss of hopes and ideals.

Underlying the specifics of Bardamu's experiences will be three
interrelated lessons, as it were, invariants of Céline's universe. One of
these lessons is that human existence is an absurd "ecstasy," in the Heideg-
gerian sense of a standing out (*ex-stasis*) against the various phenomena of
entropic disintegration that must inevitably triumph over all individual
existence and, for Céline, over all human constructs as well, except perhaps
for art.

Individual existence, according to Céline, is predicated upon the
need to maintain a stable identity despite the tendency toward dispersion in
time and space:

Tout notre malheur vient de ce qu'il nous faut demeurer Jean, Pierre ou Gaston coûte que coûte pendant toutes sortes d'années. Ce corps à nous, travesti de molécules agitées et banales, tout le temps se révolte contre cette farce atroce de durer. Elles veulent aller se perdre nos molécules, au plus vite, parmi l'univers ces mignonnes! Elles souffrent d'être seulement 'nous', cocus d'infini. On éclaterait si on avait du courage, on faille seulement d'un jour à l'autre. Notre torture chérie est enfermée là, atomique, dans notre peau même, avec notre orgueil. (p. 333)

[All our misfortune comes from our having to remain Jean, Pierre, or Gaston, whatever the cost, year in and year out. Our body, a costume of agitated, banal molecules, is rebelling all the time against that terrible farce of lasting. They want to go get themselves lost, our molecules, as quickly as possible, amid the universe, those cute things! They suffer from being only "us," cuckolds of the infinite. One would burst into smithereens, if one had the courage, one just misses doing it from one day to the next. Our dear torture is enclosed there, atomic, under our very own skin, along with our pride.]

For Céline's hero, conscious of this tension, there is constant temptation to yield to that dispersion. And this desire, displaced, manifests itself in his fascination with the associated qualities of softness and liquefaction, which constitute with respect to man as well as man's constructs, the dissolution of form, the material sign of destruction in time as the surface appearance of an oozing of "hemorrhaging"—to use Jean-Pierre Richard's term—emanating from within.[1]

A second lesson, one that we have already seen articulated by the Bardamu of *l'Eglise* in his preference for the sick, for humans in a weakened state of dependence, is *homo hominibus lupus:* "C'est des hommes et d'eux seulement qu'il faut avoir peur, toujours" [It's men and men only that one must fear, always] (p. 19). Humans, according to Céline, have a vicious nature, a propensity for destroying themselves and those about them. Another tension complements the one discussed earlier—a constant and conscious effort, notably on the part of those who have some insight into human nature, to resist yielding to natural impulses:

La grande fatigue de l'existence n'est peut-être en somme que cet énorme mal qu'on se donne pour demeurer vingt ans, quarante ans, davantage, raisonnable, pour ne pas être simplement, profondément soi-

même, c'est-à-dire immonde, atroce, absurde, Cauchemar d'avoir à
présenter toujours comme un petit idéal universel, surhomme du matin
au soir, le sous-homme claudicant qu'on nous a donné. (p. 407)

[The great fatigue of existence is perhaps, in sum, only the enormous
difficulty one assumes in order to remain reasonable for twenty years,
forty years, even longer; in order not to be simply, profoundly, oneself
that is to say foul, atrocious, absurd. The nightmare of having to
present, as a little universal ideal, superman from morning to night, the
limping sub-man with which we've been endowed.]

The third lesson, also announced in *L'Eglise* and consonant with
those I have briefly delineated above, is the primary importance of death—
the "source" of Céline's night and the "ultimate support" of his writing,
according to Julia Kristeva.[2] Death is ubiquitous in *Voyage,* as in all of
Céline's fiction, and takes on an obsessive tangibility that recalls the Middle
Ages. It is the great leveler of social and economic difference, an ultimate
and ineluctable vengeance against one's enemies. And death rarely comes
as the just conclusion to a heroic life. It is usually a rather sordid affair—a
disemboweled soldier or a woman bleeding to death as the result of a
criminal abortion—or it appears in hallucinatory visions in which those
already dead reappear as grotesque reminders of the past. "La mort court
après vous" [Death runs after you] (p. 240), Bardamu discovers. One's
relationship with death is not passive and as such establishes yet another
tension. One may make a pact with death, yielding to the void it creates
within life, by sustaining its diverse manifestations such as war, murder,
greed, calumny, persecution; or one may attempt to outrun it by means of a
lucid perception of its ubiquity and its power, by means of a refusal to
partake of its embodiment in life. As we will see in *Voyage,* this tension
with regard to death will be depicted in the "play" between Bardamu and his
double Robinson.

Bardamu's deflowering is initiated by his participation in World War
I. The novel opens with Bardamu and a friend, Arthur Ganate, sitting on
the terrace of a cafe. After denigrating the fighting ability of their countrymen, the state of the government, love—the latter disparaged as "l'infini mis
à la portée des caniches" [the infinite within the reach of poodles] (p. 12)—
Bardamu is overcome with patriotic fervor upon seeing a cavalry regiment
pass in the street and considering the enthusiasm with which soldiers have

been leaving for the front. He enlists and quickly discovers that he has been the victim of a deception.

In Céline's depiction of Bardamu's experience of the war there is no mention of the causes that might have provoked the conflict between France and Germany; nor is there any evocation of great battles, gas attacks, trench warfare, etc. Even the circumstances of Bardamu's heroic feats, in the course of which he is seriously wounded and for which he will be subsequently decorated, are never described. Céline is, of course, not interested in offering a historical account of the war; but, more important, even within the fiction he is elaborating, he is quite obviously avoiding presenting the war as an occasion for heroism. That sort of depiction would, in effect, serve only to affirm the patriotic slogans and spectacles that had lured Bardamu into enlisting and which continue, as propaganda, to maintain the morale of the soldiers. From Céline's perspective, the war is politically incomprehensible. He views it not as a geopolitical conflict but, rather, as a sort of universal conspiracy. The war is abetted, but not occasioned, by the leaders of those countries involved in it. War sanctions an individual and societal pact with death: millions of soldiers, the cannon fodder without which wars cannot be fought, give vent to their inherent desire to kill, "plus enragés que les chiens, adorant leur rage (ce que les chiens ne font pas)" [madder than dogs, worshipping their madness (which dogs don't do)] (p. 17).

War invests the Flanders countryside with all its fury, transforming it into a landscape of destruction and devastation. At times this landscape is depicted as "full," saturated with the presence of the conflict, as Céline magnifies certain effects of the war so that they fill the landscape or are assimilated to natural forces. Whatever the case, Céline depicts Bardamu as reduced by comparison with this plenitude to an insignificant element, "inutile" [useless] amid this "immense universelle moquerie" [immense, universal mockery] (p. 36). Thus the summer afternoon is filled with the "vibration" not of myriad insects but of countless bullets. The night becomes "énorme" and "épaisse" [thick], acquiring, in Bardamu's imagination, a spatio-temporal indeterminateness and a sort of viscosity. Both aspects of the night are correlatives of its containing (as it conceals) "innombrable volontés homicides" [innumerable murderous wills] (p. 26) that collectively constitute the "délire" [delirium] (p. 19) of European society at war. The night is sometimes illuminated by immense conflagrations that replace the moon and the stars, fires that link earth and sky as they "lick" the clouds (p. 32). The rain that frequently falls in the region becomes an "eau sale" [filthy water] that the fields "bavaient" [slobbered] (p. 22), as if the entire countryside were exuding the excretia of war or had been transformed into an immense slavering beast.

At other times, the landscape of war is characterized by the opposing qualities of emptiness and isolation: "fermes désertes au loin" [deserted farms in the distance] (p. 16), "églises vides et ouvertes" [empty, vacant churches] (p. 16), "hameaux évacués" [evacuated hamlets] (p. 27), "les grands carrés et volumes des maisons, aux murs blanchis de lune, comme de gros morceaux de glace inégaux, tout silence, en blocs pâles" [great squares and volumes of houses, with walls whitewashed by the moon, like large, irregular chunks of ice, all silence, in pale white blocks] (p. 40). On this dehumanized landscape, Céline captures the absurdity of the war in a "panoramic shot" that blurs the identities of the combatants as it reduces them to a derisory scale: "Tout au loin sur la chaussée, aussi loin qu'on pouvait voir, il y avait deux points noirs, au milieu, comme nous, mais c'était deux Allemands bien occupés à tirer depuis un bon quart d'heure" [Far away on the road, as far as you could see, there were two black dots, in the middle, like us, only they were two Germans, busy shooting for a good quarter of an hour] (p. 15).

Concomitant with this revelation of Bardamu's insignificance is his discovery of his own fragile materiality. The latter is conveyed most forcefully, though indirectly, through the metaphor of the field abattoir:

> Sur des sacs et des toiles de tentes largement étendues et sur l'herbe même, il y en avait pour des kilos et des kilos de tripes étalées, de gras en flocons jaunes et pâles, des moutons éventrés avec leurs organes en pagaïe, suintant en ruisselets ingénieux dans la verdure d'alentour, un bœuf entier sectionné en deux, pendu à l'arbre, et sur lequel s'escrimaient . . . les quatre bouchers du régiment pour lui tirer des morceaux d'abatis. (p. 24)

> [On sacks and tent canvases spread wide, and on the grass itself, there were pounds upon pounds of guts on display, fat in pale yellow flakes, disemboweled sheep with their entrails in a jumble, oozing curious little streams into the surrounding greenery, there was a whole ox, split in two and hung from a tree, on which four regimental butchers were toiling . . . to extract parts of the organs.]

This makeshift slaughterhouse, spread out on the field of battle, implicitly reminds Bardamu, and the reader, of the slaughter of men. But it also conveys to Bardamu an image of human destiny—the dissolution and liquefaction to which the flesh must ineluctably fall heir. Both connotations of the abattoir metaphor appear to be at play in Bardamu's reaction to this spectacle—he suffers a fit of vomiting and then faints. Both acts mark his visceral reaction to what he has seen; both acts are "magical" (in the Sartrean sense) in that they permit the victim to provisionally escape from the cause that occasioned them. Small wonder, then, that Bardamu will choose the asylum over the battlefield, exchanging one form of delirium for another but one that provides shelter from war's insanity and which, finally, allows Bardamu to be demobilized.

Here and there on the landscape of *Voyage* one finds places of apparent refuge—hospitals and, in particular, insane asylums. It is the latter that will interest us here, for the role of the asylum is linked to one of the major themes of Céline's fiction—the theme of delirium. *Délire* and the verb *délirer* appear frequently in Céline's novels. Cognitively, delirium signifies the expression of ideas contrary to reality, usually accompanied by a state of excitement of agitation. To this literal definition we must add a second, archaic meaning, poetic frenzy, the heightened state of sensibility that permits artistic creation. Although distinctions between insanity and delirium are often blurred in Céline's works, notably in *Voyage,* the two will be distinguished in subsequent novels on the basis of degree: insanity is the limit of delirium; delirium is an "imperfect" form of insanity.

I noted that the asylum was a place of apparent refuge, apparent because the value accorded to delirium is not always clear. On the one hand, delirium will result in protective enclosure, a shelter from external reality and its attendant horrors. On the other hand, that same protecting enclosure posits a refusal of lucidity, a retreat from the voyage. Of course, the temptation that the asylum offers is predicated upon the view that the world is an asylum which differs from the institution in that the often destructive penchants of the institution's inhabitants are moderated, defused as it were, by virtue of their having been turned inward and by virtue of separation and supervision.

Délire may also be any lie, mania, or evasion that permits one to still remain in society while denying or diminishing the reality of existence—the greater delirium—such as Céline conceives it, war, poverty, misery, dissolution in time, etc. Céline conveys this modality of *délire,* as he will convey certain of its other modalities, by means of a spatial image: "Où aller dehors, je vous le demande, dès qu'on n'a plus en soi la somme suffisante de délire" [Where do you go, I ask you, once you no longer have within yourself a sufficient quantity of delirium] (p. 199). This opposition between within (the lies one tells oneself) and without (external reality) establishes the function of delirium, in this benign form, as the elaboration of a sort of portable asylum, a self-fabricated refuge. A variation on this same opposition is founded upon the desired dualism of mind and body—the latter in the world, the former attempting to detach itself from the body and thus the ills, temporal and physical, to which the body succumbs: ". . . les miteux ça délire facilement. Il y a un moment de la misère où l'esprit n'est plus déjà tout le temps avec le corps. Il s'y trouve vraiment trop mal. C'est déjà presque une âme qui vous parle. C'est pas responsable une âme" [Those who are wretched rave easily. There is a point in misery when the mind and the body are no longer always together. It is too painful for it to be found there. It is already almost a soul that speaks to you. A soul is not responsible] (p.224).

If the delirium of the poor—those who are most in need of it—is pathetic, for it supposes that they must live on whatever meager illusions they can find and sustain, the delirium of those in power can be both comical and deleterious. Their caprices and their *idées fixes* transform them into Bergsonian automatons as they pursue their goals oblivious to the reality around them. But in so doing they may contribute to the "délire ordinaire du monde" [the ordinary delirium of the world] (p. 87)—that is to say, its fascination with war, its indifference to death, poverty, and suffering. Thus Bestombes, the chief-resident of the hospital in which Bardamu is placed after he suffers his nervous breakdown, constantly delivers long-winded patriotic speeches to his soldier-patients. He exhorts them to make even greater sacrifices for *la patrie* when, already broken in mind and body, already the victims of the slogans used by public officials, all they seek is a refuge from the war.

Bardamu's own breakdown, his personal manifestation of delirium, occurs during his leave from the war when, in the course of an outing with his mistress Lola, an American girl in charge of preparing the donuts the Red Cross distributes to the soldiers, he comes across a shooting gallery appropriately named Le Stand des Nations. The sight of its bullet-riddled targets transforms the gallery in Bardamu's imagination into an image of the war itself. Shortly thereafter, Bardamu begins to have visions, seeing himself and everyone around him imprisoned within a vast shooting gallery and destined to become targets. Bardamu screams an alert: "On va tirer! Foutez le camp tous!" [They're going to shoot! Everyone get the hell out!] (p. 61). The police are summoned to take this "crazy" soldier to a hospital.

Bardamu's stay in the hospital in which are mixed the wounded, those suffering from nervous disorders, and the supposedly insane, permits him to confirm what he has already learned at the front—namely, that the war is a global insanity and those who refuse to participate in it should be judged sane: "Quand le moment du monde à l'envers est venu et que c'est fou que de demander pourquoi on vous assassine, il devient évident qu'on passe pour fou à peu de frais" [When the world comes to the point when it has been turned upside down and it is crazy to ask why you're being killed, then it is obvious that you can easily pass for insane] (p. 64). In such a world, ethics and values no longer have their usual meaning; cowardice and insanity become positive virtues, according to Bardamu: "Alors je suis tombé malade, fiévreux, rendu fou, qu'ils ont expliqué à l'hôpital, par la peur. C'était possible. La meilleure des choses à faire, n'est-ce pas, quand on est dans ce monde, c'est d'en sortir? Fou ou pas, peur ou pas" [Then I fell sick, feverish, made crazy, they explained at the hospital, by fear. That was possible. The best thing to do, isn't it so, when you're in this world is to get out of it. Crazy or not, fear or no fear] (p. 61).

Bardamu has received the respite he sought from the war. But he realizes that so long as he remains in France and the war continues, he risks being returned to the front. He loses his mistress Lola who, imbued with patriotic fervor, becomes disgusted and dismayed when Bardamu exclaims in her presence "vivent les fous et les lâches" [long live the crazy and the cowardly] (p. 66). He loses another mistress, named Musyne, a violinist, who forsakes him for the company of wealthy Argentinians. Fearful of the war, alone and without a job, Bardamu decides to leave Europe to take a position as manager of a trading post in Africa. The firm that employs him is called La Compagnie Pordurière du Petit Congo. Pordurière evokes *ordure* 'filth,' 'excrement.' As Bardamu will discover, the company is aptly named.

Bardamu embarks for Africa upon the *Amiral Bragueton. Bragueton* suggests *braguette*, 'a fly (of a pair of pants),' and it is just this unbuttoning of one's fly, the exposure not of the passengers' privates but their murderous inner selves, that will take place. Having fled the incomprehensible carnage of the war, Bardamu will find himself once more the victim of circumstances. This time the landscape is that of a circumscribed space—not merely the confines of the ship but the ship as enclosed by an increasingly stifling atmosphere as the rusty hulk steams southward. The image of the "étuve" [steam-room] reappears frequently, to characterize both the atmosphere of the ship and, later, that of the colonies to which it is heading. In Céline's lexicon, the *étuve* suggests a kind of stewpot, whose human contents simmer in their own juices. As the passengers leave the coast of Portugal, the pot—as constituted by the ship and its cover of heat and humidity—begins to heat up: ". . . étuve infiniment tiède, inquiétante. L'eau dans les verres, la mer, l'air, les draps, notre sueur, tout, tiède, chaud" [an incredibly warm and disquieting steam bath. The water in the glasses, the sea, the air, the sheets, our sweat, everything warm, hot] (p. 112). With the increase in heat and humidity a "vil désespoir s'est abattu sur les passagers de l'Amiral Bragueton" [an ugly despair settled upon the passengers of the *Admiral Bragueton*] (p. 112). The inhumanity of the passengers emerges from within, rising to the surface like the perspiration of their bodies. Although Bardamu has offended no one, he is viewed as different from the other passengers, who have already served in the colonies. He becomes the target of the rage of the passengers, some of whom, officers in the colonial army, pursue him, hoping to provoke him into a fatal duel. He becomes their safety valve, the *pharmakos* whose destruction will appease the anger of his fellow travelers and permit their society to return to a state of (precarious) equilibrium.[3] Their behavior is juxtaposed with that of the soldiers Bardamu has just left; once the necessary controls have been removed, people—now unbuttoned, naked—fall victim to their natural penchant for destruction:

> l'angoissante nature des blancs, provoquée, libérée, bien débraillée enfin, leur vraie nature, tout comme à la guerre. Etuve tropicale pour instincts tels crapauds et vipères qui viennent enfin s'épanouir au mois d'août sur les flancs fissurés des prisons. (p. 112)

> [the atrocious nature of the white man, aroused, liberated, finally unclothed, as in the war. A tropical steam room for baring human instincts, like the heat of August brings out toads and vipers on the cracked walls of prisons.]

Having managed to evade his pursuers for several days, Bardamu is at last cornered and summoned to defend his honor. Bardamu's defensive strategem, abhorrent as it may be to the reader still imbued with the belief in the nobility of heroic action, is consonant with what Bardamu has learned from his wartime experience. "Lâcheté devient une magnifique espérance à qui s'y connaît" [Cowardice becomes a magnificent hope for the person who knows what it's all about] (p. 119), Bardamu reasons; and from this fear is born the desperate flattery with which Bardamu placates his would-be assassins. Expounding upon the glories of combat and of the colonial administration, he, self-consciously and creatively, abandons his own self-esteem in order to flatter the egos of the others. His words, abetted by ample quantities of alcohol, prove too much of an intoxicant, and the murderous instincts of his pursuers are reabsorbed, as it were, into the inner recesses from which they had emerged. Bardamu is able to steal from the ship and disembark on the African shore.

Like the Africa of *L'Eglise,* that of *Voyage* constitutes a vast hot-house in which organisms grow in luxuriant profusion and where the white man's presence is a vain struggle against a hostile environment that exposes his fragility at every turn. It is an environment where a small vegetable garden produces plants that grow "deliriously" (p. 140) huge, where the blinding heat of the sun literally "cooks" (p. 135) a person's eyes, where fevers, digestive ailments, and skin diseases befall virtually all the white settlers (who find it exciting to wager on whose fever will attain the maximum temperature), where one is constantly besieged by snakes, scorpions, and insects of all sorts, especially mosquitoes. Echoing Pistil's description of life in the colonies in *L'Eglise,* the narrator states:

> La vie ne devient guère tolérable qu'à la tombée de la nuit, mais encore l'obscurité est-elle accaparée presque immédiatement par les moustiques en essaims. Pas un, deux ou cent, mais par billions. S'en tirer dans ces conditions-là devient une œuvre authentique de préservation. Carnaval le jour, écumoire la nuit, la guerre en douce. (p. 126)

> [Life only becomes barely tolerable at nightfall, but, even so, the darkness is immediately seized by mosquitoes in swarms. Not one, two, or one hundred, but by the billions. To pull through under such conditions is a true feat of self-preservation. Carnival by day, sieve by night, the war in miniature.]

Given these conditions, Bardamu discovers that the colonial hospital offers the only refuge, from the climate, from the insects, and from the indifference and pettiness of the white settlers.

The image of the *étuve* reappears frequently to characterize this hostile African landscape. The constituant elements of everyday existence break down and begin to dissolve one into the other like the ingredients of a stew that has been overcooked. This process of dissolution resembles the molecular dispersion that, according to the narrator, menaces humankind and its creations:

> On avait à peine le temps de les voir disparaître les hommes, les jours et les choses dans cette verdure, ce climat, la chaleur et les moustiques. Tout y passait, c'était dégoûtant, par bouts, par phrases, par membres, par regrets, par globules, ils se perdaient au soleil, fondaient dans le torrent de la lumière et des couleurs, et le goût et le temps avec, tout y passait. Il n'y avait que de l'angoisse étincelante dans l'air. (p. 147)

> [You hardly had time to see them disappear, men, days, things, in that greenery, that climate, the heat and the mosquitoes. Everything went through it, it was disgusting, by bits, by phrases, by members, by regrets, by globules, they became lost in the sun, dissolved in the torrent of light and colors, and with them taste and time, it happened to everything. There remained only a sparkling anguish in the air.]

Insofar as the white settlers are concerned, they too are "stewed." They are portrayed as undergoing a slow process of liquefaction as the effects of the climate cause a dissolution of flesh and identity. Women are "fondantes . . . en interminables règles" [melting in endless menstruation] (p. 142) while their children "se dissolv[ent] par la chaleur en diarrhée permanente" [are dissolved by the heat in a continuous diarrhea] (p. 144); Europeans are described as substances that easily melt, "sorbets" [sherbets] (p. 143) "beurre" [butter] (p. 144), "morceau de sucre dans du café" [a sugar cube in coffee] (p. 144).

The moral aspect of this process of liquefaction—that which oozes to the surface—is the emergence of the inner self of the colonizer as manifested in the treatment accorded the native population. Economic exploitation, corruption, cruelty, and apathy come to characterize the colonial administration. The environment in which it operates makes it a natural theatre for the expression of humankind's penchant for wickedness. The softness—literal and figurative—of the white settlers, the narrator notes, is part of a process of vitiation brought about by the availability of ice (we may recall Pistil's fascination with that substance). With an abundant supply of ice the colonizer need face nothing more rigorous than the afternoon apéritif.[4] One conspicuous exception to the fate of the Europeans concerns a certain Sergeant Alcide, who patiently and good-naturedly endures renewed tours in Africa so that he can support a crippled niece whom he has never seen. Such altruism is indeed a rare commodity in Céline's fiction.

After a long trip upriver into the bush, Bardamu assumes his position as manager of an isolated trading post. There he quickly finds himself suffering the same fate, physically, as his fellow countrymen. "Stewing" (p. 173) in a constant fever, constantly vomiting up the papayas and melons with which he attempts to nourish himself, he stays at his job, refusing to yield to the temptation of abandoning his trading post for fear of having to render accounts to the company. But, finally, the African landscape begins to overwhelm him: "La factorie et moi, on s'enfonçait. On allait disparaître dans la boue après chaque averse plus visqueuse, plus épaisse" [The trading post and I, we were sinking in. We were going to disappear into the mud, after each downpour, ever more viscous, more thick] (p. 175). Bardamu rebels against this dissolution by means of a ritual act of purification— setting fire to the trading post. That fire is subsequently interiorized as Bardamu succumbs to a high fever, accompanied by delirium, and is carried out of the jungle by bearers.

The circumstances of his departure from Africa are "explained" by the hallucinations Bardamu's fever produces. Realism gives way to fantasy—having arrived in Africa on a ship that became a prison for him, Bardamu departs as a prisoner on the *Infanta Combitta,* described, anachronistically, as a Spanish galley complete with galley slaves, whose number Bardamu will join. Ironically, he is freer on the *Infanta Combitta* than he was on the *Amiral Bragueton.* The galley slaves can look forward to a pension at the end of their service and are even permitted to vote—but on Sundays only. Céline may be satirizing here the welfare state, as Allen Thiher has suggested.[5] However, if we juxtapose this "unreal" voyage not only with that of the *Amiral Bragueton* but with an earlier description of the ship of state as a "grand galère" [great galley] (p. 13)—with the poor rowing and the rich and powerful on the bridge—another aspect of the voyage emerges. Hallucination, or delirium—to use Céline's preferred term for this mode of perception—can make existence palatable, can provide an escape from it. But the price that one must pay is the refusal of lucidity, the renunciation of the voyager's self-imposed mission to experience life in all its horrors and subsequently relate his story. Thus Bardamu will leave the security of the ship to take his chances in America.

Bardamu's departure from Africa and his arrival in America mark not only his passage from the most primitive "biological" landscape to the most modern, most civilized, one, but also a return to a more northerly climate. The polarity of North and South will assume major significance in Céline's novels—one of which will be entitled *Nord* —his pamphlets, and in the life of the author.[6] *Voyage* announces the biological basis of this polarity, which is apparent, of course, in Céline's treatment of Bardamu's journey on the *Amiral Bragueton* and the European's situation in Africa:

> Dans le froid d'Europe, sous les grisailles pudiques du Nord, on ne fait hors les carnages, que soupçonner la grouillante cruauté de nos frères, mais leur pourriture envahit la surface dès que les émoustille la fièvre ignoble des tropiques. C'est alors qu'on se déboutonne éperdument et que la saloperie triomphe et nous recouvre entiers. C'est l'aveu biologique. Dès que le travail et le froid ne nous astreignent plus, relâchent un moment leur étau, on peut apercevoir des blancs, ce qu'on découvre du gai rivage, une fois que la mer s'en retire: la vérité, mares lourdement puantes, les crabes, la charogne et l'étron. (pp. 112-13)

> [In the cold of Europe, under prudish Northern fogs, we only glimpse, apart from the slaughters of wartime, the swarming cruelty of our fellow men. But their rottenness rises to the surface as soon as they are aroused by the ignoble fever of the tropics. It is then that the frenzied process of unbuttoning begins and that filthiness triumphs and takes hold of us completely. It's a biological confession. As soon as work and cold weather no longer constrain us, release their stranglehold somewhat, you can see in the white man what you see on a charming shore when the tide goes out: the truth, stinking stagnant pools, crabs, carcasses, and turds.]

Thus, in the "play" between within and without, man's disgusting, ignominious nature is, under the proper conditions, revealed in an accelerated fashion. Northerner or Southerner, man is a "sac de larves" [a bag of maggots] (p. 115), physically and morally; only in the Southerner those "larva" multiply more readily. This "biological confession" (p. 113) will be metaphosed into a "racial confession" in the pamphlets. There the Jew, of

Mediterranean origin, will be condemned as a Southerner. He will be identified, pejoratively, as negroid and portrayed as a maggot insidiously working its way into, and corrupting, Aryan society.

When Bardamu arrives at the trading post he has a brief meeting with his predecessor. The latter is in the process of leaving the post—and Africa—with most of the proceeds of the enterprise but decides to delay his departure in order to tell his successor about the deplorable conditions that he has inherited: the dilapidated trading post with its shoddy goods, the unhealthy food and water, and the frightful sound of native music that he can expect to hear at nightfall. Their conversation takes place mostly in the darkness (lights would, of course, attract enormous numbers of insects). Bardamu is convinced that he knows the man to whom he is speaking, that it must be a certain Léon Robinson whom he met on the battlefield of Flanders and subsequently on leave in Paris. However, by the time Bardamu has convinced himself that the stranger is indeed Robinson, the man has already departed. After Bardamu has set fire to the trading post, he will follow in Robinson's footsteps. As if anticipating the nature of the path Robinson has elected and future encounters under equally unhappy circumstances, Bardamu baptizes the man "ce Robinson de tous les malheurs" [this calamity-ridden Robinson] (p. 146).

Darkness is indeed Robinson's element, for throughout the novel he will lead the way into the "night" and to the "end of the night" as Bardamu's double, his alter ego. He will represent the concretization—or at least projection—of the dark side of Bardamu's thoughts and desires. The initial encounter between the two men had also taken place in darkness. Bardamu, "deflowered" by his experience of the war, had been musing that one way of escaping from the horrors of the conflict would be to have himself taken prisoner by the Germans—"un tout petit peu d'espoir, celui d'être fait prisonnier" [a tiny bit of hope, that of being made prisoner] (p. 40). Shortly thereafter, in the course of a reconnoitering mission, Bardamu meets Robinson and is surprised and fascinated when Robinson tells him that he too had been contemplating allowing himself to be captured by the Germans so he would no longer have to fight in a senseless war—"ça m'intéressait soudain, plus que tout, son projet, comment il allait s'y prendre lui pour réussir à faire paumer" [it suddenly interested me, more than anything, his plan, how he was going to arrange to succeed in getting himself pinched] (p. 144).

Robinson apparently does not succeed in being picked up by the Germans, for when Bardamu meets him many months later in Paris, he indicates that he is still a soldier in the French army. The circumstances of this second meeting indicate once again that Robinson is able to anticipate Bardamu's sentiments, notably concerning the shady aspects of existence. Bardamu accompanies a friend to the home of a grieving mother who has lost a son in the war. The friend will feign having known the son in the hope of receiving some money from the mother; and Bardamu is content to accompany him if he can also profit from the mother's loss. When Bardamu arrives at the house, he meets Robinson, who informs him that he had been writing to the mother in order to eventually get some money from her. No one receives anything this time because the mother, unable to bear the death of her son, has hanged herself.

"Je reçus tout près du derrière de Lola le message d'un nouveau monde" [I received in the area of Lola's behind the message of a new world] (p. 55). This message that Bardamu receives from the body of Lola, his American mistress, is a desire to forsake the terrors and stupidities of World War I, the inequities of a French army all too ready to use soldiers like Bardamu for cannon fodder, and come to the United States with its promise of a new and better life.

As we have seen, the relationship between Lola and Bardamu lasts only so long as Bardamu plays the fearless, patriotic French soldier. Bardamu's interest in Lola is, as we might suspect, primarily sexual. His delight with her body is enhanced by his perception of her as a typical American woman. And his easy enjoyment of her favors convinces him that the means to success in America will be found through the bodies of Lola's female compatriots:

> Je n'en avais jamais assez de parcourir ce corps américain. . . . un pays apte à produire des corps aussi audacieux dans leur grâce et d'une envolée spirituelle aussi tentante devait offrir bien d'autres révélations capitales au sens biologique il s'entend. Je décidai à force de peloter Lola d'entreprendre tôt ou tard le voyage aux Etats-Unis comme un véritable pèlerinage et cela dès que possible. Je n'eus en effet de cesse et de repos . . . avant d'avoir mené à bien cette profonde aventure, mystiquement anatomique. (p. 55)

> [I never tired of caressing this American body. . . . a country capable of producing bodies of such startling grace and tempting spiritual elevation

would offer many other essential revelations, biologically speaking to
be sure. My petting with Lola led me to decide to undertake, sooner or
later, a voyage to the United States as a real pilgrimage, and just as
soon as possible. I could find, in fact, no peace or rest . . . before
having concluded this profound, mystically anatomical adventure.]

Bardamu's project takes shape presumably during the moments he and Lola
spend in bed. We can read "parcourir [le décor] américain" for "parcourir
ce corps américain," since the exchange between Lola and America is
predicated upon Bardamu's assumption that Lola's horizontal, submissive,
penetrable body will be the model for the "body" of America. This series of
metonymic exchanges—Lola's body for that of the American woman, for
America itself and an assumed way of life—reveals more than just a simple
project of conquest with comically mystical overtones. The passage from
Lola's body to that of America is indeed a *passage* —a text, of course, by
the protagonist-turned-narrator but also a voyage. Insofar as Bardamu's
plans to travel to America are concerned, he postulates a return to the
pleasure he enjoyed with Lola, in the form, ultimately, of a secure and
financially comfortable existence in that New World. The attainment of that
goal would, according to these premises, eliminate the further need for
passage —text or voyage.

Bardamu's trip to America is delayed, of course, by his substitute
voyage to Africa. When Bardamu finally arrives in New York on board the
Infanta Combitta, he is both surprised and disconcerted by the architecture
of this American city as contrasted with its European counterpart. As was
the case in *L'Eglise,* where Bardamu had a similar perception of the differences between European and American cities, the dissimilarity between the
two landscapes is conveyed by sexual metaphors. Whereas the European
city is depicted as feminine, the American city, which Bardamu had
expected to be equally feminine as an extension of Lola's body, turns out to
be masculine in nature:

> Figurez-vous qu'elle était debout leur ville, absolument droite. New
> York, c'est une ville debout. On en avait déjà vu nous des villes bien
> sûr, et des belles encore, et des ports et des fameux même. Mais chez
> nous, n'est-ce pas, elles sont couchées les villes, au bord de la mer ou
> sur des fleuves, elles s'allongent sur le paysage, elles attendent le
> voyageur, tandis que celle-là l'Américaine, elle ne se pâmait pas,

non, elle se tenait bien raide, là, pas baisante du tout, raide à faire
peur. (p. 184)

[Imagine that it was standing up, their city, absolutely erect. New York
is a city standing up. Of course, we'd already seen lots of cities, and
fine ones at that, and ports and even famous ones. But at home, cities
lie down alongside a coast or a river, they stretch out on the landscape,
awaiting the traveler; whereas the American one does not swoon, no,
she stands stiff, not at all ready to be laid, stiff enough to scare you.]

Bardamu's masculinity appears to have been diminished, transferred in part
to the landscape with its phallic verticality. Indeed, the overpowering effect
of the landscape on Bardamu suggests that he has become impotent, that he
is no longer confident he possesses the will and drive to complete his
"pilgrimage." And we may suspect that there will be an attendant
transformation of Bardamu's role—from active to passive, from conqueror
to victim.

Another aspect of the New York landscape reinforces the disparity
between it and Lola's body. Whereas the latter was open to penetration,
entry into New York's buildings—a house or building is, of course, a
traditional Freudian symbol of the female body—is obstructed for the poor
and shabby-looking Bardamu by a "système de contraintes" [system of
restraints]. Not only is Bardamu frightened by the "system," but he also
"caves in with shyness" [m'effondrais de timidité]—this last notation
suggesting detumescence:

Mais à la pensée d'avoir a pénétrer dans une de ces maisons je m'effarais
et m'effondrais de timidité. . . . Pour eux c'était la sécurité peut-être
tout ce déluge en suspens tandis que pour moi ce n'était rien qu'un
abominable système de contraintes . . . en couloirs, en verrous, en
guichets, une torture architecturale gigantesque. . . . (p. 205)

[But at the thought of having to penetrate one of these houses, I grew
frightened and caved in with shyness. . . . For them this suspended
deluge perhaps meant security, whereas for me it was nothing but a
system of restraints . . . hallways, bolted doors, entrance gates, a
gigantic architectural torture.]

He has entered a wasteland characterized by the qualities of vertical rigidity,
hardness, and closure.

Since Bardamu has predicated the satisfaction of his desire on the
repetition of the pleasure he once enjoyed with Lola and has made women
the mediators of his conquest of America, he is at first delighted to see all
around him numerous substitutes—or so he thinks—for his ex-mistress:
"Souvenir de Lola! Son exemple ne m'avait pas trompé. C'était vrai. Je
touchais au vif de mon pèlerinage" [Souvenir of Lola! Her example had not
deceived me. It was true. I was getting to the heart of my pilgrimage]
(p. 193). Appearances are, however, deceptive. The women are as imposing as the architecture around him. Those at the Laugh Calvin Hotel (the
name may be a reference to the very serious Calvin Coolidge, president
1923-29), where Bardamu is staying, have the same sort of mechanical,
rigid symmetry, hardness, and impenetrability as the facades of Manhattan's
buildings. They are jewellike objects to be venerated, as if the lobby were a
temple, rather than be sexually exploited. Such a setting excludes the
possibility of laughter as it literalizes the term "pilgrimage":

> . . . plongées en de profonds fauteuils, comme dans autant d'écrins.
> Des hommes attentifs autour, silencieux à passer et repasser à certaine
> distance d'elles, curieux et craintifs, au large de la rangée des jambes
> croisées à de magnifiques hauteurs de soie. Elles me semblaient ces
> merveilleuses attendre là des événements très graves et très coûteux.
> Evidemment, ce n'était pas à moi qu'elles songeaient. (p. 196)

> [. . . sunk in deep armchairs, as in so many jewel-cases. Attentive men
> all around them, silent, passing back and forth at a certain distance from
> them, curious and timid, giving a wide berth to the line of crossed legs
> revealing magnificent heights of silk. It seemed to me that these
> marvelous creatures were awaiting events of a serious and costly nature.
> Clearly, they were not thinking of me.]

Bardamu joins the other worshippers of these women who resemble, with
their cold, statuelike beauty, the movie stars that appear on the posters and
in the films of the movie houses he has begun to frequent—"parfaites, pas
une négligence, pas une bavure, parfaites . . . mignonnes mais fermes et
concises en même temps" [perfect, without a fault, without a blemish,
perfect . . . delicate but, at the same time, firm and concise] (p. 201).
    The one unknown woman in New York that Bardamu dares
approach shares these same attributes of cold, hard perfection, and ultimately, lifelessness. In this case the woman herself is not described but

rather the environment in which she works—a modern cafeteria—and whose material qualities she shares. In the cafeteria Bardamu must perform his "rite alimentaire" [feeding ritual] (pp. 205-06) according to the prescribed rules, which forbid fraternization between customers and employees. This religious motif recalls the hotel and the movie theatre as temples where women serve as objects of veneration. Having gained entrance to this formica shrine, Bardamu will try to "pick up" one of the busgirls. The light that illuminates the cafeteria is harsh and glaring, reducing everything to a blinding play of surface reflections, transforming the food into something resembling the plastic and metal of which the cafeteria is constructed. "Mes fraises sur mon gâteau" [the strawberries on my cake], Bardamu remarks, "étaient accaparées par tant d'étincelants reflets que je ne pouvais pas me résoudre à les avaler" [were caught by so many shimmering reflections that I couldn't bring myself to swallow them] (p. 207).

The sterility of such a decor is reinforced by the imagery of the hospital that appears in the description of the cafeteria. It is compared to an "operating room" and its employees garbed in immaculately white uniforms are depicted as "nurses" (p. 206). Hitherto positively valorized as a refuge from the war or, in the case of Bardamu's stay in Africa, as a shelter from the heat and humidity, the image of the hospital is, in our present context, negatively valorized. Bardamu's approach to the girl in question is less an attempt to seduce her than a despairing effort to extract some sign of life from the landscape of which she is a part: "J'en avais assez d'être seul! Plus de rêve! De la sympathie! Du contact!" [I had enough of being alone! No more dreaming! Some sympathy! Some contact!] (p. 208). But Bardamu receives no response from the girl, and the incident, which David Hayman has compared to a "dumb show reminiscent of the early Chaplin films," ends with Bardamu's polite ejection from the premises.[7] Having failed to act according to the rules, the "system of restraints," having tried to rebel against the dehumanization that characterizes the environment of the cafeteria, he is shown to the door by the bouncer "comme un chien qui vient de s'oublier" [like a dog that has just forgotten himself] (p. 208).

"C'était peut-être la Grèce qui recommence" [It was perhaps Greece reborn] (p. 193), Bardamu had thought to himself upon first seeing the beautiful women of New York, their perfect forms evoking in his mind the ideal of Classical Greece.[8] But, to recall Nietzsche's *The Birth of Tragedy*—which, as I have noted, Céline had probably read—however beautiful these women may be, they are, as Bardamu has discovered, flawed; for they embody the Apollonian extreme, perfection of form, self-control, distance, plasticity, without the Dionysian element of overflowing life. According to Nietzsche it is the synthesis of Apollo and Dionysus that produces great art. And for Céline, one essential manifestation of that synthesis can be found in the dance. Bardamu will later meet a woman who approaches the Célinian ideal—Molly, the beautiful prostitute with a heart of gold and the body of a dancer.

Masturbation becomes a means of profaning those temples in which female beauty is worshipped, of breaking the "system of restraints." Exchanging the "sweet" and "warm" (p. 205) space of the movie theatre for the intimate confines of his room at the Laugh Calvin Hotel, the movie projector for his mind's flow of images, Bardamu masturbates himself to sleep. By means of fantasy, he is no longer excluded from the life around him; he eliminates the distance between himself and external reality by transforming the latter into a world of satisfied desire.

Another form of masturbation concerns the use of money. As we have seen, a principal "restraint" under which Bardamu is obliged to operate is that of poverty. In America, Bardamu had been warned, "c'est tout millionnaire ou tout charogne! Y a pas de milieu" [you're either a millionaire or a stiff! There's no in-between] (p. 186). In the heart of the city he discovers the temple of money, a temple more forbidding than the others. Through the use of ecclesiastic motifs, Céline explicitly condemns the commercial orientation of this New World. Manhattan is characterized as a "borough of gold," into which "one enters only on foot" (p. 192). The dollar is a "Saint-Esprit," a "host" not to be eaten but "placed on the heart," as one places a billfold in the interior pocket of a jacket (p. 192). The barred window of a bank teller is compared to the grille of a confessional, with the Dollar becoming the priest receiving the confession (p. 192).

Bardamu's attempt to "pick up" the girl in the cafeteria links that formica sanctuary with the temple of money in a masturbatory fantasy, for his approach to the girl is preceded by a reverie that transforms him into a wealthy man, able, by means of his money, to have the woman he desires: "ça doit faire un drôle d'effet, pensais-je, quand on peut se permettre d'aborder ainsi une de ces demoiselles au nez précis et coquet 'Mademoiselle, lui dirait-on, je suis riche, bien riche . . . dites-moi ce qui vous ferait plaisir d'accepter . . .' " [It must have a strange effect, I thought, when one can take the liberty of approaching one of these girls with their neat, coquettish noses "Miss, one would say to her, I am rich, very rich . . .

tell me what you would care to accept"] (p. 206). The use of money to make reality conform to one's desires, derived according to Freudian theory from the child's attribution of magical powers to his feces during the anal stage of development, is analogous here to Bardamu's activities in his hotel room. Bardamu's fantasy is completed by the vision of a world that is antithetical to the hostile landscape of New York: "Tout se transforme et le monde formidablement hostile en vient à l'instant rouler à vos pieds en boule sournoise, docile et veloutée" [Everything is transformed, and the formidably hostile world comes in a moment to roll at your feet in a clever ball, docile and velvety] (p. 206).

The connection between money, sexuality, and excrement leads us to yet another of the metaphoric temples that dot Bardamu's New York landscape and mark the route of his "pilgrimage." Unlike the others, this one is located below the surface of the city—in an underground mens room. Bardamu gains access to it from the street. Penetrating between the "monsters of houses" (p. 192) that border it, houses from which Bardamu and others like him are excluded, the street is a *passage,* not only by virtue of its physical configuration but also by virtue of its opening onto other paths of a similar nature. There would seem to be no end to the misery Bardamu has discovered, for the street points "vers le bout qu'on ne voit jamais de toutes les rues du monde" [toward the end one never sees of all the world's streets] (p. 192). One link between this perspective and the project that originally brought Bardamu to America is established by the image of the street as a "triste plaie" [sad wound] (p. 192), with its connotations of a negatively valorized female orifice.[9] To enter that "wound" is to confront the subterranean aspects of existence, to explore a system that is peristaltic, excremental rather than sexual in nature. Bardamu enters the lavatory through a "hole" in the street, down a staircase of "pink marble" (p. 195).

The activities that take place within this mens room contrast radically with the sort of existence one finds above ground:

> Ce contraste était bien fait pour déconcerter un étranger. Tout ce débraillage intime, cette formidable familiarité intestinale et dans la rue cette parfaite contrainte! J'en demeurais étourdi. (p. 196)

> [This contrast was just the thing to disconcert a foreigner. All this intimate exposure, this extraordinary intestinal familiarity, and in the street that perfect restraint. I remained overwhelmed by it.]

The opposition between "débraillage intime," "familiarité intestinale" and "parfaite contrainte" recalls and anticipates other aspects of Bardamu's voyage. During the trip to Africa on the *Amiral Bragueton,* when Bardamu had become the *pharmakos* for the ship's passengers, "débraillage" had been negatively valorized as the 'venting' (literally 'unbuttoning') of man's propensity for violence toward others, exacerbated in this instance by the tropical heat. As for excrement and the sharing of toilets, both will later be negatively valorized as, for example, in the case of the overflowing privies that characterize the Parisian *zone,* where Bardamu will sporadically practice medicine, and which symbolize the moral and physical corruption of its inhabitants. For Bardamu in New York, "débraillage" and defecation, associated thematically and syntagmatically, are depicted as forms of liberation, signs of life that become means to human contact. The men on line waiting their turn to enter the stalls are no longer the solitary figures they were in the streets above. A spirit of camaraderie links these total strangers—whose only bond might be their exclusion from the temple of the dollar—as they anticipate the pleasure of relieving their needs, "la perspective . . . paraissait les libérer et les réjouir intimement" [the prospect . . . appeared to liberate them and give them an inner pleasure] (p. 195).

As for the act of defecation itself, we know from Freudian theory that the child passes through an anal stage during the course of his development, when libido is concentrated in the anal zone. Thus the release of tension inherent in the act of defecation is erotic. As evidence by the joyous attitude of the men on line, the pleasures of defecation serve as a regressive substitute for genital satisfaction in this constipated, commercial society. Céline refers to this coming together of men for the purposes of defecation, men who in the streets above are alienated from themselves and from one another, as the "communisme joyeux du caca" [the joyous communism of crap] (p. 196). This expression with its felicitous alliteration sums up, as it were, this entire episode as an attack against a psychologically repressive— and thus neurotic—society founded upon privilege and possession, a society which, as we have seen, worships the dollar. The episode could serve as an illustration of Norman Brown's thesis that modern capitalistic society is structured by sublimated anality taking the form of the love and manipulation of material goods and money.[10]

Bardamu's attitude toward this "scatalogical rite" (p. 196), one that serves as the underground response to the rites of the other temples he has discovered, remains ambiguous. On the one hand, he is attracted by the communal pleasure of those in the city who, like Bardamu, are victims of New York's "systems of restraint." On the other hand, he is disgusted by the odors resulting from that activity. Unaware at this point that the W.C., like the "sad wound" of the street, will open on to other scenes of elimination, other underground aspects of existence, he is not ready to share the fate of those around him, to resign himself to a limited existence with limited pleasures.

Whatever other interpretations we may give to "débraillage" and defecation, they are unmistakably signs of life in an otherwise sterile, lifeless environment. This function is reinforced by Céline's use of the associated imagery of secretion. When Bardamu decides to visit Lola, having finally found her address in New York, he longs for the presence of a French-style concierge in the building, for she would be able to tell him what sort of existence Lola has been leading since he last saw her. The gossip with which a concierge might enlighten Bardamu—permitting him a penetration of the New York landscape hitherto impossible—is depicted as a kind of ooze emanating from all parts of the building and channeled through her. What would be disgusting in other contexts becomes "tasty" when compared to the "insipid" ambiance in which Bardamu has been struggling: "Détritus, bavures à suinter de l'alcôve, de la cuisine, des mansardes, à dégouliner en cascades par chez la concierge, en plein dans la vie, quel savoureux enfer" [Leavings, salivations that drip from the alcove, from the kitchen, from the attic rooms, to spill in cascades through the concierge's place, immersed in life, what a tasty hell] (p. 211).

Bardamu's decision to see Lola again is a tacit admission that his project to conquer America has thus far been a failure. Musing on being able to once again have sexual relations with her, Bardamu employs the image of burglarizing a building, breaking through the "system of restraints": "Un corps luxueux c'est toujours un viol possible, une effraction précieuse, directe, intime dans le vif de la richesse, du luxe . . ." [A luxurious body always makes for a possible rape, a precious break-in direct and intimate, into the heart of wealth, of luxury] (p. 212). As for Lola, her opinion of Bardamu remains unchanged. She still considers him a loathsome coward, a thoroughly despicable person, and wishes to rid herself of him as soon as possible. His departure is delayed by the arrival of some of Lola's women friends. Consonant with the passivity Bardamu had acquired upon landing in New York, it is Lola's friends, and not Bardamu the Frenchman, who direct the conversation about France. Not only do they tell Bardamu about Le Chabanais and Les Invalides, they inform him as well about the merits of various Parisian brothels.

Although Bardamu is unable to effect the sexual "break-in" with Lola that he desires, he finds another means of penetrating her defenses. When Lola relates that her mother is being treated for cancer of the liver by the best and most costly specialists and that a cure is expected, Bardamu, putting to use some of the medical knowledge he has acquired, demolishes her prospects for the future by telling her categorically that her mother's ailment is fatal. "Je la tenais" [I had her] (p. 221), Bardamu says to himself, noting Lola's fright upon hearing his words. No longer passive, Bardamu now can dominate his ex-mistress. Now he is prepared to use language to commit the "effraction" he desired. He tells Lola that cancer is hereditary: ". . . je la voyais devant moi blêmir Lola, faiblir, mollir" [I saw Lola before me grow pale, weaken, soften] (p. 221). "Faiblir" and "mollir" contrast with the rigidity and hardness that Lola previously shared with the New York landscape. Her near collapse recalls as well the submissive Lola of Paris. It is only by means of threatening Bardamu with a gun—with its obviously phallic connotations—that Lola is able to reassert her "firmness" and put an end to Bardamu's verbal assault. Bardamu escapes with some satisfaction and enough money to permit him to leave town.

Having abandoned New York for Detroit and the possibility of employment in the Ford automobile factory. Bardamu discovers that he has forsaken the sterile landscape of New York for an equally sterile factory setting:

> Partout ce qu'on regarde, tout ce que la main touche, c'est dur à présent. . . . Il faut abolir la vie du dehors, en faire aussi d'elle de l'acier, quelque chose d'utile. On l'aimait pas assez telle qu'elle était, c'est pour ça. Faut en faire un objet donc, du solide, c'est la Règle. (pp. 225-26)

> [Everywhere one looks, everthing one's hands touches, is at present hard. . . . Outside life must be abolished, also made into steel, something useful. It was not loved enough as it was, that's the reason. Hence it's got to be made into an object, into something solid, that's the Rule.]

Bardamu once again longs for a female body whose qualities would be antithetical to those of this surroundings—"un vrai corps que je voulais toucher, un corps rose en vraie vie . . . molle" [I wanted to touch a real body, a pink body endowed with real life . . . soft] (p. 226). And it is by means of money that Bardamu is able to fulfill his wishes, by purchasing the services of prostitutes in a brothel on the outskirts of the city.

One of those prostitutes is named Molly, a name derived from the Latin *mol,* meaning 'soft.' Physically, she resembles the ideal Célinian woman, for she is both flesh and perfect form; specifically, she shares the qualities of the dancer by virtue of her splendid legs—"jambes longues et blondes et magnifiquement déliées et musclées, des jambes nobles. La véritable aristocratie humaine, on a beau dire, ce sont les jambes qui la confèrent, pas d'erreur" [long, blond legs, magnificently supple and muscular, noble legs. True human aristocracy, despite what others say, is conferred by the legs, no mistake about it] (pp. 227-28). The elasticity of Molly's legs "corrects" her softness. That which is elastic yields but returns to its former shape, thus courting but not succumbing to the flaccidness that is a sign of inevitable decomposition—flesh and form exist in harmonious equilibrium.[11] Given Molly's profession, one can take this concept of elasticity one step further: her legs are supple enough to permit her to assume the horizontal, submissive position required by her customers but quickly return her to the erect, noble carriage of the dancer; she is a prostitute, available to anyone who can afford her, but her kindness and generosity are freely given; she can continue to exercise her profession and yet offer Bardamu a sincere love and a genuine interest in his self-betterment, in his making a success of himself in America. Molly thus represents a synthesis of the qualities of the American and European landscapes, hitherto opposed. Bardamu's deepening relationship with Molly appears to arrest the displacement instituted by desire, to conclude the passage that brought him to the United States.

But the possibility of Bardamu's successfully realizing his project bears with it the seeds of its destruction. Molly's many virtues transform her into a kind of Circe who enchants her Odysseus with the lure of an idyllic existence—a *soft* life. Their existence together takes on a dreamlike quality as symbolized by the landscape that becomes the setting for their afternoon strolls. As opposed to the urban or factory landscape, this new setting is pastoral—the countryside that borders the city: "Des petits tertres pelés, des bosquets de bouleaux autour de lacs minuscules, des gens à lire par ici par là . . ." [Little scalped hills, clumps of birches around tiny lakes, people reading here and there] (p. 231). A threatening note intrudes upon this landscape, an image of the fragility of the relationship between

Bardamu and his prostitute with a heart of gold—"le ciel tout lourd de nuages plombés" [the sky heavy with leaden clouds] (p. 231). Bardamu becomes uneasy in the presence of Molly, disturbed by the stirring of another desire; he wishes to resume the journey upon which he knows he is embarked, to explore existence in all its manifold aspects. Life itself becomes the ultimate mistress:

> Comme si la vie allait emporter, me cacher ce que je voulais savoir d'elle, de la vie au fond du noir, pendant que je perdais de la ferveur à l'embrasser Molly, et qu'alors j'en aurais plus assez et que j'aurais tout perdu au bout de compte par manque de force, que la vie m'aurait trompé comme tous les autres, la Vie, la vraie maîtresse des véritables hommes. (pp. 231-32)

> [As if life were going to triumph, to hide from me what I wished to know of it, of life in the depths of darkness, while I lost my fervor kissing Molly, and then I would not have enough left, and I would have lost everything in the end through lack of strength, and life would have deceived me like all the others, Life, the true mistress of real men.]

Bardamu's encounter with Robinson, his alter ego, gives him a further insight into the nature of that all-encompassing "mistress." Whereas Bardamu's walks with Molly take place during the day, his meeting with Robinson occurs, as did their previous encounters, during the night. Robinson had become in Bardamu's eyes the master hustler, someone who would be certain to find success in America. Robinson's namesake, Robinson Crusoe was, we may recall, able to master the hostile environment of his desert island with the aid of the instruments of his civilization and the zeal of a capitalistic entrepreneur. "Il n'était pas un type dans mon genre Robinson. Il devait en connaître des trucs et des machins sur l'Amérique" [He wasn't a guy of my sort, Robinson. He was supposed to know the ins and outs of America] (p. 205). The discovery that Robinson has failed to live up to his expectations profoundly shocks and disappoints Bardamu. Robinson has become one of the faceless souls that constitute the "Foreign Legion of the night" (p. 233), an after-hours cleaning man in Detroit's office buildings. Unlike Bardamu, he can penetrate the American landscape, but only to perform the menial tasks required of him. And since cleaning the bathrooms is part of his job—he remarks that "lavatory" and "exit" are the only English words he has learned—we can link Robinson's failure with the "scatological rite" that Bardamu witnessed but was not ready to perform. Robinson cannot permit himself such fastidiousness or such pride—and nor can Bardamu once he has left Molly. Bardamu has but one alternative—to leave America and return to France. The architecture of the novel reinforces the illusory aspects of Bardamu's attempts to make a new life for himself first in Africa and later in America by framing these "exotic" adventures between the sections dealing with France.

The disillusionment that Bardamu has experienced in America will result in a modification of his role as protagonist. He will be less the focus of the action than an observer-witness, particularly with respect to his relationship with Robinson. No longer will Robinson be the guide in whose footsteps Bardamu will attempt to follow. Instead he will become the exemplary victim whose ineffective struggles to rise above the misery and mediocrity of his situation can be recorded but not imitated.

Bardamu's return to Paris "closes" the frame within which the contrasting voyages to Africa and America are juxtaposed. This ordering of the landscapes traversed by the protagonist appropriately stresses the permanence of his European experience, the failure of the voyage to materially change Bardamu's situation. The landscape to which he returns is not, however, the same as the one he had left. The Parisian setting changes from that of the faded, wartime elegance of the city of light to the poverty of the *zone*. It is there that Bardamu, having completed his medical studies, fitfully attempts to start up a practice. The Bardamu of *L'Eglise* is a far more dedicated, far more professional and successful doctor than the Bardamu of *Voyage,* who is more concerned with collecting his fee (which, in fact, he rarely does) than he is with the health of his patients. The area in which Bardamu practices is baptized Garenne-Rancy. The name is significant, for *garenne* is the word for 'rabbit warren' and *Rancy* evokes *rance,* 'rancid.' Garenne-Rancy is indeed a place of crowded squalor and fetid odors. But more than just its poverty, absence of good housing, and proper sanitation, Garenne-Rancy evinces, given the nature of its socio-economic conditions, those forces of destruction and dissolution that attack both its residents and its material structures. Garbage, excrement, bad odors, and secretions of various kinds mingle together in Céline's portrait of the *zone,* and once again they assume their negative valorization as manifestations of a corruption working its way to the surface from within:

... cette espèce de village qui n'arrive jamais à de dégager tout à fait de la boue, coincé dans les ordures et bordé de sentiers où les petites filles trop éveillées et morveuses, le long des palissades, fuient l'école pour attraper d'un satyr à l'autre vingt sous, des frites et la blennorragie. Pays de cinéma d'avant-garde ou les linges sales empoisonnent les arbres et toutes les salades ruissellent d'urine les samedis soirs. (pp. 328-29)

[this sort of village which never succeeded in completely freeing itself from the mud, sunk in garbage, and bordered by paths where little girls, sharp beyond their years and with runny noses could be found along the fences, running away from school and picking up from dirty old men, some change, french fries, and gonorrhea. An avant-garde film setting, where dirty laundry poisons the trees and all the lettuce patches drip with urine on Saturday nights.]

On this landscape of squalid misery, Doctor Bardamu is a figure little better than some of his patients. Poor and ill, he is called in because his fee, when he gets it, is lower than that of the other doctors in the area. Most of his cases are of a gynecological nature, and there is little he can do, or cares to do, to relieve them. Sex and alcohol are, as always, the principal diversions of Céline's poor. Only in one instance does he become truly involved in a medical problem, that of a child named Bébert who has contracted typhoid. Children possess a special innocence in that they have not yet acquired, though they probably will, the viciousness that for Céline characterizes the majority of adults: "Tant qu'il faut aimer quelque chose, on risque moins avec les enfants qu'avec les hommes, on a au moins l'excuse d'espérer qu'ils seront moins carnes que nous autres plus tard" [As long as you have to love something, you run less of a risk with children than with adults, you at least have the excuse to hope that later they will be less rotten than the rest of us] (p. 242). But Bardamu's efforts are as impotent in the case of Bébert's typhoid as they have been elsewhere, and the boy dies.

One day a familiar visitor appears in Bardamu's waiting room— Léon Robinson. Although Robinson is indeed suffering from a lung ailment, Bardamu cannot be sympathetic toward the renewal of his relationship with his old friend. Indeed, he is singularly distressed by the visit, for a resumption of their acquaintanceship poses the possibility that Bardamu may become infected with the "espèce de maladie" [kind of sickness] (p. 268) that Robinson is carrying. The illness in question is not medical but, rather, moral. Bardamu is aware, since their encounter in America, that Robinson is an embodiment of the misery that he—Bardamu—has been attempting to transcend. Robinson, an obvious link between the landscapes Bardamu has crossed in his quest for a better life, is thus a mirror of Bardamu's own failures. But Bardamu is also aware of the distance that now separates him from his alter ego. He perceives in Robinson's expressed desire for freedom, a freedom from care that only financial security can bring, that Robinson is willing to do anything that might alleviate his misery. For Robinson, morality and ethics are obfuscations that blind one to the realities of self-interest. Robinson, with his burden of resentments, misery, and petty hatreds, has made a pact with death; in his search for the satisfaction of his desires he has become both destructive and self-destructive. Bardamu fears that he will become contaminated by or implicated in this play of forces. Unable to rid himself of Robinson's presence, no longer desirous of following in Robinson's footsteps but still aware of the attraction of Robinson's destructive amorality, he will become a relatively passive witness to his friend's voyage to the end of the night.

     In frequenting Bardamu's office, Robinson has become friendly with an elderly bourgeois couple, the Henrouilles, whose dreary life has been spent pinching pennies in order to pay the mortgage on their house. They enlist Robinson's aid in ridding themselves of the troublesome presence of the husband's mother. Bardamu had already refused to help the couple put the still sprightly old woman in an old age home. Robinson, having no scruples whatsoever, has agreed to build a rabbit hutch whose door will be attached to a shotgun, a booby trap ostensibly placed to ward off thieves. The Henrouilles hope that when the mother opens the hutch to feed the rabbits the shotgun blast will kill her. They can then claim that the mother had been warned about the device, but senility had made her forget. Having made murder his vocation, Robinson has become a pitifully shrunken creature of the darkness: "Il se recroquevillait tellement dans le noir pour tousser sur lui-même que je ne le voyais presque plus si près de moi, ses mains seulement je voyais encore un peu, qui se rejoignaient doucement comme une grosse fleur blême devant sa bouche, dans la nuit à trembler" [He curled himself up so much in the darkness in order to cough that, as close as he was to me, I could hardly see him any more. Only I still saw a little bit of his hands, which were lightly clasped together, like a big pale flower, in front of his mouth, to tremble in the night] (p. 302). But Robinson's mediocrity prevents him from being a successful accomplice to murder. During the course of rigging the trap, the shotgun goes off, and Robinson is struck in the face and blinded.

Robinson's blindness is a form of darkness, and thus his accident can be linked to both the novel's title and to a broader thematic opposition between darkness and light. Having made one of the tenets of his "philosophy" the absence of illusions, Robinson's desire to "see clearly" (p. 383) has helped bring about his blindness. But now that his quest for freedom has temporarily come to a halt as he is submerged in his "noir tout à lui" [his very own darkness] (p. 323), he will experience no insight, no realization of the dangers of the path that he has taken. It is Bardamu, however, who, though more concerned with the attention that the accident might bring from the police than the crime itself, is enlightened by Robinson's example. He is reminded once again that Robinson has opted for complicity with death. Bardamu expresses his own position with a play on blindness and opening one's eyes: "Maintenant qu'il s'agissait d'ouvrir les yeux dans la nuit, j'aimais presque autant les garder fermés. Mais Robinson semblait tenir à ce que je les ouvrisse, à ce que je m'en rende compte" [Now that it was a matter of opening my eyes in the night, I'd have liked as much to keep them shut. But Robinson seemed to insist that I open them, that I become aware] (p. 310). Robinson is finally sent off to Toulouse, to continue his recuperation from the accident and to stifle any suspicions his accident might have provoked. But death lingers in his presence, in the form of the mummified bodies in the crypt of a church, a tourist attraction for which Robinson sells tickets. Ironically, Mère Henrouille, his intended victim, has been given the concession for the crypt, whose revenue supports her and Robinson.

Bardamu decides to pay his friend a visit, to make sure that the situation there is stable. In the course of his stay he, Robinson, and the latter's fiancée, Madelon, decide to spend a day seeing the countryside surrounding the city. During the outing Bardamu and Robinson make a last "journey," this time together. They—along with Madelon—are invited aboard a houseboat anchored on a river as a goodwill gesture by the boat's owner after his dog annoys Robinson.

Inventing an African experience to replace the miserable one he had endured, Robinson informs his well-to-do hosts that he had served as an agronomist for the Pordurière Company. As for Bardamu, he presents himself as a distinguished physician from Paris. Thus the two travelers transform their respective journeys into successes. In so doing, they have permitted themselves a moment of delirium, one that is consonant with sunshine, good food and drink, and agreeable company: "La vérité ne demande qu'à vous quitter. Il s'en faut toujours de très peu pour qu'elle vous libère. On n'y tient pas à sa vérité. Dans cette abondance soudaine d'agréments le bon délire mégalomane vous prend comme un rien" [The truth asks only to leave you. Very little is ever needed for it to liberate you. We don't value our truth very much. Amid this sudden abundance of amenities, a proper megalomaniacal delirium takes hold of you like nothing] (p. 396).

Such moments of self-delusion are, by necessity, short-lived. Robinson's "truth" awaits him in Toulouse. Two days later, just as Bardamu is preparing to take the train for Paris, someone calls to him from the street to come attend an accident victim. The old woman, Madame Henrouille, has fallen off the rickety stairway leading to the crypt. But Bardamu, suspecting that what has transpired is no accident, ignores the summons (and his Hippocratic oath) and departs from the city. As Robinson will later admit, it was he who pushed Madame Henrouille, causing the fatal accident. The crypt has symbolized the permanence of Robinson's pact with death. And it is in this land of the dead that he will finally succeed in killing his victim. The murder coincides with the return of Robinson's vision. So long as he remained blind, he was dependent upon the good will of others and helpless without it. But apparently the loss of his sight did not permit him to see clearly into the night that was enveloping him, and, ultimately, his blindness will serve only as an alibi for murder—at the time of the "accident" he was supposedly still blind. The recovery of his sight marks the renewal of his journey to the end of the night. His killing of Madame Henrouille has no profit motive—despite Robinson's financial gain from receiving her portion of the concession. Instead, the murder is occasioned by Robinson's disgust with seeing himself victimized by others: although the income from the crypt is small but sufficient, Robinson is disgusted by the payoffs he must make to church officials in order to keep the concession and he is equally revolted by Madelon's imperiousness. Madame Henrouille becomes the focus for this resentment, for it was her escape from the original murder plan that put Robinson in his present position. Thus Madame Henrouille's continuing existence became an obsession, and that presence filled Robinson's field of vision as a correlative of his blocked situation, "je ne voyais plus qu'elle" [I saw nothing but her] (p. 438).

After Bardamu decides to abandon his practice, he takes a position as the assistant to the director and owner of a private mental asylum, a

certain Doctor Baryton. I have already noted how asylums and hospitals
have been positively valorized in *Voyage* as a refuge from the insanity and
sickness of the so-called real world. Insanity, as the narrator has already
suggested, is the "limit" of delirium; that is to say, it constitutes the farthest
advance one can make beyond those relatively minor delusions one may
entertain as a means of mitigating the horrors of everyday existence. But
Bardamu, as will all his future incarnations, opts ultimately for lucidity—the
lucidity that emerges from experience and observation. The final destination of these perceptions lies in their transposition in the form of the novels
in which they are depicted. Even Molly with her good nature and her magnificent dancer's body was unable to keep Bardamu from pursuing this
mission.

We can recall that Bardamu was himself a patient in a mental
hospital, after his breakdown at the shooting gallery in the Bois de
Boulogne. Now that he has become a resident physician, he must resist
the temptation to share the world of the patients, to yield to the "vertigo"
(p. 417) that draws him into the dreamlike existence of those whom Beckett
called the "microcosmopolitans." Indeed, Bardamu wonders how far he
might penetrate into that realm and still be able to return to reality. The
world of the insane, its dangers and temptations, is depicted as an ill-
defined region of blurred outlines, soft structures, quicksand-like terrain,
just the opposite of what Bardamu discovered in New York. It is a
landscape where identities and categories tend to dissolve into a comforting
amorphousness:

> Je me tenais au bord dangereux des fous, à leur lisière pour ainsi dire, à
> force d'être toujours aimable avec eux, ma nature. Je ne chavirais pas
> mais tout le temps, je me sentais en péril, comme s'ils m'eussent attiré
> sournoisement dans les quartiers de leur ville inconnue. Une ville dont
> les rues devenaient de plus en plus molles à mesure qu'on avançait entre
> leurs maisons baveuses, les fenêtres fondantes et mal closes, sur ces
> douteuses rumeurs. Les portes, le sol mouvant . . . L'envie vous prend
> quand même d'aller un peu plus loin pour savoir si on aura la force de
> retrouver sa raison, quand même, parmi les décombres. Ça tourne vite
> au vice la raison, comme la bonne humeur et le sommeil chez les
> neurasthéniques. On ne peut plus penser qu'à sa raison. Rien ne va
> plus. Fini de rigoler. (p. 417)

[I held myself on the perilous edge of the insane at their border, so to speak, by virtue of always being agreeable with them, my nature. I did not go over the edge, but I always felt myself in danger, as if they had cleverly drawn me into the districts of their unknown city, a city whose streets become increasingly softer as you advanced between their runny houses, their windows melting and poorly closed to doubtful noises. The doors, the shifting ground . . . But you feel a longing nonetheless to go a little farther so that you'll know whether you're strong enough to return to reason, nonetheless, among the ruins. Reason quickly turns to vice, like good humor and sleep among neurasthenics. It's all over, the fun is ended.]

Bardamu encounters another soft landscape at the asylum, a living one in the form of a desirable attendant named Sophie, who serves as an occasional lover. Bardamu, the student of anatomy, is astounded by the "elasticity" (p. 463) and "suppleness" (p. 464) of her body, by her "aerial grace" and "precision" (p. 464), by the nervous energy that vibrates through her. Although Sophie is not a dancer, she partakes of those physical qualities that distinguish the dancer and which Bardamu so admired in Molly. But this is a different Bardamu from the one who was tempted to settle down with his purehearted prostitute. Sophie's feline grace projects a health and an optimism that "trouble" (p. 463) him, for they are not consonant with his more pessimistic view of the human condition that sees the body as flaccid, corrupted, invaded by the canker of time. In short, he must somehow demonstrate that Sophie is no different from himself, from all the others, that she, as Michel Beaujour has noted, is "organic matter that is in the process of decomposition."[12] He fulfills his desire to "humanize" (p. 463) her by stealing into her room while she is asleep and observing her. He discovers what he had set out to find—that the relaxation afforded by sleep causes Sophie's body to become a mass of amorphous flesh, no different from any other, flesh that in its limpness already anticipates the decay to which it must inevitably succumb:

C'était alors un tout autre spectacle Sophie, familier celui-là et tout de même surprenant, rassurant aussi. Sans parade, presque pas de couvertures, à travers du lit, cuisses en bataille, chairs moites et dépliées, elle s'expliquait avec la fatigue . . . (p. 463)

[It was a very different sight Sophie presented, familiar this one, nevertheless surprising, reassuring too. Without display, almost no blankets, crosswise on the bed, thighs askew, moist and unfolded flesh, she was having it out with fatigue.]

In the course of his relationship with Sophie, Bardamu tells her about his friend Robinson and, in particular, about his encounter with Madelon, the fiancée Robinson acquired in Toulouse. Shortly after the death of Madame Henrouille, Robinson had left Toulouse and the relatively good life it promised with the prospect of marrying Madelon and managing the concession to the mummy crypt. As we might expect, Robinson turns up at the asylum and asks Bardamu to help him find a job. Bardamu finds work for him in the asylum but begins to grow uneasy about Robinson's presence when he perceives Madelon in the vicinity. He fears that a quarrel between the two might lead Madelon to denounce Robinson to the police as a murderer and thereby implicate Bardamu, who has learned from his friend how Madame Henrouille was pushed to her death. Bardamu's attempt to "hide" Robinson by finding another job for him proves fruitless, and he must finally confront Madelon in person. When he tells her to stay away from Robinson, she appears to mock his words and, yielding to impulse, he slaps her. Madelon and Robinson are subsequently seen together on several occasions, and when Sophie suggests that Bardamu might as well make the best of the situation and finds a means of reconciliation with Madelon, he proposes that the four of them spend an evening together at a local carnival.

However, the carnival fails to function for them as it does for others—as a means of temporary escape from the problems of life, as a form of delirium.[13] The disintegration of the carnival atmosphere is precipitated by Madelon's discovery of a maggot in one of the chestnuts she is eating. Her anger at having discovered it and Robinson's displeasure at watching her spit it out brings the animosity between them to the surface. The maggot is, of course, symbolic. Bardamu had already referred to man as a sack of maggots, and this time it is Robinson who becomes the vehicle for a vision of man's impotence and depravity. His journey, he states, has taken him too far to be saved by Madelon's love, a love that is itself a form of delirium in that it hides the ugly absurdity of existence. Existence, Robinson tells her, is something that he can no longer swallow, no matter how "palatable" one tries to make it:

Tu veux en bouffer de la viande pourrie? Avec ta sauce à la ten-
dresse? . . . Ça passe alors? . . . Pas à moi! . . . Si tu sens rien tant
mieux pour toi! C'est que tu as le nez bouché! Faut être abrutis
comme vous l'êtes tous pour pas que ça vous dégoûte . . . Tu cherches
à savoir ce qu'il y a entre toi et moi? . . . Eh bien entre toi et moi, y a
toute la vie . . . (p. 483)
[Do you mind eating rotten meat? With your tenderness sauce? Does it
help it go down? Not for me. If you don't smell anything so much the
better for you! Your nose must be blocked up! You've got to be a
numbskull like you all are for it not to disgust you . . . You want to
know what there is between us? . . . I'll tell you, between us there's all
of life . . .]

Robinson's disgust with life can only be resolved by death, which offers no
solution but at least terminates the voyage that Robinson has undertaken.
Having pushed Madelon to the breaking point, Robinson has, in a sense,
elected to commit suicide, though of course he would lack the courage and
skill to take his own life. And as if to answer Robinson's outburst about
the indigestibility of existence, Madelon shoots her fiancée in the stomach.
She then jumps from the taxi in which they have been riding and disappears
into the night, that same night that has now become Robinson's eternity.
As Robinson lies dying, at peace at last, he seems to radiate an "espèce de
calme" [a kind of calm] (p. 485).

Paradoxically, perhaps, Robinson's death permits him to once more
resume his role as guide: this time not as a moral and ethical misfit, but as
an example of human limits, and, more specifically, as a reminder to
Bardamu of the limits of his own journey, both spiritual and geographic.
Bardamu is left to make the best of a situation that promises no amelioration
as it permits no self-deception. Robinson has come "home" from his "pays
atroce" [horrible country] (p. 487); Bardamu is left behind to ponder and
then to describe the nature of its landscape:

Là-bas tout au loin, c'était la mer. Mais j'avais plus rien à imaginer
moi sur elle la mer à présent. J'avais autre chose à faire. J'avais beau
essayer de me perdre pour ne plus me retrouver devant ma vie, je la
retrouvais simplement. Je revenais sur moi-même. Mon trimbalage à
moi, il était bien fini. A d'autres! . . . Le monde était refermé! Au
bout qu'on était arrivés nous autres! . . . (p. 489)

[Over there, far in the distance, lay the sea. But now I had nothing left to imagine about the sea. I had something else to do. I had tried in vain to lose myself so as not to find myself face to face with my life, I kept finding it again. I kept coming back to myself. My wandering was over. Let others carry on! . . . The world had closed me in! The rest of us had come to the end! . . .]

The conclusion of the novel images Bardamu's admission that his days of wandering are over and he must now confront, where he is, the debris of his life. He perceives, receding in the distance, a tugboat pulling a barge down the nearby canal. The sound of its whistle, experienced by Bardamu as a call to further voyages with their seeming possibility of a new and better life, only serves to remind him that such prospects are but a form of self-delusion.

De loin, le remorqueur a sifflé; son appel a passé le pont, encore une arche, une autre, l'écluse, un autre pont, loin, plus loin . . . Il appelait vers lui toutes les péniches du fleuve toutes, et la ville entière, et le ciel et la campagne, et nous, tout qu'il emmenait, la Seine aussi, tout, qu'on n'en parle plus. (p. 493)

[In the distance the tugboat sounded its whistle; its call passed one bridge, another arch, yet another, the lock, another bridge, far away, still farther . . . It called toward it all the barges on the river, all, and the entire city, and the sky and the countryside, and us, everything it was leading away, the Seine too, everything, let us speak no more about it.]

3
A Legendary Childhood: *Mort à crédit*

IN *MORT À CRÉDIT,* HIS SECOND NOVEL, Céline adopts a set of
"opening signals" that, save for the two volumes of *Guignol's Band,* he
will employ, with some minor variations, in all of his subsequent novels.
Delirium will be the instrument by which the onset of the narrative is
effected, a movement from present to past, from narrator-protagonist to
protagonist-tending-toward-narrator, from "reality" to fiction in the form of
the past recalled through re-creation. In the case of *Mort à crédit,* it is
Bardamu's youth—Bardamu who now bears the name Ferdinand—that will
be depicted.

The text begins on a note of melancholy and isolation. The narrator
relates that the concierge of his building has just died—an elderly woman
who lived alone. Her death causes the narrator to meditate upon his own
situation; he too is alone, growing old (perhaps prematurely so), and facing
a not-too-distant death. He is isolated in his room, a room that can readily
be interpreted as a metaphor of the mind, for its space is filled with memories of past encounters, memories that are as fragmented, as dispersed in
time and space as the people and events that occasioned them. His present
circumstances and the languages used to describe them have a distinctly
Beckettian flavor:

> Nous voici encore seuls. Tout cela est si lent, si lourd, si triste . . .
> Bientôt je serai vieux. Et ce sera enfin fini. Il est venu tant de monde
> dans ma chambre. Ils ont dit des choses. Ils ne m'ont pas dit grand'
> chose. Ils sont partis. Ils sont devenus vieux, misérables et lents
> chacun dans un coin du monde. (p. 501)

> [Here we are still alone. All that is so slow, so heavy, so sad . . .
> Soon I will be old. And it will finally be over. So many people have

come into my room. They told me things. They didn't tell me very
much. They've departed. They've become old, miserable, and slow,
each in his own corner of the world.]

This "we" refers both to those people the narrator has encountered and to
the various selves of the narrator, scattered in time and space. We can
anticipate here the "play" that will take place between the older narrator and
the narrator as young hero. The latter's apprenticeship of life will inform
the narrator's tale. And, as Charles Krance has indicated, the "ce" of "ce
sera enfin fini" links the survival of the narrator—"biographical time" with
his narrative "autobiographical time"—as it articulates the relationship
between living and writing.[1] The narrator survives so that he may tell all.
And he has already identified himself as the author of *Voyage* as well as that
of *Le Roi Krogold,* a tale of war and vengeance and lust set in the Middle
Ages, portions of which will appear in *Mort à crédit.*

The stage is set for a return by the narrator to his past when he
recalls that two days before the death of the concierge, he had decided to
pay a visit to Gustin, his cousin and a fellow doctor. This visit serves as an
occasion for the narrator to juxtapose the practice of medicine with the
writing of literature. Writing is depicted in part as a compensatory activity,
a means of escaping from the unending struggle against alcoholism and
venereal disease that characterizes the doctor's lot in the Parisian *zone.*

But there is another reason, besides an escape from the difficulties
of practicing medicine, that engages Ferdinand in the activity of writing—
the after-effects of the head wound he suffered in the war. He informs us
that his inability to sleep, resulting from a buzzing in his ears, has led him to
take up writing. "Si j'avais bien dormi toujours, je n'aurais jamais écrit
une ligne" [If I had always slept well, I would have never written a line]
(p. 505). Bardamu, we may remember, had been trepanned, and Céline
claimed to have undergone the same procedure as a result of his own injuries in World War I. We know that Céline himself had not been trepanned.
Whatever may have been the true extent of his injuries, the head wound will
reappear in one way or another in all of Céline's novels. Why should Ferdinand's head wound, manifesting itself, variously, in the form of buzzing,
internal orchestra, delirium, hallucinations (often associated with recurrent
attacks of the malaria Ferdinand contracted in Africa) be connected with
writing? We can mention several possible links at this point. The wound
serves as a self-conscious transitional device by which the narrator shifts

from present to past in order to capture memories resurrected by delirium; hallucinatory visions initiate a re-creation of experience, yielding deeper insights into reality; recalling the opening of the skull—trepanation—the narration constitutes an emptying of the skull's contents, the "spontaneity" of delirium becoming a mask for meticulous craftsmanship as Céline's manuscripts indicate; lastly, writing, seemingly an "accidental" and "irrational" activity—as opposed to medicine—is revealed to be a necessary concomitant of Ferdinand's personality.

We noted that the narrator was the author of two very different kinds of texts: the contemporary concerns of *Voyage* as opposed to what Allen Thiher has called the "heroic poetry" of *Le Roi Krogold*.[2] The discussion that he holds with his cousin as to what sort of literature he should be writing is not based exclusively upon aesthetic concerns but anticipates the future association of the narrator-author's position in society with the sort of writing he will practice. "Tu pourrais raconter des choses agréables" [You could relate agreeable things] Gustin tells him (p. 502), but he falls asleep when portions of *Krogold* are read to him. It is clear that the direction taken with *Voyage* will be pursued, that such writing is perceived as more relevant to the human condition than *Krogold,* whatever the latter's merits may be as a historical fiction. The price to be paid for the narrator's commitment to writing a novel like *Mort à crédit,* and those novels that will follow it, will be the opprobrium that he will incur. In an image that recalls the dispersion of people, places, and events of which the narrator was the locus in his room-mind—a dispersion which is opposed by memory—the narrator now sees himself as a target: "J'en raconterai de telles [histoires] qu'ils reviendront exprès, pour me tuer, des quatre coins du monde" [I will tell such (stories) that they will return to kill me, from the four corners of the globe] (p. 502). This "ils," one can be certain, does not refer to specific individuals, who might be mentioned in future works, but doubtless refers to those other companions scattered in time and space—the readers of Céline's fiction, writings whose insights and style will shatter comfortable assumptions and thereby arouse hatred. The fictions that distort and mutilate the protagonist and narrator will serve the same function for the reader: "Hypocritical reader," Baudelaire wrote in the introductory poem to *Les Fleurs du mal,* "my fellow-man, my brother." The prophecy uttered by the narrator-author will, of course, be best realized in the case of Céline himself, in the confusing of his literary works with his anti-Semitic pamphlets and articles in the collaborationist press.

Having chosen the sort of literature to which he will commit himself, the narrator changes the subject of his conversation to a topic seemingly unrelated to writing. Ferdinand recounts that Mireille, the niece of the woman who types his manuscripts, has jeopardized his job at the clinic where he works by spreading stories about his supposedly disreputable character—such as his arranging orgies with his patients. In order to put an end to this malicious gossip, Ferdinand decides to take this splendidly endowed but apparently perverse girl for a stroll in the Bois de Boulogne in order to persuade her to desist from recounting stories about him. Attempts to amuse her by reciting portions of *Le Roi Krogold* fail; and slaps and threats seem to have no effect. Mireille is primarily interested in discussing lesbianism and surprising couples making love in the Bois— which is teeming with them. Ferdinand slaps her around once again, and she runs off crying.

While chasing her, Ferdinand undergoes hallucinations, later ascribed to the malaria he contracted in Africa and to troubles emanating from his head wound. Ferdinand's "visions"—however they are triggered— reflect the sexually charged atmosphere of the Bois, reinforced by Mireille's conversation. The couples making love become increasingly numerous. They, Ferdinand, and Mireille converge at the Arc de Triomphe, where Mireille's clothes fly off, and an Englishwoman encountered along the way bites her in the breast, sending up a fountain of blood. Finally, the flame at the Tomb of the Unknown Soldier becomes a gigantic pyre, covering everyone with fire. Flames are stuffed under clothes as the couples fall asleep one upon the other. Ferdinand wakes up in bed, attended by his mother.

One need not dwell very long on the sexual aspects of this hallucinatory landscape: the orgiastic mingling of bodies, the violent lesbian action of the Englishwoman, the pursuit of Mireille, the fires of lust as well as those of fever. We may recall that in *Voyage* the convergence of fire and fever served as a transitional device by means of which the passage from Africa to America was effected. Here too we have a passage: a break with the narrator's present and a return to the room which, as we saw earlier, was populated with the ghosts of the past and in which the narrator's principal activity was writing. The passage in question will, of course, be a narrative. It will also be a voyage into the past, one that will take the narrator back to the *passage* de Bérésinas, the arcade where he grew up. That his mother should be present at his bedside when he awakens adumbrates the direction that his journey will take.

While he is in bed, Ferdinand's delirium continues. The noises he hears in his head are, as usual, described as music, an internal orchestra. "Ma grande rivale" [my great rival], Ferdinand remarks, "C'est la musique" [is music] (p. 525). The mention of music in a text so conscious of its own elaboration immediately suggests to the reader that the narrative to be generated from this delirium will have its own specific musicality. This transition from internal to external music is emphasized by the other "noises" Ferdinand hears—not his own but those of a student above him practicing his piano playing. Both the student and the narrator are undergoing an apprenticeship. However, whereas the student plays another's composition, the narrator will create his own music, his own "opéra du déluge" (p. 526).

Although the narrator had clearly distinguished between the two modes of writing in which he had been engaged—the "escapism" of *Krogold* as opposed to the "realism" of *Voyage*—these alternatives reappear. Recalling segments of *Krogold,* he begins to masturbate to them, using them to shape a world of satisfied desire. But he soon abandons this evasion in order to undertake a more perilous journey—a fictional voyage into his own past as announced by the image of a ship. At first he sees in his hallucinatory visions a large sailboat filled with the dead. That one ship is then transformed into a multitude of smaller vessels, each filled with a dead person, each containing a story to be told by the narrator. The centrifugal image of scattered memories that we examined earlier has now been replaced by a centripetal image. The narrator's memory has been stimulated by the experience he has just undergone. The mother berates her wayward son, and he answers her by vomiting on her crippled leg. The nature of his response reveals a continuing revolt against the childhood he led—or was forced to lead. Juxtaposing *dégueuler* [puke] with *gueuler* [scream], we can anticipate the violence of the language with which the narrator will describe his past and perhaps interpret such a telling as a form of self-purgation. With the words announcing his birth, his rebirth in the fiction he is about to relate, "le siècle dernier je peux en parler, je l'ai vu finir" [the last century, I can speak about it, I saw it end] (p. 533), the recounting of the narrator's childhood begins.

Although born in a small town on the outskirts of Paris, Ferdinand grows up in Paris itself, in the Passage des Bérésinas. As I noted in my "biographical introduction," this sort of *passage* (the type can still be seen) is a covered street, usually quite narrow, lined with shops and enclosed by gates at both ends. This particular one is, typically for the period, protected by a thick glass awning that protrudes from above the shops. The latter occupy the ground floor of the buildings in which they are located and above them there are apartments, often inhabited by the shop owners, and frequently linked by a stairway to the stores below.

Ferdinand's mother, Clémence, owns a shop in which old lace is sold and repaired and an occasional piece of antique furniture sold as well. Although Ferdinand's father Auguste helps Clémence with running errands and an occasional furniture delivery, his principal occupation is that of a secretary-copyist—he is an educated man—in an insurance company. The store occupies the ground floor and the family lives on the two floors above—all three floors being linked by a narrow spiral staircase.

Life in the Passage recalls the underground lavatory in New York that was described in *Voyage*. On the street level, under the glass canopy, the occupants lead almost an underground existence, imprisoned within the narrow confines of a space filled with the asphyxiating odor of gas lamps and the smells and sight of dog excretia and human expectoration. The Passage is termed a "genre d'égout" [a kind of sewer] (p. 561), from which the only escape becomes an occasional trip to the country in the company of Uncle Edouard, Clémence's brother. Although Ferdinand will later fear and detest Nature, in *Mort à crédit* the traditional opposition between the nefarious life of the city and the simpler, more salubrious life of the country will be maintained.

Physical asphyxiation outside finds its correlative in the familial suffocation within the store and apartment. Ferdinand's mother, dragging her crippled leg from one end of the shop to another and from floor to floor in the narrow stairway, is the paragon of the scrupulously honest bourgeois shopkeeper, convinced that hard work will permit her eventually to succeed in a world that no longer values the quality of handmade lace. Her martyrdom to the work ethic carries over to the raising of her son. She attempts at all costs to make him submit to a code of petit bourgeois conformity: education, proper dress, cleanliness, a modest job with a secure future. Even more intolerable for Ferdinand is his relationship with Auguste. The latter, trapped in a position whose responsibilities and salary are not commensurate with his education or expectations, is a man of violent rages, particularly as concerns his son. He becomes convinced that Ferdinand is not only incapable of maintaining the family's sense of bourgeois respectability but is a worthless shirker, bent upon ruining his parents financially and morally.

Confined within the narrow limits of the apartment, Auguste's fury becomes even more explosive; as he vents his rage he bounces from wall to wall, from object to object, demolishing the fragile order of the household. The magnification of the damages he causes leaves no doubt in the reader's mind as to the comic element present in the narrator's portrayal of this inept figure: "Il plonge dans le buffet . . . Il rebondit dans la crédence. . . . Tout le bazar nous flanche sur la gueule . . . Toute la vaisselle, les instruments, le lampadaire . . . C'est une cascade . . . une avalanche" [He dives into the sideboard . . . He rebounds into the buffet. . . . The whole business comes down on our heads . . . All the dishes, the silverware, the lamp . . . It's a cascade . . . an avalanche] (p. 685).

His father's anger does, as we have just seen, take the form of physical violence. But more frequently, Auguste's rage expresses itself in a purely verbal manner—long chains of curses, threats, imprecations, as for example:

> Bordel de Bon Dieu de saloperie! Qu'avons-nous fait ma pauvre enfant pour engendrer une telle vermine? pervertie comme trente-six potences! . . . Roué! Canaille! Fainéant! Tout! Il est tout calamité! Bon à rien! Qu'à nous piller! Nous rançonner! Une infection! (p. 804)

> [Good God, what crap! My poor dear, what did we do to produce such vermin? He's as corrupt as three dozen gallow-birds! . . . Profligate! Scoundrel! Idler! You name it! He's calamity in the flesh! Good for nothing! Except to clean us out! To fleece us! A plague!]

These verbal explosions serve to silence Ferdinand and, eventually, will cause him to reject language. They serve as well to inform the narration, for the narrator's verbal energy can be seen as an inheritance of his father's outbursts. But Auguste's anger is not always properly vented. At times, neither willing nor able to express himself spontaneously, Auguste attempts to contain his rage, causing him, in Ferdinand's eyes at least, to swell up like a balloon that is ready to take flight—"il se serait envolé, tellement il était sursoufflé" [he would've taken off, he was so overinflated] (p. 674). If the pressure is suddenly released, Auguste ricochets around the room, as might a balloon whose air was suddenly expelled. On the other hand, farting is the sign of a more gradual decrease of pressure. These images of Auguste as a balloon are indeed comical. But they have another purpose as well, for they foreshadow the activities of Ferdinand's substitute

father, Courtial des Pereires, editor of a journal for inventors, inventor
himself, prolific author of do-it-yourself manuals and self-study books on a
vast variety of topics. Courtial too, as we shall see, is possessed of an
overabundance of verbal energy. He is also a balloonist.

Clémence's store is a "musée sale" [dirty museum] (p. 543) with its
piles of old lace and antique furniture. It is the supply of lace that
constitutes the principal merchandise of the family business, and wherever
one turns, one finds still more piles of lace. The space of the store mingles
with that of the apartment as parts of the latter are used as storage space.
The disorder of the objects in question is a reflection of the disorder of the
life of the family and of human existence in general We may recall, insofar
as the latter is concerned, the image in *Voyage* of the individual struggling
to maintain a coherent self as the molecules of which he is made tend to
become random and fly off into the surrounding space. Clémence continues
to increase her filthy, ill-smelling stock hoping that the changing tastes of
fashion will once more make handmade lace attractive. But these hopes are
futile, for such luxury items belong to a world that is unraveling, so to
speak, as Clémence struggles to maintain it. And the more she struggles to
succeed, and thereby create more order, financial and otherwise, in the
family, the more disorder she establishes. The end of handmade items and
the small stores that sell them is not far off, as Clémence herself can see.
Department stores are in the ascendancy, and they sell machine-made
goods. Their clientele possesses no "estime pour les choses du fin travail,
pour les ouvrages tout à la main . . . Plus que des engouements dépravés
pour les saloperies mécaniques" [no consideration for fine workmanship,
for goods made entirely by hand . . . Nothing but depraved infatuation with
machine-made crap] (p. 760). Despite her infirm leg, Clémence will
eventually be forced to sell her shop and work as a door-to-door saleswoman for one of the very department stores that have put her out of
business.

August finds himself in circumstances that are analogous to his
wife's. Although an educated man and a dutiful employee, Auguste's
bosses—for reasons that are not explained—constantly subject him to indignities. The worst insult they can hurl at him is that he is a "calligrapher"
(p. 764), that is to say a man whose only skill—that of being an excellent
penman—is no longer relevant to the needs of the marketplace. When a
vacancy arises at a rival insurance company, Auguste decides to apply for
the job. However, his candidacy depends upon his being able to type. He

bangs away night after night on a rented machine but fails to master this new technology. The *galerie des machines* that had frightened Auguste by its noise and movement during a family visit to the International Exposition was the harbinger of an age in which a man such as Auguste would be an anachronism on the job market.[3] As is the case with Clémence, Auguste's struggle against disorder leads only to more disorder. Fear of losing his job and rage at his own incompetence will gradually transform Auguste into a sick man, both physically and mentally. An eruption of boils will be an external manifestation of the changes taking place within him. He reaches a point where he can no longer distinguish between the real and the imaginary, and it is only with Clémence's aid that he is able to continue working. Insanity would be the ultimate escape from the pressures to which Auguste is being subjected; it lies at the further limit of the delirium that affords a temporary escape from existence or, in the case of the narrator, that permits a deeper insight into the nature of reality. "Pour se défendre contre la vie faudrait des digues dix fois plus hautes qu'au Panama" [In order to defend yourself against life you need dikes ten times higher than those of Panama] (p. 519), the narrator had remarked. Insanity is just such a dike, but Auguste hovers on its edge, trapped by pride and poverty just outside its protection.

The values which Ferdinand's parents attempt to live by and inculcate into their son are, as we have seen, unable to shield the family against the disorder from within and the disorder from without. Indeed, the awning that presumably protects the Passage appears to function as a magnifying glass, enlarging their problems. If Ferdinand is to escape the Passage, if the Passage is to point the way out from asphyxiation and disorder, then Ferdinand, faithful to the precepts of his parents, must find himself a job. But conditions outside the Passage will be such that he will constantly find himself returning to it—because he loses the few jobs he is able to find and because he discovers in those spaces outside the Passage many of the same attributes he found within it.

Ferdinand becomes the locus for the interplay between order and disorder. He becomes the means by which the disorder lurking behind the superficial appearances of order will be made manifest. Before he begins to look for a job—a job that will be, in fact, nothing more than an apprenticeship in one trade or another, as arranged by his mother—Ferdinand must be properly attired. As André Smith remarks, throughout the novel Ferdinand will have a problem with clothes—he grows out of them or tears them so

that they become unwearable. They fit him as poorly as he fits the positions
his mother finds for him.[4] As we might expect, the clothes that his mother
purchases for him are bought with the intent that they should last indefinitely. They they are heavy, armorlike outfits which, along with the requisite tight celluloid collar, constitute a kind of portable prison. The shoes he
is forced to wear are so constricting that he removes them whenever he can
in order to relieve the pain they cause. His "wounded" feet link him to his
crippled mother; he is hobbled by the existence she has chosen for him.

Ferdinand's first job is with the firm of Monsieur Berlope, a seller
of ribbons and trimmings. He is employed as a stockboy, responsible for
bringing samples of goods to the salesmen. In order to find those samples,
Ferdinand must sort through several floors of merchandise which exist in
the same sort of confusion and disorder that typified his mother's shop.
There is a constant danger of an avalanche, of goods spilling down upon the
stockboys. Moreover, he works within a space that is essentially vertical in
nature, as is his parents' store-apartment, with articles stockpiled on several
levels. Like Clémence dragging herself wearily up and down the stairs of
the apartment, Ferdinand is forced to go up and down constantly with his
aching feet in order to fulfill the salesmen's needs. And like the tapping
made by Clémence's crippled leg, more an object than a living part of her
body, Ferdinand's ill-fitting shoes cause him to make a similarly disagree-
able sound as he goes about his job. The disturbance draws a reprimand
from his supervisor:

> Il a encore trouvé à redire de mes grolles, que je faisais avec trop de
> bruit dans les escaliers. Je talonnais un peu c'est exact, le bout me
> faisait un mal terrible surtout arrivé sur le soir, ils devenaient comme
> des vrais tisons. (p. 626)

> [He even complained about my clodhoppers, that I made too much
> noise on the stairs. It was true that I tended to walk on my heels, my
> toes hurt me something awful, especially toward evening, they felt just
> like hot coals.]

Having brought an element of discord into the store, Ferdinand is
confronted with the resultant oppression—a situation analogous to the one
he finds at home when Auguste becomes ever more enraged with a son who
does not fit into the established mold. Ferdinand's oppressor at Berlope
and Company is Monsieur Lavelongue ('Longwash'), who decides to keep

a close watch over the young apprentice in the hope of finding a pretext for firing him. He succeeds when he spies Ferdinand telling stories to a fellow stockboy and concludes that Ferdinand is impairing the boy's morals. In fact, Ferdinand is simply amusing his companion with stories he had memorized from popular magazines about *King Krogold*. Not only do such stories provide an escape from time and space in the form of a historical fiction replete with castles, cathedrals, and body-strewn battlefields, but they also present a world in which order is established unambiguously by the cross and the sword.

Finding another job for Ferdinand is no easy matter. Once again he must be properly outfitted, despite Auguste's protests that money thus spent is money wasted. This time Ferdinand's mother attempts to find a position for him in the jewelry trade. The Paris they explore in search of a job is a space that is essentially vertical in nature, a space traversed through a movement up and down stairs that recalls Ferdinand's job at Berlope and Company as well as Clémence's activities in the family apartment: "Tout ce parage-là [the Marais, among other *quartiers*] on peut le dire, on l'a dépiauté par étages" [Believe me, we covered that whole neighborhood, floor by floor] (p. 642). The little, cell-like workshops they enter recall the businesses in the Passage with their clutter of unsalable merchandise and their mingling of business and family life.

It is Uncle Edouard who finally finds a job for Ferdinand. Edouard is just the opposite of Ferdinand. He has the self-assurance that Ferdinand lacks and is also an inventor and a successful businessman. Here, as throughout the novel, Edouard will be a sort of *deus ex machina,* saving Ferdinand from impossible situations, mending rifts with his family, never scolding the adolescent, always believing in giving him yet another chance. His saving Ferdinand each time the boy appears "bogged down" in another set of intractable circumstances gives the narration a forward, metonymic impulse, thus assuring the continuing apprenticeship of the hero an apprenticeship that will not only introduce him to a trade but, more important, one that will initiate him into the injustice, despair, and disorder of existence in general.

When Ferdinand arrives at his next place of employment, the shop of the jewelrymaker Gorloge, he finds himself in familiar circumstances. Like Ferdinand's parents, Gorloge and his wife occupy an apartment in which living quarters and workshop are combined. Ferdinand sees them eating noodles—a frequent item in the menu of Ferdinand's family.

Gorloge's specialty, chiseled jewelry, like Clémence's lace, is a product that has gone out of style. And like Clémence's stock, Gorloge's collection consists of a confused mass of ugly, outmoded, unsalable items:

> Toute la formation terrible des épouvantails . . . L'insomnie d'un monde entier . . . Toute la furie d'un asile en colifichets . . . J'allais du tarte à l'atroce . . . Même au magasin de Grand'mère, rue Montorgueil, les rossignols les plus rances, c'était de la rose à côté . . . . (p. 648)

> [The stuff that nightmares are made of . . . The insomnia of the whole world . . . The manias of an insane asylum in the form of trinkets . . . I was going from the insipid to the atrocious . . . Even in my Grand-mother's shop on the rue Montorgueil, the most putrid white elephants were beauties by comparison . . .]

And once again Ferdinand's forced submission to his mother's system of values is revealed by his performance on the job. This time the link between mother and son is manifested by the large tray of jewelry, supported by a strap around his neck, that Ferdinand will trundle from shop to shop in search of a buyer. His mother will carry a similar tray, piled with lace, when she attempts to reduce her stock by selling door to door in the country, during one of the family's so-called vacations, and, later, after her shop has failed, when she becomes a saleswoman, selling machine-made lace for one of the department stores. Moreover, the potential buyers that Ferdinand visits resemble his mother—entombed in their dying commerce like so many mummies:

> Ils avaient aussi modèles . . . presque identiques, assez pour se faire mille cercueils et d'autres colliers mythologiques. . . . Ils en avaient jusqu'aux épaules . . . Ils disparaissaient, ils devenaient déjà égyptiens. (p. 650)

> [They also had their models . . . almost identical, enough to make themselves a thousand coffins and many more mythological collars. . . . They were shoulder-deep in the stuff . . . They were disappearing, they were already becoming Egyptians.]

Voyeurism becomes a means for Ferdinand of escaping the tedium of his job, and of acquiring further knowledge. And one can add that this voyeurism points toward the protagonist-turned-narrator who, in peering into other lives in the course of his narration, must, perforce, also be a voyeur of sorts.[5] What Ferdinand sees through a hole in the wall of the Gorloge bedroom is the disorder of his employer's marriage as Madame Gorloge and Antoine, the atelier's foreman, take advantage of Gorloge's absence for military service. So long as Ferdinand remains outside the bedroom, glued to his spy-hole, he can remain a disinterested spectator of the Breughelian comedy taking place within. There the gargantuan Madame Gorloge and her lover indulge in a comedy of uninhibited sexuality, falling over one another and dragging the various objects in the room with them. But this elephantine coupling, comical though it may appear, has a more serious, threatening aspect. Having participated vicariously in the spectacle, Ferdinand will soon become one of the players, for, unknown to him, his spying has been arranged by Madame Gorloge. And once he enters the room, seduced by the colossal temptress, he will participate in a disorder far more serious in its consequences than what took place at the Berlope Company.

Madame Gorloge is the first of Céline's dominant women, an overpowering creature more monster than human: she has huge breasts, a "furnace" for a vagina, "des cuisses comme des monuments, des énormes piliers et puis alors du poil au cul, tellement que ça remontait la fourrure, ça lui recouvrait tout le nombril" [thighs like monuments, enormous pillars with hair even on her ass, her bush was so overgrown that it even covered her navel] (p. 669). Ferdinand's sexual initiation is less a seduction than an assault in which he is devoured by the enormous woman after she invites him into her room and locks the door.

Ferdinand's experience is not simply a transition into manhood but also, recalling *Voyage,* a passage that ultimately assumes the form of a journey, the first of many that Ferdinand will eventually take. His sexual encounter with Madame Gorloge is in fact part of an elaborate plot to steal an expensive ring that had been made up for a client and entrusted to Ferdinand for safekeeping. The ring is hidden inside Ferdinand's pants. After Ferdinand removes his clothes, Madame Gorloge steals the ring. As a result of this escapade, in which he becomes the patsy, he is precipitated back into the confusion of his parents' household, to confront the rage of his father. He is finally rescued by his uncle Edouard, who convinces his parents that a stay in England will remove him from the temptations of Paris, and the acquisition of English will make him a more attractive job applicant. This is the first of the voyages Ferdinand undertakes in search of a better life, though in fact this is not his first trip to England. Before examining in detail Ferdinand's change in landscape we need to note briefly the nature of that earlier voyage. But in order to approach that subject we must first examine the role of the ship in *Mort à crédit,* for it is here, rather than in *Voyage,* that we discover the first elaboration of this fundamental theme in Céline's writings.

As I noted in my study of the "opening signals" in *Mort à crédit,* the materials that the narrator will use in his story are depicted as conveyed in little boats propelled by lies. The voyage of the narrative, that which transports both reader and writer outside of the room, the mental space of the narrator, becomes the textualization of those materials. However, given the nature of the latter, the boat becomes a symbol of liberation only insofar as it remains a fantasy within the narrative. The voyages Ferdinand actually takes on ships are failures. *Voyage* gave us a variation on this opposition. The journey on the *Amiral Bragueton* was marked by oppressive heat and persecution. The hallucinatory voyage on the *Infanta Combitta* constituted a liberation, emphasized by the seemingly contradictory position Bardamu occupied as a happy galley slave.

It is Auguste who transmits his love for and knowledge of boats to the young Ferdinand. "Je pense à Auguste" [I think about Auguste], the narrator remarks, "il aimait aussi les bateaux. C'était un artiste au fond . . . Il n'a pas eu de chance" [he also loved ships. Deep down he was an artist . . . He had no luck] (p. 533). Auguste is not merely an artist by virtue of his poetic reveries about ship voyages, for he also paints boats in watercolors. From the highest room of the apartment he looks out over Paris as if he were a ship's captain gazing at the sea from the bridge. It is not by chance that the room in which these imaginary journeys take place as well as the one in which he does his paintings, the concretization of his longings, belongs to Ferdinand. The young Ferdinand uses that room for masturbation, voyages into an imaginary world of satisfied desire. And it is from an analogous room that the narrator will receive his "fleet" of memories.

The sort of deception that lies in store for Ferdinand insofar as his "real" journeys by boat are concerned is perhaps adumbrated by the catastrophic trip the family takes to England. The voyage is a one-day excursion from the Normandy coast, where Clémence has taken the family in order to sell her lace at some of the seaside resorts. Shortly after their departure, they encounter rough seas on the Channel. Most of the passengers including Ferdinand and his mother but not Auguste—true sailor that he is—become violently seasick. There ensues an epic exchange of vomit between the passengers, described in sumptuous detail by Céline, that leaves everyone covered with someone else's lunch. One of these exchanges offends Auguste, who gets into a fight with the culprit and is soundly thrashed.

When the family finally arrives in England, they discover that their suitcase is missing and that the smiling countryside they had expected to find seems, in the darkness and driving rain through which they stumble, to resemble the chaotic sea they had just crossed: "La pluie d'Angleterre c'est un océan suspendu . . . On se noie peu a peu" [The English rain is the ocean suspended in air . . . One drowns little by little] (p. 615). Far from the protective confines of the Passage, soaked, dirty, vomit-covered, the three figures look like vagrants, the very antithesis of the bourgeois respectability that Clémence and Auguste treasure.

Ferdinand's second voyage to England begins on a different note. Upon disembarking in the small town adjacent to Meanwell College—the name is suggestive of future disillusionment and disappointment—Ferdinand at first discovers an atmosphere as suffocating as that of the Passage when he is enveloped in the smells and smoke that surround the area of the station, "ça devenait de plus en plus tenace, plus enveloppant" [it was becoming more and more persistent, more enveloping] (p. 691). This extension of the Passage serves to remind Ferdinand that a *passage* has indeed been effected, for no sooner does he realize where he is than he feels the intoxication of the *dépaysement* that comes with the knowledge that in changing landscape one loses—or so it seems— one's former identity: "Ça me semblait tout d'un coup qu'on ne me rattraperait plus jamais . . . que j'étais devenu un souvenir, un méconnaissable, que j'avais plus rien à craindre, que personne ne me retrouverait jamais . . ." [It suddenly seemed to me that they'd never catch up with me any more . . . that I'd become a memory, unrecognizable, that I had nothing more to fear, that no one would ever find me again] (p. 696).

The college itself occupies a "magnificent site" (p. 707). Set on a hillside outside the town, it dominates the surrounding area. In this setting it is swept by the wind, by the fresh air that was unavailable in the Passage. Stimulated by this healthy ambiance, Ferdinand will grow rapidly. However, it is a growth that takes place concomitant with Ferdinand's isolation—as imaged by the winter landscape that surrounds the college in banks of fog, cutting it off from visual contact with its surroundings: "On voyait plus rien de la ville, ni du port, ni de la plaine au loin . . . ! Toujours le brouillard, un coton énorme" [We couldn't see anything of the city or of the port, or of the plain in the distance . . . ! There was always fog, an enormous ball of cotton] (p. 714).

Ferdinand's isolation is self-imposed; he retreats into his own thoughts as a means of rebellion. An essential aspect of this isolation concerns language. Ferdinand has been sent to Meanwell College to learn English but once there he retreats into almost total silence. It is not English that Ferdinand rejects but, rather, language itself. Given the opportunity, Ferdinand opts not to speak at all, for he distrusts language—which has been the weapon of those who have oppressed and exploited him: the lies and schemes of his employers, the pious admonitions of his mother, the vituperations of his father. Ferdinand makes his decision with great lucidity and determination: "J'avais un bon truc pour me taire, une occasion vraiment unique, j'en profiterai jusqu'à la gauche" [I had a good thing for being silent, a truly unique opportunity, I will get the most mileage out of it] (p. 720). The only linguistic appreciation that Ferdinand will develop during the course of his stay at Meanwell will be a sensitivity to the "musicality" of the English language as it is spoken by Nora Merrywin, the beautiful, ethereal wife of the owner and headmaster of the school.

In certain ways Nora is just the opposite of the ogrelike Madame Gorloge with her enormous bulk and engulfing sexual organs. Ferdinand things of Nora as a "fairy" (p. 727) and associates her with certain aspects of existence at Meanwell in which she is properly spiritualized: playing the piano, saying prayers with the students at bedtime, and, particularly, attending chapel, where she becomes an object of veneration: "Dans l'église, Nora me faisait l'effet d'être encore plus belle que dehors, moi je trouvais du moins. Avec les orgues, et les demi-teintes des vitraux, je m'éblouissais dans son profil . . . " [In the church, Nora seemed to me to be even more beautiful than she was outside it, at least I found it that way. With the organ and the half tones of the stained glass windows I was dazzled by her profile] (p. 727). However, Nora's status as an idealized woman is a precarious one. Ferdinand's attempt to keep her at a distance is constantly menaced by his desire to touch her and, indeed, to consume her. His depiction of her beauty as "des réussites de la viande" [carnal triumph] (p. 727) indicates the intrusion of the materiality of desire into Ferdinand's aesthetic appreciation. At times, alone with his mixed emotions concerning Nora,

Ferdinand gives himself over to furious bouts of masturbation as he thinks of devouring that "viande"—literally 'meat':

> Je la mangeais Nora dans toute la beauté, les fentes. . . . Je lui aurais arraché la moule, si j'avais mordu pour de vrai, les tripes, le jus au fond, tout bu entièrement . . . je l'aurais toute sucée. . . . (p. 727)

> [I devoured Nora in all her beauty, every crack and cranny. . . . I would have torn out her cunt, had I really bitten into it, her entrails, every bit of juice, entirely drunk up . . . I would have sucked her dry. . . .]

But after a time Ferdinand comes to realize that sexual desire, and the sex act itself, lead to a dispossession of self, a loss of identity, and thus he attempts to stop masturbating:

> J'aimais mieux . . . brouter entièrement les linges . . . que de me faire promener par la Nora ou par une autre! J'avais compris . . . le cul c'est la farandole! C'est la caravane des paumés. Un abîme, un trou, voilà! . . . Je me l'étranglais moi, le robinet . . .

> [I preferred . . . to chew up the bed linen . . . rather than be taken in by Nora or by another! I had understood . . . ass is a merry-go-round! The caravan of losers. An abyss, a hole, that's all there is to it! . . . I choked off my faucet . . .]

As we will soon see, Ferdinand's resolve will be put to a crucial test shortly before he leaves Meanwell College.

With some additional money from home, Ferdinand is permitted to remain at Meanwell during the spring. But the extension of his stay coincides with the rapid decline of the school. When the coming of spring permits Ferdinand to take long walks across the beautiful English countryside, that landscape is marred by the discovery that a new school is being built in the vicinity—the Hopeful Academy, whose splendid facilities will outstrip by far anything Meanwell has to offer. As Ferdinand's departure date draws near, Meanwell increasingly loses students to the new institution; and as that necessary source of revenue dries up, the meals at Meanwell become skimpier, and the furniture and fixtures are progressively sold off in order for the school to remain open.[6] Ferdinand will leave Meanwell with nothing—neither a command of English nor an improvement in his character so that he can conform to the ideals his parents set for him. During his final days at Meanwell, Ferdinand will once again find himself implicated in a situation in which order yields to disorder, though he is not the immediate cause of the transformation.

It is the hitherto unapproachable Nora who enmeshes Ferdinand in the demise of Meanwell. On the night before his departure, he is sexually attacked by Nora in a desperate attempt to lose herself in sexual passion as her existence at Meanwell disintegrates. Perhaps the deteriorating financial situation of the school has exacerbated her seeming lack of compatibility with her older, somewhat decrepit husband. The reader is never informed of the motivation underlying Nora's assault on Ferdinand. Some form of madness seems to have seized her, for her attack on Ferdinand while he is asleep in the dormitory bears a resemblance to Madame Gorloge's "seduction" of the young apprentice: "Je me trouve étreint dans l'élan! . . . congestionnné, raplati sous les caresses . . . Je suis trituré, je n'existe plus . . . " [I find myself grasped in her impulse! hardly able to breathe, flattened under her caresses . . . I'm ground to nothing, I'm wiped out] (p. 753). Ferdinand "defends" himself by replying to Nora's attack. He fulfills his desire to "devour" her: "Je ne fais qu'un dans sa beauté. . . . Je croque en plein dans son nichon! . . . Je suce tout." [I'm one with her beauty. . . . I bite her right in the tit! . . . I suck everything] (p. 754). Nora's insanity terminates in her suicide as she throws herself into the nearby Medway River. Ferdinand's last sight of her is of a "a bit of white" (p. 756) in the darkness, as she disappears, Ophelia-like, into the swirling waters.

Destitution, madness, and disorder have usurped the utopia that Ferdinand had expected to find upon arriving at Meanwell. One last image of that chaos greets Ferdinand when he enters the headmaster's quarters and attempts to impress upon Nora's husband that his wife has killed herself. But the headmaster is too drunk to realize what Ferdinand (mustering his limited resourses in English) is saying. Rising from his chair, he scatters bottles of whiskey and jars of marmalade onto the floor. He takes a step, only to slip in the mess and slide across the floor, collapsing in a heap. Not only does the headmaster's office mirror the chaos that has entered the school, it also anticipates Ferdinand's return to the Passage and his parents' apartment, where Ferdinand has encountered a similarly chaotic landscape as the product of his father's outbursts of anger.

Ferdinand returns to the Passage as unemployable as he was before he left. But Ferdinand has changed: he is bigger, older, and more indepen-dent. The freedom he experienced in England, imaged by the long walks he took across the open English countryside, has made it difficult for him to readapt to the confines, physical and mental, of the Passage. "Dans cette putain d'Angleterre j'avais perdu l'accoutumance de respirer confiné" [In that son of a bitch England I had lost the habit of stifled breathing] (p. 776). Instead of looking for a job, Ferdinand takes to spending his time in open squares with other jobseekers, between whom there is an exchange of gossip and lice. One substitute for the English countryside is the Tuilerie Gardens, where Ferdinand and other Parisians come to take refuge from the August heat. One evening Ferdinand, having exchanged the provisions he bought for his family's dinner for bottles of wine, has a hallucinatory experience in those same gardens. He imagines that the crowds of people seeking relief from the heat have become an immense mob, drinking the ornamental pools dry in order to quench their thirst.[7] Having passed out after too much wine, Ferdinand awakens in the now deserted Gardens, long after the dinner hour has passed.

Ferdinand's belated return to the confines of the apartment leads to an ultimate scene of disorder in which all the elements of his chaotic home life are present. Auguste alternately swells and vents his rage; Clémence, crippled and helpless to stop her husband, lies useless on the bed. At one point, August turns away from cursing his son to vent his rage against the typewriter that he had rented and was never able to master. It, like his son, symbolizes his inability to control his existence. Ferdinand, still drunk, finally can stand no more and throws the typewriter at his father, knocking him down. He himself also falls down and while on the floor begins to strangle his father. Ferdinand's attack is directed against his father's verbal energy, a revolt against his father's use of language to browbeat him: "Je vais lui écraser la trappe! . . . Je veux plus qu'il cause . . ." [I'm going to smash in his mouth! . . . I don't want him to talk any more] (p. 806). Ferdinand finally strikes Auguste's head against the floor, knocking him unconscious. Alerted by the maid, a group of neighbors arrives, and Ferdinand is driven into a downstairs room where he is locked in. There Ferdinand expels his remaining fear, anger, and nausea in the form of vomit and defecation. This violent activity metaphorically tears Ferdinand apart— "on dirait que tout se décolle, que tout se débine en morceaux" [everything seemed to be coming unstuck, everything was going off in pieces] (p. 808)—for it is Ferdinand's identity that is coming apart as the price of his rebellion against his father. We may also equate his vomiting (*dégueuler*) with his father's shouting (*gueuler*). Having silenced his father, the latter's verbal energy can now be arrogated by his son.

Once again it is Uncle Edouard who saves the day by rescuing Ferdinand from the room and taking him home. As we might expect, Edouard's apartment, Ferdinand's present refuge, contrasts radically with the space of the family dwelling:

> Chez l'oncle, son logement, c'était gentiment situé, c'était riant, agréable . . . Ça dominait sur les jardins rue de Vaugirard. . . . Y en avait des ribambelles de petits bosquets, de potagers devant et derrière. . . . Je ne me sentais plus du tout traqué au domicile de l'oncle Edouard. (p. 811)

> [My uncle's place was nicely situated, it was cheerful, pleasant . . . It looked out over the gardens on the rue de Vaugirard. . . . There were rows of little copses, of kitchen gardens in front and back. . . . I didn't feel myself hunted any longer at Uncle Edouard's house.]

Edouard's apartment is, however, a temporary refuge at best, a mini-utopia outside the framework of existence in which Ferdinand is condemned to operate. He knows he cannot return to the family residence nor stay with his uncle indefinitely. He must find a job, and his uncle finds one for him with Roger-Martin Courtial des Pereires, the editor of the *Génitron,* a magazine for investors. Ferdinand will be only an errand boy and receive no wages, but he will be lodged and fed at the review's offices, also called the Génitron.[8]

Courtial and his periodical are indissociable, for the substance of the review consists of Courtial's descriptions of and opinions upon the inventions that his subscribers submit to him. His scientific knowledge is prodigious in its scope. Unlike Ferdinand, he has an answer to every question, an opinion on every invention submitted to him—"il avait toujours réponse à tout et jamais embarrassé, atermoyeur, déconfit" [he always had a reply for everything, and he was never one to be embarrassed, to procrastinate, to become disconcerted] (p. 816). However, never lacking for an answer, having a command of a staggering variety of scientific and quasi scientific subjects does not necessarily mean that Courtial is able to operate effectively in the world outside the offices of the *Génitron.* Indeed, as we shall discover, Courtial is a manipulator of words, the master of a utopian, pseudo-scientific rhetoric that will produce tragi-comic consequences when applied to reality.

Physically Courtial is small and solidly built and in excellent condition. This last attribute apparently derives from the physical exercises he performs every day in the little gymnasium he has set up in the offices of the review. He keeps in shape, he tells Ferdinand, so he can meet the physical demands of being a balloonist. His balloon, called the *Zélé*, the *Zealot,* is so delapidated as to hold barely enough air to enable it to fly above the church steeples of the towns in which Courtial, for a fee, puts on his exhibitions of lighter-than-air flight during fairs and celebrations. Like one of Beckett's characters, Courtial never removes his overcoat, no matter what the weather; the overcoat will symbolize the closed system within which he will attempt to function.

Courtial vulgarizes his prodigious knowledge by writing a great number of do-it-yourself and self-study books, on subjects ranging from bicycles, to electricity, to the observation of heavenly bodies. Underlying this abundant publication is a utopian project. Like Mallarmé who wished to write the quintessential poem that would sum up the universe, Courtial's project is to encapsulize all knowledge, "mettre l'univers dans une bouteille, de l'enfermer par un bouchon et puis tout raconter aux foules" [to put the universe in a bottle, to enclose it with a cork and then tell it all to the multitudes] (p. 821). The comparison between Mallarmé and Courtial is suggested by the narrator himself, who, in juxtaposing the two, deflates all claims to absolute knowledge by attributing the printing of Courtial's best known manual—the one on the mechanics of the bicycle—to a certain Berdouillon and Mallarmé.

Although Ferdinand is impressed and, at times, awed by Courtial's extraordinary knowledge, his admiration for his employer is tempered by his awareness of the unscientific, disorderly side of the man—his inability to perform even the simplest mechanical tasks, his exposing himself in front of children, his frequenting of brothels for the purpose of flagellation, and, above all, his inveterate gambling on horse races. Disorder and chance thus exist in tension with Courtial's vocation. In order to keep his journal running despite his gambling losses, Courtial is obliged to undertake yet another disorderly activity—organizing fraudulent contests in which inventors pay an entry fee with the hope of earning substantial prize money. These contests—one of them, for example, offers a prize for the invention of a perpetual motion machine—result in complaints to the police. Fortunately for Courtial, there has never been sufficient evidence for prosecution. For his part, Ferdinand is quite happy to work for Courtial: his job as errand boy, office caretaker, balloon repairman, etc., is not at all taxing, permits a great deal of independence, and satisfies his material needs. Moreover, given Courtial's penchant for dispensing scientific knowledge—or what passes for it—Ferdinand receives additional compensation in the form of the lectures Courtial delivers to him on various and sundry topics.

The contradictions within Courtial are reflected in the space he occupies. Like all of Céline's great eccentrics, Courtial creates a landscape that is an extension of his personality. The locus of Courtial's affairs is the group of rooms that make up the Génitron. This name suggests several possibilities, all of which will be applicable in one way or another to the nature of the space in question and to the activities that emanate from it: *générer/ génération* [generate/generation], *génie* [genius], *nid* [nest], *étron* [turd]. In the cellar of the offices reposes Courtial's balloon, the *Zélé*. That the balloon should be found there, at the bottommost level of the Génitron, is significant, for the balloon is in such a state of disrepair that Ferdinand spends a good deal of his time patching it. Despite his efforts, its capacity to fly is sorely limited. It is among the folds of his balloon that Courtial will retreat for his naps, dreaming perhaps of the time when he soared above the heads of the crowd. The cellar also provides a handy retreat when creditors or angry investors are looking for him. On the mezzanine level there is a "bureau tunisien," an office decorated in North African style, where Courtial can receive and impress important guests. Above the offices there is a "chambre de bonne" where the pigeons that Courtial releases during his balloon flights are kept. Their flights contrast with the feeble ascents Courtial is able to make in his *Zélé*.

But the heart of the Génitron is to be found on the first two floors. Both spaces are filled to overflowing with mounds of brochures, notices, copies of the journal, manuscripts, etc. This material is piled so high and with such precarious balance that the least shock might result in a massive avalanche. This sort of disorder recalls the family store as well as the Berlope trimmings company:

> Les bureaux du 'Génitron' en fait de terrible désordre, de capharnaüm absolu, de pagaye total, on pouvait pas voir beaucoup pire . . . Depuis le seuil de la boutique jusqu'au plafond du premier . . . c'était qu'enfoui sous les papelards, les brochures, tous les invendus à la traîne, un méli-

mélo tragique tout crevassé, décortiqué, toute l'œuvre à Courtial était là,
en vrac. . . . On pénétrait au petit bonheur . . . on enfonçait dans une
ordure, une fuyante sentine . . . dans la tremblotante falaise . . . Ça
s'écroulait tout d'un coup! . . . Ça déclenchait d'autres avalanches, un
effroyable carambole de toute la paperasse bouilloneuse sur un ouragan
de poussière . . . un volcan foireux d'immondices . . . Ça menaçait la
digue de rompre chaque fois qu'on vendait pour cent sous! . . . (p. 828)

[It would be difficult to find a more terrible disorder than the one in the
offices of the 'Génitron,' an absolute junk shop, a total mess . . . From
the doorway of the shop to the ceiling of the second floor . . .
everything was buried under papers, brochures, unsold copies littered
about, a desperate clutter, all cracked, split apart, the complete works of
Courtial were there, scattered everywhere. . . . You'd dig into it at
random . . . you'd sink into a pile of crap, a leaking bilge into a
swaying cliff . . . Suddenly it would cave in! . . . That set off other
avalanches, a frightful collision of papers bubbling in a hurricane of
dust . . . a crappy volcano of filth . . . The dike threatened to burst each
time we sold a buck's worth of stuff.]

Unlike Ferdinand's real parents, who attempt to construct a dike of
bourgeois morality against the encroachment of disorder, Courtial, whom
one can consider a substitute father, takes a much different approach to the
disorder represented by the monumental clutter of his office. When
Ferdinand complains that he, unlike his boss who finds his way effortlessly
through the chaos, cannot locate anything in all the mess, he is treated to a
sermon on the subject of disorder and the nature of the universe. Courtial
tells his young employee: ". . . le désordre. . . . c'est la belle essence de
votre vie même! de tout votre être physique et métaphysique. . . . Toute la
nature! Une fuite dans l'impondérable!" [disorder is the perfect essence of
your very own life! of your entire physical and metaphysical being. . . . All
of nature is a flight into the imponderable] (p. 829). On the basis of this
view of reality, Courtial compares the chaotic state of the Génitron offices to
a "cerveau" [brain] (p. 830). Both, he claims, are proteiform, forever in
movement, changing. Thus Ferdinand would be foolish to operate on the
basis of reason, order, categories. True wisdom, Courtial continues, lies in
living in "harmonie" (p. 830) with things as they are. And the proof of
Courtial's harmonious existence would thus be his uncanny ability to locate
materials amid the "chaos vertigineux" [dizzying chaos] (p. 839) that

surrounds him. How do we reconcile Courtial's metaphysics with his self-appointed role as scientist and vulgarizer of science? Courtial explains that his task is to understand and demonstrate how things work, how certain laws operate within that overall framework of disorder, but never to impose an order or rectify matters. "Tout l'ordre est dans les ideés" [the only order is in ideas], he states, "dans la matière pas une trace" [not a trace is to be found in matter] (p. 829).

After the failure of his perpetual motion contest and his subsequent attention from the police, a frustrated Courtial decries his "imprisonment" in the material world, "la vie matérielle me ligote" [I am bound by material life] (p. 896). Courtial is here putting into philosophical terms what others would consider far more prosaic; namely, his inability to run his journal and still pay his gambling debts. However, Courtial's statement taken at its face value points toward more serious contradictions in his outlook and character. Despite his knowledge and despite his position as an editor of a journal for inventors, Courtial is on the one hand as "bound" by the inflexibility of certain of his ideas as he is by his financial concerns. On the other hand, certain of his ideas afford him the freedom he seeks only so long as they remain speculative. Let us first examine Courtial's rejection of progress in aviation.

Progress can be a vehicle of disorder, for it ultimately destroys those who are unable to adapt adequately to change. Progress has undermined Ferdinand's real family—his mother's business has been destroyed by machine-made lace, his father's employment is threatened by his inability to use a typewriter. A similar phenomenon occurs with his substitute family (Courtial has a wife whom we will discuss shortly). Courtial is no less attached to the (disappearing) world of the artisan than are Clémence and Auguste. Courtial is the artisan-inventor trapped in a world that has ceased to honor the individual tinkerer. His position is clearly shown in his rejection of the airplane in favor of the balloon. Despite the number of articles defending the balloon that Courtial churns out, he is powerless to stop the progress of aviation and the subsequent decline in the number of offers he receives to perform at fairs. And as those offers decrease so does Courtial's income, thereby jeopardizing the existence of the journal as well as the mortgaged house he owns in the suburbs. The progressive deterioration of the *Zélé* in the basement of the Génitron offices symbolizes Courtial's losing battle with the airplane and adumbrates the collapse of the structure the balloon supports.

The inability of the *Zélé* to rise more than a few feet above the ground corresponds as well to the deflation of the "zealous" windbag that Courtial has become. Whereas Courtial readily floats in the realm of far-fetched ideas, he is easily grounded when he attempts to apply those same notions to the material world. That he should be using pieces from his first balloon, the *Archimède,* to patch the *Zélé* puts Courtial's decline into sharper relief. The *Archimède* recalls better days when competition from the airplane did not exist. The name of the balloon also suggests to the reader the career of the Greek inventor Archimedes. We can recall his famous proposition that given a suitable place to stand and a lever long enough he might move the earth. Courtial's reveries are, as we shall shortly see, no less idealistic.

It is the loss of the *Zélé,* which has become so tattered that it is uninflatable, that sets the stage for the emergence of the many contradictions we have noted in Courtial's outlook and personality. Irène, Courtial's wife, finally visits the offices of the Génitron in order to examine the financial situation of her husband. Of particular concern for Mme Courtial is the possibility of foreclosure on their house. Unlike the monstrous Madame Gorloge or the ethereal Nora Merrywin, this substitute mother poses no sexual threat to the young Ferdinand. A hormonal deficiency caused by a hysterectomy has given Irène masculine traits—mustache, beard, bushy eyebrows.[9] With no income from balloon flights and Courtial dispensing all the money that comes into the journal for bets on losing horses, Irène is desperate to save their house, for which she has been saving for many years. As if to answer her prayers, one day a clergyman named Fleury comes into the office to consult with Courtial on a matter of great urgency.

Fleury has a project that immediately attracts Courtial's attention: he proposes that the *Génitron* organize a contest to design a diving bell that will permit the recovery of sunken treasure. Needless to say, he has come equipped with a map showing the locations of various treasure ships. Unlike the previous contests Courtial had organized for the purpose of bilking his inventor-subscribers, this contest can be legitimate because Fleury has brought with him enough money to pay for the expenses of the contest as well as for a special issue of the review to publicize it. No reader of the novel could doubt for a moment the fantasy of such a project. But Courtial is immediately enthusiastic—about the money he can make and about the "scientific" possibilities inventing the necessary recovery equipment presents. He becomes inflated with a sort of verbal delirium as the enterprise begins to take shape in his mind. The *Zélé* may be in shambles, but Courtial can soar on his own enthusiasm: "Déjà il avait son topo tout prêt dans l'esprit . . . tout baveux . . . complètement sonore! . . . Il nous éblouissait d'emblée sur la question des plongeurs!" [He had his subject already prepared in his mind . . . full of juice . . . fully resonating! . . . He dazzled us straight away on the question of the diving apparatus] (p. 119).

Despite the competition for the best design of a diving bell, Courtial establishes himself as the final authority concerning the nature and operation of the equipment. His ideas on the matter spill forth in a torrent of scientific terminology—"ferro-magnétique au sommet" [ferro-magnetic at the top] (p. 925), "surcharge galvanoplastique à pivolet centrifuge" [galvanoplastic overload with centrifugal pivot], "éclairage radio-diffusible" [radio diffusible lighting] (p. 926), etc. But Courtial's plans for construction of the diving bell are utopian; they exist in the world of ideas, as a quasi-scientific rhetoric that constitutes a closed system. And that system will be self-sustaining provided that it remains impermeable to the material world.

Not only does Courtial wish to design the diving bell, he also plans to make the first descent. Having failed as a balloonist, Courtial wishes to substitute water for air, descent for ascent, to become a "pilleur des abîmes" [a pillager of the depths] (p. 924). Upon hearing of Courtial's intentions, Irène calls her husband crazy and reminds him that he is first and foremost a balloonist. The juxtaposition of these two activities reinforces the suggestion that just as Courtial failed in the air he will fail under the sea. That deflation comes when Fleury returns to the *Génitron,* supposedly to examine the progress of the special diving bell number and bring additional money. So sooner does Courtial begin to discuss the project with him, than the clergyman begins pinching his own face convulsively; then he gets down on all fours and barks like a dog as he scatters piles of papers and brochures. Two policemen arrive and drag the man out of the office. They inform Courtial, with Irène and Ferdinand standing by, that Fleury is a madman—he is a real clergyman (a canon) but steals from his family and the church to support his fantastic projects.

That Courtial should be fooled by a crazy man is, of course, no happenstance. Fleury's insanity is just a step beyond Courtial's self-deluding delirium. The "dikes" that Fleury has constructed around himself to shut out the outside world are more solid than those Courtial has erected by means of his scientific—pseudo-scientific—ideas and jargon. The arrest of Fleury will put the strength of those "dikes" to the test. As soon as

Courtial's inventors hear of the cancellation of the diving bell project they assemble in the vicinity of the *Génitron* offices to protest what they assume to be yet another fraud on the part of the journal. Finally, a group of the most disgruntled inventors, led by a man carrying a prototype of a diving bell, marches upon the office. Courtial takes shelter in the *cave,* but this time the inventors expend their anger upon the journal. Using the model of the diving bell as a battering ram, they destroy the *Génitron* offices. The latter ultimately collapse in an avalanche of plaster and papers. The "harmony" upon which Courtial had prided himself has yielded to disorder; the verbal closed system he had constructed has been breeched by reality. The sign of that closed system, the overcoat which Courtial never removed, is destroyed as he struggles to free himself from the ruins of his enterprise. He emerges from the rubble "défroqué" [defrocked] (p. 944).

As for Ferdinand, as gullible as the others with regard to the sunken treasure project, he is content to observe the destruction of the *Génitron* from across the street. Once again Ferdinand is witness to the loss of his employment when a (provisional) system of order is destroyed by the disorder lurking within it. A brief visit to the Passage that Ferdinand makes at this time emphasizes this process of destruction. Ferdinand discovers that Auguste has become so fearful of losing his job with the insurance company (we may recall his inability to master the skill of typing and thus find other employment) that he has become paranoid, hovering on the edge of insanity with only Clémence's ability to guide him to work every day separating him from going insane. Auguste is obviously not privileged, the way Fleury is, to avoid any responsibility for his actions and find refuge within insanity.

With the collapse—literally— of the *Génitron,* Ferdinand will go with Courtial and Irène to the country where they will attempt to establish a new mode of existence. I have hitherto only briefly mentioned the opposition between city and country. However, that opposition constitutes an important theme in *Mort à crédit* as well as a recurring pattern in Ferdinand's movements. After Ferdinand was falsely accused of stealing the ring made up by Monsieur Gorloge, he "retreated" to the English countryside; after the fight with Auguste he took refuge in his Uncle Edouard's house, which is situated in a rural-like landscape; and now, when the *Génitron* has been destroyed, he is once again heading for the countryside. In each case the country has afforded an escape from the suffocating complexity of urban existence. However, as we shall shortly see, this time the escape to the countryside will not work. Like all such opportunities for relief from the contingencies of existence, this one too will be destroyed. The name of the hamlet in which the three settle, Blême-le-petit, adumbrates the catastrophe that awaits them. *Blême* literally means 'pale' and, by metonomy, it evokes 'death.' And it is indeed a 'little' or 'slow' death that their new existence holds in store for them. The general appearance of the property they buy adds to these expectations: they move into a delapidated farmhouse in a desolate countryside where they are surrounded by hostile neighbors. Their presence constitutes an intrusion into the narrowly limited life of the rural community.

Having lost his balloon, having failed to become a great undersea explorer, Courtial has but one domain to conquer—the earth. Courtial intends to accomplish this conquest by raising giant vegetables. His technique will be to "irrigate" them with electromagnetic waves. In order to do this, Courtial must give each plant a small electrical charge by means of a grid of wires implanted in the soil and connected to an electric generator. Never at a lack for words, Courtial "demonstrates" the truth of his method whenever he can find an audience. However, having sold all of his possessions in order to move to the country, Courtial does not have enough capital to implement his project. He therefore decides to transform the farm into a combination school and summer camp. His advertisements stress the healthy climate of the country as opposed to the "pourritures citadines" [urban rot] (p. 989), an antithesis we have already seen at work in the development of Ferdinand.

Fifteen children are sent by their parents to take advantage of Courtial's offer. Like Ferdinand at the Meanwell Academy, the children thrive in the outdoors. And part of their good health derives from the labor they provide in planting Courtial's experimental potato crop, the potato being the first vegetable that Courtial will grow by means of radio-telluric waves. While they await this first harvest, Courtial's financial situation grows increasingly worse, and the children take to roaming the countryside in search of food with which to supplement their meager diet. They quickly become expert scavengers, stealing every bit of produce they can find from the surrounding farms. And as the children pick the countryside clean, Courtial, perceiving that his harvest will not meet his expectations, refuses to confront the reality of the situation. Instead, he soars skyward on flights of scientific rhetoric about the movement of heavenly bodies—"il promenait les mains dans les voies lactées" [he caressed the milky way] (p.

999)—far from the terrestrial disorder that threatens to destroy his project.

His impending doom is reflected in the changing nature of the countryside. Its cold and desolation and hostility begin to close in upon the farm as the children, forced to undertake ever more risky food-gathering missions, are picked up by the authorities one by one. A state of siege finally settles upon the farm as their victimized neighbors grow ever more threatening. Huddling together for warmth and protection behind closed shutters, the inhabitants of the "camp" face the very real possibility of starvation.

Finally, the time to harvest the potato crop arrives—and the result is catastrophic. Not only have Courtial's potatoes failed to grow to giant size, they are rotten and filled with maggots as if Courtial's radio-telluric waves had accelerated the decay they evidence. The peasants in the area believe that Courtial has succeeded in producing not a new breed of potatoes but rather a new species of maggot, capable of infesting the entire region. The rot that has attacked Courtial's potatoes can be interpreted metaphorically as the decay that lies at the very heart of existence, the maggots as the canker that gnaws at the heart of every project. And Courtial, who has kept his head in the clouds, in whose head was formed the idea for growing potatoes by means of radio waves, commits suicide, appropriately, by blowing his head off with a shotgun.[10] The "harmony" of which he had once boasted has yielded to figurative as well as literal confusion as scattered bits of his brain mingle with the soil—the disorder within merges into the disorder without. Courtial the balloonist, the windbag, the dreamer, has become earthbound. What is left of his head has become stuck to the road which he chose as the site of his suicide—"ça faisait un pavé compact avec la route" [it made a compact paving stone with the road] (p. 1021).

Irène perceives the "justice" of the circumstances of her husband's death: "Il n'a rien dans le corps le pauvre homme! ... Puisque c'est tout dans la tête ... Ça se voit au premier coup d'œil mon Dieu!" [He's got nothing in his body, the poor man! ... Since it's all in his head ... My God, you can see that right away!] (p. 1038). Pried from the ground, Courtial's remains are shrouded in the remaining piece of the *Archimède,* as if to recall the good old days when Courtial could survey existence from the lofty heights to which his balloon and his ideas were able to carry him.

In the final analysis, Courtial's delirium was but a provisional dike, unable to shield him from the encroaching flood of contingent existence. Insanity—of the pathological kind—would have constituted a truly impermeable system. Despite Courtial's suicide, there is a strong analogy between his situation and that of Auguste—both of whom have served as "fathers" to Ferdinand. Both men were windbags, both men were unable to cope with a changing society, both men hovered on the brink of insanity but were unable to go that one step further that would have provided them refuge. Fleury appears at Blême, after Courtial's death, as the embodiment of that protective extreme represented by insanity. Fleury's immunity to the sort of disaster that has befallen Courtial is conveyed by his final gesture of plunging his hand into Courtial's skull, that source of "harmony," and destroying what remains of Courtial's brain:

> Il rentre les deux mains dans la viande . . . il s'enfonce dans tous les trous . . . il arrache les bords! . . . les mous! Il trifouille! . . . il s'empêtre! . . . Il a le poignet pris dans les os! . . . Y a une espèce de poche qui crève! . . . Le jus fuse! gicle partout! Plein de la cervelle et du sang! . . . (p. 1055)

> [He sticks both hands into the meat . . . he sinks them into all the holes . . . he tears the edges! . . . the soft places! He digs around! . . . He gets stuck! . . . He's got his wrist caught in the bones! . . . There's some kind of pouch that bursts! . . . The juice pours out! spurts everywhere! Full of brains and blood! . . .]

Ferdinand leaves Irène to care for the final arrangements and, his employment having been terminated with the death of Courtial, takes the train for Paris. Once again he finds himself a prisoner of the city, whose streets become a dark *passage* symbolizing enclosure and entrapment:

> Toutes les façades, tout ça si fermé, si noir! Merde! . . . si peu baisant . . . c'était encore pire que Blême! . . . J'en avais les grolles par tout le corps . . . et surtout au bide . . . et à la tête! J'en aurais tout dégueulé . . . Ah! Je pouvais plus repartir du tout! (p. 1065)

> [All the facades, all so closed, so black! Shit! . . . what a turn-off . . . it was even worse than Blême! . . . It gave me shivers through my whole body . . . and especially in the belly . . . and in the head! I could have puked it all up . . . Ah! I just couldn't move on!]

Vomiting permits Ferdinand to purge his fear and anxiety, with respect to what has happened to Courtial and to what awaits him in Paris. He hears the voice of Courtial as he staggers through the streets of Paris, but it is a voice that speaks of a realm that Ferdinand cannot attain, that Courtial could not attain, for it can only discourse about constellations and planets. As we have come to expect, it is with his uncle Edouard that Ferdinand will seek refuge. But whereas the apartment and the almost bucolic landscape surrounding it once constituted an escape from the Passage and all it represented, Ferdinand realizes that such evasions are no longer possible. He makes no mention of the landscape this time. As for the apartment, he now finds it cramped, and the cot on which he once comfortably slept is now too small. Ferdinand has, of course, grown physically, but the "shrinking" of the apartment must be interpreted metaphorically as the sign of another sort of growth. Ferdinand realizes that he cannot hide in his uncle's house as if he were a child. Vomiting, wracked with chills, he decides that the only option left to him is to join the army, for all he has known is misery and disappointment.

The final images of Ferdinand semi-delirious in his uncle's apartment recall the attack the older Ferdinand suffered after his experience with La Mireille. The similarities between the two permit us to better measure the distance between the narrator and the protagonist, the difference between their respective orders of experience. As we saw in the case of the narrator, delirium afforded a breakdown in the everyday life he was leading and subsequently served as a *passage* toward his youth, coextensive with the transformation of memories into narrative. That transformation constitutes an apprenticeship of writing, by means of which an order is imposed upon the disorder of experience. As for the final delirium of the protagonist, it marks the end of a certain innocence. Whatever trials lie before him, he has already witnessed hatred, fear, stupidity, ridicule, death, suicide; he has already glimpsed the precariousness of ideas, systems, institutions; he has already perceived that existence is a "death on the installment plan."

Lastly, we might compare the narrator's head wound with Courtial's. As a manipulator of language Courtial functions as an alter ego of the narrator in a manner analogous to the way in which Robinson functioned as an alter ego of Bardamu. Courtial's destiny is exemplary as was that of Robinson (who, by provoking Madelon, can be considered as also having committed suicide). Bardamu was a witness and a survivor as is Ferdinand: both endure in order to become narrators of the respective stories in which Robinson and Courtial appear. Whereas Courtial's head wound is fatal and results from an intrusion of reality into the order of his ideas, the narrator's head wound leads to a re-creation of reality; it transforms him into a "super-seer" (as he will refer to himself in a later novel, *D'un château l'autre*). And it is this creative delirium that permits him to encompass and transcend the delirium of a Courtial or an Auguste as well as the insanity of a Fleury. Or, in another sense, the novel as creative delirium offers the reader an insight into the delirium and insanity of existence:

> Elle a couru derrière moi, la folie . . . tant et plus pendant vingt-deux ans. C'est coquet. Elle a essayé quinze cents bruits, un vacarme immense, mais j'ai déliré plus vite qu'elle, je l'ai baisée, je l'ai possédée au finish. (p. 525)

> [It pursued me, insanity . . . so much and more for twenty-two years. That's cute. It tried fifteen hundred noises, an incredible din, but I raved more quickly than it did, I screwed it, I came out ahead at the finish line.]

4
Down and Out in London:
Guignol's Band I,
Guignol's Band II: Le Pont de Londres

GUIGNOL'S BAND BEGINS WITH A SERIES of prefaces which situate the narrator-author, Ferdinand, at two different moments in time subsequent to the period that will be described in the novel. Two of these prefaces treat the critical reception the author's preceding works, notably *Mort à crédit,* have received and anticipate what sort of reception the present work will, in its turn, be accorded. In these prefaces Céline introduces for the first time in his works a narratee, a reader whose assumed antagonistic attitude toward the author will be parried within the text itself. The other three prefaces, framed by the two mentioned above, provide a thematic introduction to *Guignol's Band* in that they deal with the ravages of war. The war in question is World War II, but the carnage described by the narrator anticipates the events of the novel, which are set against the background of World War I. As we shall see, Ferdinand has fled to England in 1916, after having been wounded in the Great War and having spent time in several hospitals. Although the war is not being fought on English soil, the country's inhabitants, and particularly its French nationals, are being swept by patriotic fervor and are joining the army in droves. Ferdinand is left to mock the enthusiasm of the enlistees, having experienced at first hand the insanity of war. Ferdinand's principal task is to stay on the right side of the law, for, equipped with papers of dubious authenticity, he runs the risk of being sent back to France and forced to return to the front.

In the first of the two "critical" prefaces, Ferdinand announces that *Guignol's Band* will occupy two volumes and asks his reader to reserve judgment until he has read both. But having solicited the patience of his reader, the narrator then has the latter state categorically that he will not read anything more by Céline, having already been exposed to earlier works. That the narrator should be referred to, disparagingly, as a "Jew" (p. 7) for "perverting" the French language in his novels is ironic, given the author's widely publicized anti-Semitic views. That irony is compounded when Céline refers to his critics as "youtrons" (p. 7), a neologism forged from the derogatory *youpin* 'yid,' 'kike' and the word for 'turd,' *étron*. In the second critical preface Céline defends his writings—and here one is not sure whether he is referring to his fiction, his pamphlets, or to both—by stating that his vilification was occasioned by his "bon cœur" [good heart] (p. 31), which made him express himself when he should have perhaps remained silent. The myth that emerges from both these prefaces is that of Ferdinand as scapegoat, the innocent victim of a tacit conspiracy on the part of society to persecute him for what he has written as well as for his inability to conform to society's norms. As for the confusion between author and narrator-protagonist, it had been encouraged by Céline through use of autobiographical materials in his fictions and through his assuming of aspects of Ferdinand's existence, such as his oppressed childhood.

In the remaining prefaces we return to the carnage of war. The focal point of the landscapes described will be a bridge, and the role of that bridge will anticipate by contrast the "pont de Londres" that will appear in the second volume of *Guignol's Band*.

The time in question is 1940. With the fall of France, Ferdinand, serving as an ambulance driver, is forced to flee the city of Orléans, under bombardment by the Germans, along with remnants of the defeated French army and a ragtag population of civilian refugees. The column finds itself stopped before a bridge leading out of the city, a bridge scheduled to be demolished by the French Army Corps of Engineers. There is a sudden rush to cross the bridge before it is destroyed. Céline depicts the band of refugees as an enormous, confused mass of people and vehicles animated by the delirium occasioned by fear, a depiction that typifies the chaos and panic that shape the French landscape during this period, "la sarabande des frayeurs, la foire par dessous les tonnerres à la rampette-dislocation" [the saraband of fright, the fear of crawling from place to place under the thunder] (p. 14).

To attempt to cross the bridge is, however, to expose oneself to the fire of the German planes flying overhead. Despite the danger, the narrator is aware of the contrast between the confusion below and the graceful

solitude of the planes above as they make their passes over the bridge.
Depicted not so much as planes belonging to a specific enemy force but as
instruments of divine punishment, they are referred to as "le méchant du
ciel" [the evil one in the sky] (p. 16), "archangels" (p. 17), mythical,
dragonlike creatures—"les petites langues de feu dardent partout. . . . Il est
gris et noir! . . . et maudit de la tête en queue" [little tongues of flame dart
everywhere. . . . It is grey and black! . . . and accursed from head to tail!]
(pp. 18-19). As the bombs explode and the machine guns rattle, vehicles
and bodies fly everywhere. The ambulance sails through the air, strikes a
heavy truck, and shatters into many pieces. Fissured by bombs, the bridge
becomes a perilous path between the planes above and the roaring river
below. Those who still attempt to cross it are depicted as engaged in a life
and death "dance," which the narrator contrasts with the postures of the
pedestrians in the popular song "Sur le pont d'Avignon." The sight and
sound of exploding bombs and cannon fire, the bodies and parts of bodies
scattered in all directions, the confused mass of men and machines, all these
elements merge in the narrator's view to create a hallucinatory effect, a
"vision féerique" [fairy story vision] (p. 22). This remark serves to remind
the reader of the self-conscious art of the narrator, of his transposition of
reality into an aesthetic product which, whatever may have been its point of
departure in reality, will have its intrinsic beauty.[1]

The events outside of Orléans serve as a bridge to the events of the
novel as the narrator will portray them, as a bridge to the past. The narrator
notes, in mock self-deprecation, that he has "plus de souffle au souvenir"
[more inspiration in relating memories] (p. 17), memory being synonymous
with re-creation. And like the bridge at Orléans, those memories are
confused and associated with the destruction of war: "Trop de monde
a passé dessus . . . comme sur le pont . . . sur les souvenirs . . . comme
sur les jours! . . . Trop de monde gueulant la bataille" [Too many people
have passed over it . . . like on the bridge . . . on memories . . . as on the
days! . . . Too many people screaming battle] (p. 17).

Thus the bridge is part of the narrator's external landscape as well as
part of his internal landscape. His consciousness is filled with chaotic, war-
scarred memories which will be sorted out and, coextensively, transposed
in the form of the narrative to which the various prefaces themselves serve
as a bridge. Those memories will create a thematic and temporal bridge
between the two wars to which the narrator has borne witness, between his
near past/present and his distant past. To create that bridge is in one sense

to blur the interval separating those two moments of history. However, to achieve that obliteration is to erase the specificity of each of those wars. One can argue that for Céline the pamphleteer, for Ferdinand the self-proclaimed innocent victim of persecution, it was the Jew who became the victim of that blurring of differences. Céline would claim that the Jew was responsible for causing France to enter once again into the folly of war. Later, in the wartime trilogy, Ferdinand-Céline will look back wistfully upon World War I as a "good" war with its cavalry charges, limited weapons, and relative security for non-combatants.

The fourth preface depicts a French soldier (possibly a Resistance fighter) who, having suffered through the disastrous defeat of his country, assassinates a German soldier and is thus transformed into a blood-thirsty avenger. These "vaillants" [valiant ones] (p. 25), as the narrator mockingly calls them, are then plunged into all the tortures of hell as they try to exorcize the demon of murder within themselves. Such men—and the narrator may very well be thinking of his own potential assassins—have by virtue of their actions internalized that landscape of war, have come to war with and within themselves. In so doing, they have lost an inner "song" (p. 25) that would signify the possibility of joy instead of a life-long condemnation to hatred and destruction.

The last of the thematic prefaces addresses itself to the lower-class Frenchman: "Français mignon, ludion d'alcool, farci gâteux, blet" [Frenchie, alcoholic leprechaun, stuffed dotard, overripe] (p. 28). This hopeless and hapless figure is portrayed as a perpetual victim, abused by the law and made into cannon fodder by the politicians. And it is with these victims that the narrator identifies himself by referring to them in the first person plural. Yet the concluding vision of the preface poses other possibilities. The victimization of the Frenchman by himself as well as by others constitutes an inferno similar to the one mentioned in the previous preface, which, once passed through, will serve to purify the victim and transform him into a "diaphanous" pure spirit (p. 29), able to float through the air. Perhaps Céline is predicting that there will arise a new race of Frenchmen, purified by the suffering they have endured. However these speculations may apply to Frenchmen in general, one can readily suppose that they would be applicable to the artist, and notably Céline, whose art and artistic self are depicted as the spiritual byproducts, as it were, of the suffering that has produced them.

London, the setting for the events of *Guignol's Band,* presents in the course of the narration a variety of landscapes that will extend and complement those depicted in the prefaces. The most important of these London landscapes will be the area adjacent to and including the docks. The harsh reality of this area with its depressing, monotonous architecture, poverty, greyness, and constant dampness is offset, in the narrator's imagination, by an element associated with light and air—the numerous children that inhabit such *quartiers.* The narrator's lyrical description of their playing in the puddle-filled streets and his transcription of some of their songs serve to idealize the children. As we saw in Bardamu's relationship with the child Bébert in *Voyage,* children offer an innocence that will perforce be corrupted as they grown into adults. In a reversal of the usual growth cycle the children become the butterflies that subsequently metamorphose not even into caterpillars but into maggots.

> mignons marmots du brouillard . . . mieux jouants allègres divins et prestes qu'angelots de rêves. . . . Et puis tant de jolies chansons fraîches et comiques et galantes qui me dansent au souvenir . . . toutes à l'essor de la jeunesse. (p. 39)

> [cute little tikes of the fog . . . more playful, gay, divine, and lively than dream cherubs. . . . And then so many pretty songs, fresh and comical and gallant that dance in my memories . . . all on the wings of youth.]

The presence of these children, as yet unspoiled by the adult world that awaits them, illuminates the landscape. They are associated with the pale "fragile sun" (p. 40) that lights the otherwise dark and dreary streets. And it is they who impart meaning to the otherwise ironic names of the streets in which they play—Lavender Street, Daffodil Avenue. The children also serve as a sort of bridge by which death, linked to this happier time of life, becomes somewhat less painful: "Ainsi sera la Mort par vous dansante encore un petit peu" [Thus thanks to you Death will still be dancing a little] (p. 40).

Another positively valorized aspect of the London landscape will be the docks. We need not linger here on the importance of the image of the ship in Céline's writings. London, and certainly the London of 1916, is a great seaport in a country whose very existence is inextricably intertwined with shipping. For Ferdinand the activity of the docks constitutes a magnificent spectacle, one that involves two movements—one centripetal and one centrifugal. The first of these concerns the products that arrive on the London docks from every corner of the globe. The narrator deploys an epic lyricism in describing the London docks as they are transformed into an immense treasure trove, a landscape of superabundance, of satisfied desire, that contrasts with the desolate streets surrounding the docks and with the down-and-out status of the narrator himself:

> Après les maisons ribambelles, après les rues toutes analogues où je vous accompagne gentiment, les murailles s'élèvent . . . les Entrepôts, . . . Falaises à trésors! . . . magasins monstres! . . . greniers fantasmatoriques, citadelles de marchandises. (p. 44)

> [After the strings of houses, after all the similar streets, where I gently accompany you, the walls arise . . . the Wharves . . . Cliffs of treasures! . . . gigantic warehouses! . . . fantasmagoric storehouses, citadels of merchandise.]

The centrifugal aspect of the docks lies in the exchange that takes place in Ferdinand's mind between the products he perceives and the distant, exotic countries from which they have come. Incoming ships elicit reveries of travel to more idyllic landscapes, of enlarged spatial circumstances as opposed to the narrow limits within which Ferdinand must function:

> Le ciel . . . l'eau grise . . . les rives mauves . . . tout est caresses . . . doucement entraînés . . . vous vous charmez toujours plus loin vers d'autres songes, vers d'autres mondes qui s'apprêtent en voiles et brumes. . . . (p. 46)

> [The sky . . . the grey waters . . . the mauve shores . . . everything is a caress . . . gently borne away . . . you beguile yourself ever farther toward other dreams, toward other worlds that ready themselves with sails and mists. . . .]

Such reveries will take the form of frantic wanderings through the streets of London and, later, when Ferdinand meets Sosthène, self-proclaimed explorer and mystic, of fanciful expeditions to Tibet.[2]

Here as so often elsewhere, Ferdinand is an underground man, and it is a group of seamy Soho bars that constitutes the principal locale of his

London existence.[3] Given the irregularities in his papers, these environs are as much a matter of necessity as of choice. Ferdinand has come to London as the result of an encounter in a hospital, where he had been sent to recover from the wounds he suffered in the war. There he made the acquaintance of Raoul Farcy, a malingerer who had shot himself in the hand in order to become unfit for military service. Ferdinand helped him write letters to Cascade, an uncle residing in England. After Raoul is executed for "treason," Ferdinand is invited to come to England by the uncle. Cascade is the "grand Caïd" [great chieftain] (p. 54) of the London underworld, and his particular trade is managing a stable of prostitutes. However, Cascade is no "godfather" figure. He, like the seedy cast of characters that surround him, will be moved by forces over which he has little or no control. They will play out their assigned roles in the comical and sometimes brutal drama—likened to a Punch and Judy Show (*guignol*)—in which Ferdinand will find himself implicated during his stay in London.

Cascade has hitherto had a proper relationship with the law, has been discrete in his dealings with friend and foe, and has led the life of a dignified gentleman. Suddenly, however, his orderly existence begins to unravel as many of his fellow pimps, notably those who are French nationals, become imbued with patriotic fervor and forsake their profession in order to enlist in the army. Cascade, himself unfit for military duty, finds that he is obliged to look after his friends' "stables" during their absence. The more girls he has, the more disputes he finds himself engaged in. Cascade's embarrassment of riches is comical. But its comedy is set against Ferdinand's condemnation of war based on realities that are masked by the enlistment propaganda to which so many succumb. Whereas London is a refuge for Ferdinand from the war, the others are only too glad to forsake it for the horrors of the front: "Les petits macs ils me faisaient sourire . . . Ils avaient mangé du bobard. . . . Je disais rien. . . . Je savais moi! . . ." [The little pimps made me laugh . . . They swallowed it hook, line, and sinker. . . . I said nothing. . . . Me, I knew! . . .] (pp. 80-81).

Cascade's second problem is Ferdinand and his friend Boro. Both possess papers of dubious authenticity and both are therefore being kept under surveillance by Matthew, a phlegmatic Scotland Yard detective. Cascade feels honor-bound to protect these two members of his band but needs to remain on good terms with Matthew. After Boro throws a bomb into a bar in order to break up a dispute, he and Ferdinand are told to lie low until the affair quiets down. The two go their separate ways, but after a time Ferdinand, penniless, decides to get some money from Boro. The latter is hiding out at the home and place of business of the pawnbroker Titus van Claben.

Boro's full name is Borokron and he is of Bulgarian or Russian descent. He has two professions—playing the piano and making (and using) bombs. Indeed, his name, as Ferdinand remarks, is onomatopoeic, evoking the sound of explosions. Boro's fondness for bombs causes Ferdinand to refer to him as an "archangel": "Moi j'ai connu un vrai archange au déclin de son aventure" [Me, I knew a real archangel as he was slipping over the hill] (p. 32). We may recall that the same term "archangel" was used to describe the German fighter planes bombing and strafing the refugees as they crossed the bridge outside Orléans. Just as those planes were the instrument of a malevolent, capricious destiny, so too, as we shall see, Boro will embody an arbitrary violence that represents the intrusion of the war's violence into the otherwise peaceful London landscape. However, Boro is not merely a bomb thrower; he is also an artist.

Boro manifests that dual occupation while he is lying low at the celebrated pawnbroker's house. The house is part of an idyllic landscape. It is in the vicinity of the docks, just outside Greenwich, and is separated from the river by a large park: "Une maison située admirable, tout un théâtre devant ses fenêtres, prodigieux décor de verdure sur le plus grand port du monde" [a house admirably situated, an entire theatre before its windows, an incredible green landscape looking out upon the largest port in the world] (p. 153). To these elements one can add enormous masses of flowers everywhere, filling the air with their fragrance. This lovely backdrop will render the frightening events that transpire in Titus van Claben's house even more sinister, for one would expect them to take place in the seedy areas which Ferdinand and Boro normally frequent.

As for Titus van Claben himself, the splendors of verdant nature are wasted upon him. An asthmatic, he closes himself indoors. But that claustration must be understood in a symbolic sense as well. Like Courtial, van Claben in his person and in his surroundings, constitutes a closed system, that form of delirium which, when penetrated by external reality, shatters with catastrophic results. Nicknamed "l'Affreux," 'the frightful one,' Titus drapes his obese body in an oriental Pacha's outfit, complete with turban. And we are informed that he never removes these clothes, even when he goes to bed. Moreover, he wears makeup and lipstick. Asexual, neither a smoker nor a drinker, his only vices, if they may be called that, are music and business. This curious being exerts an almost magical power over the usually disabused Ferdinand, creating by virtue of his presence a sort of hallucinatory effect: "... un effet fantastique, une terrible berlue, un mirage ... il me fascine" [an extraordinary effect, a tremendous distorted vision, a mirage ... he fascinates me] (p. 145).[4]

Another aspect of van Claben as a closed system—again recalling Courtial— is his residence/place of business as a "carphanaüm" [junkroom] (p. 214). He lives surrounded by immense piles of objects, a great disorder that threatens to engulf him at any moment. Titus has filled his residence with objects pawned by his clients—clothing, personal articles, musical instruments, etc. This decor constitutes an autonomous world, one that mirrors its owner. Like Courtial, with his vast accumulation of tracts and journals, only van Claben can find his way through the apparent chaos. He lives amid a contained disorder of debris from the world outside his shop, a world into which he never ventures. Appropriately garbed, he is the high priest of the temple he has created as an extension of himself:

> Titus lui se trouvait bien à l'aise au creux de l'énorme cafouillis! ...
> au cœur du négoce ... en plein cratère tohu-bohu, c'est là qu'il se
> sentait en pleine forme, en raison d'être en plein sanctuaire, derrière sa
> globe, sa lampe à l'eau. (p. 163)

> [Titus, he was completely at home in the center of this enormous mess!
> ... in the heart of his business ... right in the middle of a crater of
> confusion, there he was in full bloom, by virtue of being in the heart of
> his sanctuary, behind his globe, his water lamp.]

Titus has but one weakness, one flaw in the closed world he has created—music. He permits the potentially dangerous Boro to remain in his house so long as Boro plays the piano hour after hour:

> On aurait pas dit à sa mine en le regardant, premier abord, poussah,
> chafouin, popotame, comme ça dans sa crasse et pénombre, et pourtant
> il était sensible, influencé, ravi aux anges, dès que ça fonctionnait ...
> hypnotisé, figé, pâmant, surtout en séance continue ... (p. 159)

> [You couldn't have told by his appearance, seeing him for the first
> time, pot-bellied, weasel-faced, hippolike, that was him, in his filth and
> shadow, and yet he was sensitive, swayed, carried away, as soon as it

was turned on . . . hypnotized, transfixed, above all when it was played
nonstop . . .]

The charms of music soothe l'Affreux, transforming him to the point where
he can even forget his customers. And if music can transform the grotesque
Titus, we should not be surprised that the artist himself, Boro the anarchist
and bomb thrower, is also transformed as he plays—"franchement brutal et
pénible avec sa manie d'explosifs il devenait là tout voltigeur, tout
cascadeur, tout lutin" [frankly brutal and troublesome with his mania for
explosives, he became all acrobat, all daredevil, all imp] (pp. 157-58). A
brilliant and tireless pianist, Boro creates a "magic spell" with his "wizard
fingers" to which Ferdinand is no less immune than Titus: "Ça vous tinte
plein les soucis . . . vous triche le temps, vous tille la peine" [It jingles your
cares away . . . cheats time, eases your pain] (p. 157).

These remarks on the power of music can readily be applied to the
narrator's art. His artistic recreation of his London experiences is also a
means of abolishing the destructive passage of time. The narrator alleges
that he will be unable to return one day to the "endroits réels" [real places]
(p. 178) because he will be imprisoned or hanged, or because those places
will have been destroyed. Thus he alerts his readers: "Je suis obligé d'imaginer . . . Je vais vous faire un petit effet d'art . . . Vous me pardonnerez"
[I'm obliged to imagine . . . I'm going to create for you a slight artistic
effect . . . You will forgive me] (p. 178). Moreover, the narrator emphasizes his need to master his own emotions so that what he writes will be
more controlled and therefore have a greater impact on his reader, so that the
emotion which "disconcerts" (p. 153) him will have, recollected in
tranquillity, recreated aesthetically, the power to "disconcert" the reader.

When Boro plays his music he also drinks. The intoxication of
alcohol soon dominates the intoxication of the music, and Boro and Titus
begin to fight over the amount of money Titus is willing to pay the pianist
for his nonstop playing. During the course of the struggle, Ferdinand
opens the door to permit a customer who has become entangled in the melee
to escape, and a sudden rush of air enters the house. Titus is overcome by a
violent attack of asthma and falls prostrate to the floor, gasping for breath
and wracked with vomiting. In the aftermath of Titus's asthmatic attack we
will perceive a convergence of certain of the themes already mentioned. Art
with its particular powers of transposition and transformation will be
replaced by drunkenness, delirium, and black magic; and this substitution

will permit the manifestation of mindless greed and arbitrary violence.

However, before examining that convergence we need to note that there is a third person present among Titus's "guests" as he lies choking from his asthma attack—his housekeeper Delphine. She is a middle-aged woman who, having been fired from a teaching position, now spends her time cleaning Titus's house, in a most desultory fashion, and indulging in her passion for theatregoing. Her association with the theatre serves to foreshadow the *guignol* in which she and the others will be involved. Delphine is indeed notorious, we are told, for giving her own performances in the balconies of the theatres she frequents, and for playing these roles dressed in outlandish clothes borrowed from Titus's stock of pawned items. While Titus lies prostrate, she and Ferdinand—usually a teetotaler—begin to drink, to catch up with Boro, who is already drunk. This initial state of drunkenness will be magnified when Delphine, having gone out to obtain medicine for Titus, returns with cigarettes that are laced with hashish.

The circumstances surrounding the acquisition of those cigarettes are indeed curious. Out of the dark, foggy night, a man, jet black, drops to the street from a lamppost and informs Delphine, that he is the "heavenly physician" (p. 185), able to save the dying. In the case of Titus van Claben, with which he is familiar, he prescribes "magical leaves" (p. 185), in the form of the special cigarettes he gives her. Not only will they cure him, he states, but they will also ward off the black magic of the evil spirit Fourchu, 'the Forked One.' He then shrivels into a bit of cloth and disappears. Obviously, since the cigarettes themselves could not be produced by alcoholic hallucinations, we have here an intrusion into the text of a phenomenon that does not obey the laws of everyday logic, in short, the supernatural. Nor do we have here the sort of self-conscious rhetorical device that we have examined in other novels. Instead, the intrusion of the supernatural here in the first volume of *Guignol's Band* is associated with the kind of delirium or madness that will be consonant with the puppet show antics of the characters and illuminate the violence in which many of them will be engaged. As we will see in the second volume of the novel, the supernatural will also serve as a vehicle for the projection of repressed desires and the fear of death.

The result of smoking the cigarettes is aberrant behavior and perceptual distortion. Titus, who suddenly recovers his health, kisses Delphine; Boro makes homosexual advances toward Ferdinand; Ferdinand, attempting to repulse Boro, tries to seize a sword hanging on the wall, only to discover that it is a mirage. Ferdinand also has visions of the others being eaten by dragons as well as of killing them with that nonexistent sword. Soon a general spirit of gaiety and mirth pervades the company. But unlike the spell cast by music, that of drugs and alcohol constitutes an evasion from care that is as superficial as it is shortlived.

It is greed, given uninhibited expression, that finally leads to Titus's death. Boro insists upon being paid for past performances before playing any more music. But when Titus takes out money to pay him, he foolishly displays his sacks of gold coins for everyone to see. Titus laughs as he watches them run their hands through the money he has spilled out on the floor. However, he laughs so hard that he is rendered helpless, and Boro begins to stuff the gold pieces into him, transforming Titus from a metaphorical money bag into a literal one. The sound of music from the piano is replaced by the jingle of coins in Titus's stomach. But Boro suddenly realizes that, having stuffed all the money into Titus, he has not received what he believes Titus owes him. Geting money from the miserly Titus, literally *out* of him, is a difficult task. Moreover, Titus has now begun to suffocate from having been crammed full of coins. Ferdinand, hitherto a passive spectator of the dispute between Boro and his benefactor, now endorses Boro's decision to extract his money any way he can. He and Boro turn Titus upside down and bang his head against the floor in order to dislodge the coins. When this method does not work, they drag Titus to the top of the stairs and release him, once again allowing his head to thud against the ground. This last attempt at forcing Titus to yield the money within him is a failure: no coins have come out and Titus's skull has been split open, leaving him dying.

Thus Ferdinand has become an accomplice to an accidental murder. Given the importance of the head wound in Céline's fiction, one cannot avoid juxtaposing what has happened to Titus with the narrator's situation as a wounded veteran of the war, someone who emerged from that war "plein de trous" [full of holes] (p. 80), including a hole in his head. It is ironic that Ferdinand who has fled to the safety of England to escape the sort of violence that had given him a cracked skull, and fatally broken the skulls of so many others, now finds himself instrumental in giving just such a wound to Titus.

The delirium that occasioned Titus's death persists after the event. Boro and Ferdinand accuse each other of being responsible for the murder, but are able with the help of Delphine to push Titus's body into the cellar.

There Titus finds an appropriate tomb, surrounded by piles of objects that constitute the overflow of pawned articles from the floors above. But when Ferdinand and Delphine descend into the cellar to properly position Titus's body, Boro throws a bomb into the cellar and locks them in. Ferdinand and Delphine manage to escape from the ensuing fire. An effusive Boro greets them as if nothing had happened.

The episode with van Claben is thus framed by the two bombs Boro throws in the novel. The first bomb temporarily severed Ferdinand (and Boro) from Cascade's band; the second bomb makes that separation permanent for Ferdinand, who will be blamed for the murder by Boro and Delphine. Ferdinand becomes the suspect sought by the police in their investigation of Titus's demise. As for Cascade, Ferdinand's presence in London constitutes a grave liability for his *bande* insofar as his desire—and need—to maintain a good relationship with the police is concerned. The London that Ferdinand enjoyed as a refuge has been transformed by the murder of Titus. Ferdinand has become the victim, one sought by the police as well as by Cascade.

It is the latter who first discovers Ferdinand's whereabouts, through the efforts of one of his men called Mille-Pattes ('Millipede' by virtue of the man's dexterity in handling cards, as if he had a thousand fingers). Mille-Pattes locates Ferdinand in the vicinity of the Waterloo subway station. The name of the station, recalling the defeat of Napoleon by the forces under the command of the Duke of Wellington, suggests that Ferdinand too will be involved in a battle and perhaps a disastrous defeat. Mille-Pattes informs Ferdinand of the accusations against him and offers to escort him to Cascade's headquarters. Ferdinand agrees to come with him but when they reach the Underground station to await their train, Ferdinand suspects a trick when he sees Inspector Matthew on the opposite platform. Afraid that Cascade has decided to hand him over to the police, afraid of being imprisoned, deported, and eventually forced to return as a combatant to the war he detests, Ferdinand pushes Mille-Pattes in front of an oncoming train and flees the station. His fear of the war has become a form of madness that transforms him into an assassin and the station into a prison from which he must escape at any price: "Je suis oiseau de peur! Je jaillis de la cage dans la rue" [I'm a bird of fear! I burst from my cage into the street] (p. 242).

But Ferdinand's fear does not desert him once he finds himself back on the streets of London. It causes him to hallucinate—in the form of visions and voices, and finally leaves him with a persistent headache. That headache recalls Titus's broken skull, the immediate cause of Ferdinand's present problems, as well as his own war wound. Once again Ferdinand has been wounded—and in the head—this time by fright and guilt, and within the sanctuary he had sought. There would seem to be, for Ferdinand at least, no escape from violence and death. And consonant with his role as a puppet, Ferdinand's actions are dictated by forces over which he has little or no control. He sees himself as the victim of a plot, a sinister machination that has led to two deaths. An internal voice accuses Ferdinand of being a criminal, and another voice, perhaps that of his "mother," defends him by saying that he has been duly punished in London with torture and imprisonment. The hallucinations occasioned by Ferdinand's fear lead him to confuse the London and Flanders landscapes, and he runs down the street as if he were leading a cavalry charge against the enemy, as if he were again acquiring the wounds and the subsequent medal that once permitted him to escape from the war. Ferdinand rushes into the French Consulate, still raving, and demands a medical examination so that he can return to the front, to a legalized form of killing: "J'en ai tué deux! . . . que je recommence . . . j'en ai tué dix! . . . et j'en ai tué bien plus encore! J'en assommerai bien davantage" [I've killed two of them! . . . let me begin again . . . I've killed ten . . . and I've killed a lot more! I'll strike down many more] (p. 253). Ferdinand is finally ejected from the consulate but, as that happens, he "sees" the mutilated bodies of comrades in the war.

Ferdinand thus fails in his attempt to exchange one landscape for another, both London and Flanders having become scenes of murder, one puppet's existence for another. Stripped of his haven, hunted by both the police and the underworld, having little money, lacking proper papers, Ferdinand will attempt to find some sort of refuge in mysticism and magic. And it is perhaps ironic that this aspect of human experience, influential in the circumstances that lead to Ferdinand's present impasse, will offer him a protection from the consequences of that same murder. Ferdinand will seek that refuge through a curious individual he meets at the French Consulate, dressed in a traditional Chinaman's costume—Hervé Sosthène de Rodiencourt, miner, explorer, illusionist, Eastern mystic. After some preliminary discussion, Sosthène offers Ferdinand a position that will put to use his experiences as a quartermaster with the cavalry in World War I—to be in charge of the horses on an expedition to the mysterious land of Tibet. They will seek a mystical flower, the Tara-Tohé, by means of whose petals (consumed by the initiate) one can be liberated from contingent existence

and attain to a higher order of being. Although Ferdinand has doubts about
the existence of such a flower, his anxiety makes him willing to accept
almost any proposition that would afford him the chance to escape from his
present dilemma: "Avec la fleur magique ou non . . . en Chine! . . . au
Diable! . . . où il voulait! . . . mais nom de Dieu qu'on foute le camp" [With
or without the magic flower . . . to China! . . . to the Devil! . . . wherever
he wishes! . . . only good God let's get the hell out of here] (p. 289).
Reality, however, intrudes upon Sosthène's fantasies and Ferdinand's
desperation—there is not enough money to outfit such an expedition.

Like Courtial and Titus, Sosthène, yet another of Céline's
"maniacs," lives in a disorder that is a reflection of his own mentality:
"Chinoiseries tout partout . . . c'était plus petit que chez van Claben mais
aussi foutoir bric-à-brac, c'est peu dire" [Chinese knickknacks everywhere . . . it was smaller than van Claben's place but also a dump for bric-
a-brac, that's the least you can say about it] (p. 312). So long as Sosthène
can continue to operate in his autonomous world, there will be no threat to
his security. However, like Courtial, Sosthène does not have enough
money to sustain his autonomy and hence must inevitably confront the dangers of the penetration of reality into his closed system. The context for that
intrusion will be his hiring himself, with Ferdinand as his assistant, to an
English colonel-turned-inventor, who hopes to earn the prize money that
will be awarded by the British War Office for the best design of a gas mask.

Although Ferdinand has opted to remain with Sosthène as the only
means of staying out of the clutches of the police—and of Cascade—there is
no way to escape his obsession with death. Ferdinand is haunted by the
fear of dying on the battlefield; as we saw in his visit to the French
Consulate, his inner landscape sometimes resembles a war zone strewn with
the mutilated bodies of fallen camrades. Unlike Ferdinand, Sosthène has
been able to "domesticate" death by practicing, Chinese fashion, the cult of
the departed. Wherever he goes he transports, along with his *chinoiseries,*
a trunk containing the mummified body of his grandfather Achille Norbert.
Sosthène himself is supposedly dead, killed, he tells Ferdinand, in an
ambush organized by the mining company for which he once worked.

The reader hesitates, of course, to seriously consider mysticism or
magic as a means of transcending the contingencies of existence when the
vehicle of that transcendance is a man like Sosthène. Sosthène is undeniably a comic figure with his Chinese kimonos, his extravagant projects,
and, as we shall see later, his attempts to capture within himself the strength

of demons. Moreover, we learn that Sosthène is, among other things, an illusionist on the vaudeville circuit, performing such tricks as having his wife emerge from a supposedly empty trunk or sawing her in half. And if Sosthène possesses any truly magical power, as he believes he does, it is curiously ineffective in permitting Sosthène to transform his existence into something other than that of a harmless, amusing eccentric. However, as we saw in the case of Titus's death, there is a more sinister aspect to the function of magic in *Guignol's Band*. It serves as an expressionistic device whereby anxieties and desires, otherwise repressed, become real and tangible. I shall further explore this element in my analysis of the second volume of *Guignol's Band, Le Pont de Londres*.

Guignol's Band II: Le Pont de Londres

As we saw in the first volume of *Guignol's Band*, London had become for Ferdinand a place of danger rather than a refuge, a place where he was hunted by both the police and the underworld. Sosthène's project of hiring himself and Ferdinand to do research on the development of a gas mask for the War Office is thus useful on two accounts. If Sosthène can win his share of the prize money for the best design, it will furnish him with enough capital to outfit his expedition to Tibet. Ferdinand would like nothing better than to travel to Tibet, to get as far away from London and from the war raging on the continent as he possibly can. For the meantime, however, the house of Colonel O'Collogan on the outskirts of London, where the research and development will take place, will provide a temporary shelter.

The Colonel is a caricature of the financially comfortable, eccentric British officer. Given to fancy dressing gowns, strutting about with a lollipop in his mouth, declaiming "Pray God" and "the empire is in danger" (p. 17), he seems oblivious to the reality around him. He hires Sosthène and Ferdinand despite their outlandish appearance—Sosthène has donned his Chinese robe and Ferdinand is dressed in very shabby attire—and without examining their credentials. Once ensconced in the Colonel's house, provided with lodging and food, Ferdinand is delighted with his good fortune. Given this paradise he has found, he asks Sosthène if they have not perhaps located the "magical plant" (p. 59), just a few miles outside of London.

Ferdinand is aware, however, that his cares may be only temporarily eased. His paradise will be destroyed if Sosthène's research fails to produce the proper results and the Colonel decides to rid himself of the two Frenchmen. Even worse, they could both be turned over to the police as frauds, exposing Ferdinand to possible prosecution and deportation for his crimes. That the gas mask project is doomed to failure is, of course, immediately evident given the bizarre character of those involved in the research. The nature of the Colonel's laboratory reinforces this prediction: ". . . des monticules comme chez Claben . . . Je sors pas du désordre! . . . des hommes de carphanaüm" [. . . piles like those at Claben's place . . . I can't get away from disorder! . . . from men with junkrooms] (p. 16).

Unlike van Claben's "carphanaüm"—or Courtial's—in which order was imposed by the proprietor's mind until it was shattered by outside forces, neither the Colonel nor Sosthène is able to impose upon the materials piled up in the workroom-laboratory any semblance of coherence. And at one point in their experiments, after they have inhaled some toxic gases, they go berserk and smash everything in their lab. Ferdinand is understandably very disturbed by this turn of events. Given his awareness of the precarious situation in which he finds himself, it is he who attempts to bring some order into the gas mask project. He straightens up the lab so that they may resume their experiments, but he realizes that his efforts will no doubt only forestall the greater chaos that awaits him.

There is yet another sort of "magic" that Ferdinand discovers in the Colonel's house, one that will ultimately be associated with disorder rather than order—the Colonel's beautiful fourteen-year-old niece Virginia. Ferdinand falls madly in love with her, and his amorous delirium is reflected in the language he uses to describe her. The novel is replete with passages of ecstatic adoration in which Ferdinand verbalizes the fervor of his passion, a passion which, if reciprocal, will transform his life—for example: "Ah! quelle démarche gracieuse! . . . Ah! quelle douce majesté! . . . dans le moindre de ses gestes! . . . créature entre terre et ciel" [Ah! what graceful movement! Ah! what sweet majesty! . . . in her slightest gesture! . . . creature between earth and heaven] (p. 86). The excesses of such language undercut for the reader the ostensible sincerity of the emotions that have motivated it; that is to say, the idealization of the girl and of the romantic relationship that Ferdinand would like to impose upon her, impose because Virginia does not share Ferdinand's feelings. For the most part she is, and will remain, a distant object of veneration.[1]

The name Virginia has, of course, numerous connotations. It suggests 'virgin' which is what this fourteen-year-old is, and Virginia—a distant place where Ferdinand might live in peace with his beloved. The name of the girl also recalls the famous eighteenth-century novel *Paul et Virginie* by Bernadin de Saint-Pierre, which recounts the idyllic sojourn of a young couple on the île de Maurice.[2] Ferdinand dreams of taking a voyage with his beloved, far from the dangers of London:

> J'adore Virginia . . . je l'enlève! . . . Voilà mon totem! . . . Mon âme! mon salut! la mer Adragante! tout seuls tous les deux! . . . Hissons nos pavois. (p. 129)

> [I worship Virginia . . . I'm taking her away! . . . That's my totem! . . . my soul! my salvation! the Adragante sea! . . . all alone just the two of us! . . . Let's hoist our flags.]

But this distant journey is only a reverie. The closest they can come to the ideal landscape that for Ferdinand would be a reflection of his love as well as an escape from his problems is a stroll in the garden of the Colonel's house. Ferdinand's romantic delirium transforms the garden into an Eden, which, temporarily at least, can shelter his love from the outside world. Virginia finds a rabbit, the air is redolent of perfume, a rosebush bursts into flames. And Ferdinand, purified by his "supernatural emotion," sees himself as a "firebird" (p. 89), flying through the air. Magic and delirium merge here. For Ferdinand love becomes a means of spiritualizing his existence, permitting him, as might that elusive Tibetan flower, to enter into a higher realm of being.

This paradisical moment in the garden is shattered by sounds of destruction emanating from the workshop, for it is just at this time that Sosthène and the Colonel begin to wreck their equipment after having inhaled their mood-altering gas. This juxtaposition between the garden of love and the chaotic workshop reflects the tensions within the precarious existence that Ferdinand is leading: in the first locale, Ferdinand attempts through the magic of love to transcend the disorder lurking within his English adventure; in the second, that disorder is fully manifested.

The chaos of the workshop begins to intrude directly upon the order of Ferdinand's love when Ferdinand, in the company of Virginia, is sent to London to buy new equipment. There he meets Bigoudi, one of Cascade's prostitutes, who, enchanted by Virginia, wants to initiate her into the profession. Although Ferdinand is able to keep Virginia out of Bigoudi's clutches, his anxieties concerning his love and the possible revelation of his whereabouts compound the physical strains that he has been under in his relationship with Virginia. Ferdinand sees himself as a "Punch and Judy clown' ("guignol"), overwhelmed by elements in his existence over which he has no control:

> Virginia me tournait au guignol! . . . je savais plus trop ce que je regardais . . . tout chavirait . . . la tête au brouillard . . . ça me prenait deux, trois fois par jour. (p. 124)

> [Virginia made me into a Punch and Judy clown! . . . I hardly knew any more what I was looking at . . . everything was turning upside down . . . my head was in a fog . . . it came over me two, three times a day.]

Ferdinand's dizzy spells become hallucinations as he defends Virginia against Bigoudi. The enclosure that he has built around himself with his love has become permeable. And with that permeability he has renewed visions of death. He sees once again the body of the dead Courtial, his skull shattered by the shotgun blast with which he had committed suicide. Courtial, we may remember, had tried in vain to establish an Eden of sorts on the farm he had purchased by growing giant potatoes with radio-telluric waves. The failure of his experiment—he succeeded only in producing huge maggots in shrunken potatoes—destroyed the utopia that, ultimately, could exist only within Courtial's mind.

Yet another spectre of death returns to haunt Ferdinand—Mille-Pattes, whom he thought he had killed by pushing him into the path of an oncoming subway train. While Ferdinand and Virginia are walking down the street, Mille-Pattes mysteriously appears, his mangled body apparently sewn together, and joins them. As we have come to expect, such a phenomenon acquires an ambiguous status in Céline's fiction. Whereas Ferdinand doubts the reality of what he sees before him, Virginia shows no hesitation in accepting the resurrection of Mille-Pattes, despite the yellow glow and odor of putrescence that are supposedly emanating from the man's body. Mille-Pattes and Virginia walk arm in arm with Ferdinand trailing behind, and the juxtaposition of these two figures suggests the polarities of Ferdinand's existence. On the one hand, there is Virginia, an idealized love, the stimulus for a continuing reverie of escaping to distant places, a shelter—or so it seemed—from the problems that lurk outside his romantic Eden. On the other hand, there is Mille-Pattes, whose demise does not conform to the "simple death" that Ferdinand had encountered on the battlefields of Flanders. That sort of death has an odor, Ferdinand recalls, that is "franchement charogne" [clearly a corpse] (p. 139). The smell emanating from Mille-Pattes seems to come as much from within Ferdinand as from without, suggesting an obsession with death that is mingled with guilt—Ferdinand did, after all, push Mille-Pattes in front of the train and he was an accomplice to the death of Titus van Claben: Mille-Pattes's odor is "en douce" [barely perceptible] and "vous mine" [saps you from within] (p. 140).

It is Mille-Pattes who eventually conducts Virginia and Ferdinand to the Touit-Touit Club. There, while Mille-Pattes, like his namesake, is depicted as crawling over the walls and ceiling, Ferdinand and Virginia find themselves separated in a crowd of orgiastic revelers. A band of bacchante-like women attacks Ferdinand, and they oblige him to watch Virginia as she is accosted by a group of men. Just as the resurrection of Milles-Pattes constitutes a projection of Ferdinand's guilt for the deaths in which he has been involved, the Touit-Touit club and the activities that take place within it represent a countervailing projection—Ferdinand's hitherto repressed sexual desire for Virginia. Having at first resisted the advances of the women so that he might rescue Virginia, Ferdinand soon finds himself at ease in this dreamlike landscape in which his desires are fulfilled. He is "pris par l'ambiance" [captured by the atmosphere]; desire becomes a "magie insurmontable" [uncontrollable magic] (p 162) as the women who have captured him probe his body; and the mirrors that decorate the walls of the club cast reflections around the room of a lustful self that has finally manifested its presence.

Ferdinand's dream of sexual relations with Virginia becomes real when he finally implements that desire: he eventually manages to rescue Virginia, only to appropriate her for himself. Having witnessed his thoughts as represented by the revelries of the Touit-Touit Club, we can now juxtapose them with his subsequent course of action. No sooner does he drag Virginia outside than in rapid succession he strikes her, asks her forgiveness, and forces her to sexually yield to him. Although he possesses Virginia outside the club, he is still by virtue of his desire very much inside it. The impulses of death and life, Eros and Thanatos, juxtaposed by the intrusion of Mille-Pattes into the relationship between Virginia and

Ferdinand, now become intertwined in the act of semi-rape by which Ferdinand deflowers the once virginal Virginia. The delirium of sexual desire functions as a counterpoint to the romantic delirium that formerly constituted the mode of Ferdinand's relationship with Virginia.[3] Both are forms of escape; both seek to deny contingent reality. Ferdinand's return to the latter is signaled by the sound of Big Ben striking the hour as he and Virginia emerge from the labyrinth of streets that lead to the Touit-Touit Club, a labyrinth that functions as a metaphor for the deeper recesses of Ferdinand's consciousness. Later, when Ferdinand recalls this fantastic episode, he will attribute it to an attack of delirium occasioned by his head wound—"avec les chocs abominables tout ce que j'avais subi de la tête! . . . fracture, commotion, trépan . . . Que c'était que des vertiges?" [with terrible shocks, everything I've undergone with my head! . . . fracture, commotion, trepanning . . . Was it only dizzy spells?] (p. 190). Whereas the Touit-Touit Club may have been shaped by Ferdinand's sexual fantasies, his violation of Virginia was certainly not imagined—several weeks after the incident Virginia informs her lover that she is pregnant. The news is revealed to him in the same garden that once served as the Edenic setting for his effusions of romantic passion. And commensurate with Virginia's announcement, the garden is dark, devoid of the flame-colored flowers that once symbolized Ferdinand's ardor.

If Virginia's pregnancy has emptied Ferdinand's love of its magic, having burdened him with yet another responsibility, having made him less mobile with respect to his pursuers, there remains another element of magic in Ferdinand's existence—the curious brand of Eastern mysticism practiced by his companion Sosthène. It was Sosthène, pseudo-Chinaman, pseudo-engineer, who had brought Ferdinand to the Colonel's house, thereby providing him with a refuge. But the whole "guignol" [Punch and Judy show] (p. 97) regarding the development of the gas mask must be preserved; progress toward winning the prize from the British War Office must be maintained if Ferdinand is not to lose his fragile security. Sosthène's doubts concerning his ability to continue the charade result in frequent attacks of depression. At these times Sosthène resorts to magic: he dances naked—with Ferdinand using spoons to provide rhythmic accompaniment—according to the directions given in the book of Vedas he has brought with him. He hopes by means of his dance to capture a demon within himself and thus assimilate for his own use the demon's power. Sosthène's desire to subjugate fate by means of mysterious powers is analogous to Ferdinand's wish for transcendance through the magic of his love for Virginia. Sosthène's failure to achieve his ends will parallel the failure of his assistant.

Sosthène's ultimate dance takes place not within the privacy of the bedroom—where he has hitherto performed—but in the most public of arenas, Piccadilly Circus. Amid stalled traffic, gaping pedestrians, and temporarily stymied policemen, Sosthène appears for a brief moment to possess the magical abilities he seeks: he seems to float in the air as he zigzags around stalled buses, just beyond the grasp of the bobbies who attempt to encircle him. But just as Ferdinand's delirium with regard to Virginia was shattered by her all-too-real pregnancy, Sosthène's magic moment is destroyed by the policemen who finally close in upon him: "... j'avais vu une pagaille horrible; une vache corrida et le Sosthène bien dérouillé et les flics dessus ..." [... I had seen a terrible mess; a nasty corrida and Sosthène given a good shellacking and the cops all over him ...] (p. 259).

After the Colonel abruptly disappears one day—ostensibly on one of his habitual sprees—Ferdinand and Sosthène receive a summons to appear at Scotland Yard. Not having the Colonel to protect them, and fearing the worst insofar as the discovery of their fraudulent papers is concerned, Ferdinand and Sosthène flee the Colonel's house in the hope of eventually finding a ship that will take them far away from England. But in order to make the necessary arrangements for the future, Ferdinand must ironically, return to his past as a member of Cascade's band, the very period he is trying to flee. He decides to pay a visit to Prospero Jim, a man with many contacts, and solicit his aid in finding a ship that will take the trio to another country. We can recall that it was the bombing of Prospero Jim's bar by Boro that forced Boro and Ferdinand to leave the shelter of Cascade's *bande* and go their separate ways, only to be reunited in the murder of Titus van Claben. Ferdinand's return to the past, however circumstantial, bears witness to his continuing obsession with death, to his inability to exorcise that demon.

Since that brawl and subsequent explosion, Prospero has opened a new tavern, toward which Ferdinand directs his own little band. Their journey to Prospero's establishment takes Ferdinand once again to that privileged part of the London landscape, the docks. The enthusiasm of Ferdinand as protagonist (and as narrator) for the spectacle offered by the docks serves as a counterpoint to his troubled state. The expression of this excitement constitutes a necessary digression: "Ah! moi ça m'anime les grand fleuves! Ça m'emporte l'imagination . . . Je ne me connais plus de voir l'eau couler" [Ah! me, great rivers turn me on! They carry my imagination away . . . I no longer know myself when I see water flowing] (p. 300).

Prospero Jim's tavern is finally located, and the requisite information about sailing schedules is extracted from him. But all he can furnish Ferdinand is but one berth, that of a cook on a Norwegian ship. Ferdinand is ready to depart alone, leaving Virginia and Sosthène behind, but his sailing must be delayed when Prospero Jim informs him that Cascade's band intends to hold a party in honor of his birthday. As evening falls, the tavern begins to fill up with Ferdinand's old friends, including Cascade and Delphine. The noise inside the tavern is matched by the noise outside, as bombs begin to fall, marking the onset of a German air raid. The bombardment reminds Ferdinand of the war from which he has sought refuge; the noise inside recalls the transformation of his London refuge into a place of murder and persecution. Cascade's present for Ferdinand is the calcified mass of flesh that was once Titus van Claben. The latter's body has been stolen from the city morgue by Doctor von Clodovitz, one of Cascade's men. As a means of exculpating Ferdinand, of wiping clean the slate of the past, Cascade has ordered that Titus's body be dumped into the Thames where it can be devoured by the crabs. With the disappearance of the body, there can be no way of bringing Ferdinand to trial for murder.

Cascade does not, however, achieve the result that he desired. On the one hand a psychological burden is indeed lifted from Ferdinand—his fear of prosecution as an accomplice in the death of the pawnbroker. On the other hand, Ferdinand still bears the guilt, to some degree, for the death of Titus. Unable to tolerate alcohol, Ferdinand makes the mistake of drinking some champagne. Under the effects of the drink, he has a hallucinatory experience during which he perceives—or feels—his head and body swell to twice their normal volume, recalling the obese body of Titus, the man whose charred body has now been thrown into the Thames—"toute ma tête enfle . . . je double de volume" [my whole head swells . . . I become twice as big] (p. 384). Ferdinand becomes convinced—revealing an inner obsession and fear—that the "Greenwich affair" will not, despite the disappearance of the *corpus delecti,* readily be forgotten, and, sooner or later, the police will be back on his trail. Once more, flight becomes the only expedient left open to Ferdinand. Amid the pandemonium caused by the revelers, Ferdinand and his companions slip out of the tavern and return to the streets of London. Ferdinand's Norwegian freighter has long since departed without him.

The party held for Ferdinand also recalls the revelries at the Touit-Touit Club. On both occasions he finds himself in the middle of a frenzied celebration, during the course of which he is set upon by women who over-power him and caress his body. In the case of his *fête* it is the members of Cascade's ever growing stable that accomplish this function. In both instances he is forced to defend Virginia. This time it is Bigoudi who, once again, desires to take Ferdinand's love in hand as an apprentice prostitute. Whereas at the Touit-Touit Club Ferdinand discovered his own sexuality reflected all round him, the club functioning as a mental landscape, Cascade's party mirrors Ferdinand's obsession with death. And once again Ferdinand is forced to flee through labyrinthine streets that take him away from the psychological landscape in which he has been immersed and back to the all-too-real streets of London. One problem remains now that he has broken definitively with his past, where can he go?

The destruction of Titus's body has changed nothing insofar as Ferdinand is concerned (Mille-Pattes seems to have been forgotten). London remains a city of police and potential informers. Neither Ferdinand's love for Virginia nor Sosthène's magic can help the little *bande*. One solu-tion, but only a temporary one, remains—to return to the Colonel's house. The spectacle of the dock area through which they must walk has now become for Ferdinand a "bouffée marine" [a puff of salt air] (p. 403). That dream of a voyage toward freedom in distant lands has now been reduced to a vague wistfulness for something beyond his grasp.

The novel ends with a *passage*— across London Bridge. The wind is blowing very strongly, threatening to push the three back toward that part of London from which they are fleeing, toward all those elements that Ferdinand must leave behind. The crossing constitutes a defeat. Although the escape from persecution that his return to the Colonel's house may afford can be considered in a positive light, in fact, Ferdinand has been defeated by forces over which he has no control. The secure, relatively care-free existence Ferdinand had hoped to find in London has not been realized. Like the wind which buffets him, the bridge and those crossing it, uncontrollable forces have pushed him about, transformed him into a puppet. Neither love nor magic has been a bridge to a better life, and, moreover, Ferdinand has but increased his burden. He is now the leader of his own *bande,* one that is composed of a pregnant adolescent and an eccentric old man. The last image we have of Ferdinand is that of a "pitre" [pawn] (p. 406), obliged to amuse Virginia with grimaces as they make their way painfully toward a future with little promise.[4]

As we have seen in other contexts, it is only the narrator who is able to triumph over the events which transformed the younger protagonist into a *guignol*. His spatial and temporal remove from the events and personnages he describes, and, in particular, his younger self, creates the ironic distance that permits the reader to better comprehend Ferdinand's situation as a pawn in a game whose rules he cannot comprehend and, more generally, to appreciate the gulf that separates the disorder of life from the order of art. Once again the project of surviving to tell all is not simply a matter of revenge against enemies real and imagined but a means of triumphing over contingent existence. In an image that uses the metaphor of the writer as a maker of lace, a metaphor that appears in several of Céline's novels, the older narrator emphasizes the self-consciousness of his art as well as the distance between "hero" and writer: "Je faisais pas encore des romans, je ne savais pas tirer sept cents pages comme ça en dentelles quiproquos . . . L'émoi m'étouffait" [I hadn't yet done novels, I didn't know how to extract seven hundred pages like that, in the form of lacy exchanges . . . Emotion suffocated me] (p. 402).

5
Scapegoats and Traitors:
Féerie pour une autre fois I,
Féerie pour une autre fois II: Normance

THE PUBLICATION OF THE TWO VOLUMES of *Féerie pour une autre fois,* the first in 1952, the second—usually designated by its subtitle *Normance*—in 1954, was a crucial event in Céline's literary production. These were the first works to be published subsequent to Céline's indictment as a Nazi sympathizer. In my biographical introduction I have noted the events pertinent to Céline's case as well as his steadfast denial of the charges made against him. Céline's narrative persona Ferdinand will continue, in Céline's remaining works, but particularly in the first volume of *Féerie,* to refute those charges. In *Féerie* we will find a curious conjoining of an attempt at exculpation, as Ferdinand assumes the role of historical scapegoat, with a hallucinatory depiction of events. In addition to its continuing aesthetic function, hallucination in *Féerie* will serve as a "political" vehicle. Through it, Ferdinand will, paradoxically, both deny and confirm the accusation made against him. On the one hand, he will portray himself as a victim of the collectivity—French society—seeking to punish him as a means of assuaging its common guilt. On the other hand, the magnification of his role as *pharmakos* will render that self-designated identification suspect, given the historical realities of the situation.[1] One might add another factor to this complex "play" of self-delusion and self-justification: Doctor Destouches will receive the judgment meted out to the pseudonymous Céline—not only as the alleged author of anti-Semitic pamphlets and collaborationist articles but also as the writer of novels subversive of bourgeois culture, like *Voyage au bout de la nuit* and *Mort à crédit.* We may recall the narrator's anticipation of persecution in *Mort à crédit,* long before the pamphlets were conceived. His prediction would be more amply realized than he could have imagined.

Féerie I is related from the perspective of the narrator and protagonist Ferdinand, incarcerated in a Danish prison while awaiting extradition to France, to be tried there as a Nazi sympathizer. He attempts to make a virtue of necessity by viewing himself not as someone charged with a specific crime but as a writer gaining an insight into the human condition by means of his imprisonment: "C'est le fond des sociétés humaines, les chiourmes, les cellules, les menottes . . . faut connaître! . . ." [It's the depths of human societies, galley slaves, prison cells, handcuffs . . . you've got to know them! . . .] (p. 63). Further, Ferdinand generalizes his situation and makes it more illustrious by placing himself in a long and glorious procession of victims over the ages, a compatriot of such notable figures as Vercingétorix, Voltaire, François I, and Oscar Wilde, victims "qu'ont payé mille fois en douleur tous les crimes qu'ils n'ont pas commis" [who paid a thousand times in pain for crimes they did not commit] (p. 153).

By portraying himself as yet another scapegoat among so many others, by depicting the persecution he has suffered as an eternally recurring sociopolitical phenomenon, Ferdinand seeks to subvert the specificity of both the charge against him and the act that engendered the charge. the History of the Third Reich with its massive destruction of European Jewry, including some 100,000 French Jews, and the story of the anti-Semitic pamphleteer do not merge into one disaster, according to Ferdinand's self-portrait. Instead, Ferdinand would have them remain disconnected both historically and linguistically, linguistically in the sense that the anti-Semitic rhetoric used in the pamphlets will be seen as pacifist, distinct from the rhetoric that was implemented as the "final solution." Ferdinand's dehistoricization of the pamphlets is analogous to the way in which the pamphlets themselves viewed the coming of World War II: it had no historical specificity; it was a repetition of World War I and all the wars before it.[2] Thus Ferdinand would slip into the ahistoricity, the timelessness, the innocence of what René Girard calls ritualistic scapegoating—the cultural regulation, by repeated imitation, of the reciprocal violence between the differentiated individual and the collectivity.[3]

Ferdinand's self-portrait as an innocent victim extends his attempt to outrun History, as it were, in his flight from Montmartre across war-ravaged France and Germany to the expected safety and financial security of Copenhagen. But it would seem that History has caught up with him. Not only is he incarcerated and under threat of extradition but he is literally "stuck"—je colle du cul [my ass sticks] (p. 189). Running sores from a case of pellagra cause his behind to stick to the stool of the cell in which he is seated. It is of course better to be "stuck" in Denmark than to be at the mercy of the French courts and possible assassins.

But if Ferdinand's body is imprisoned, his mind is still free. By means of his imagination he is able to pass through the bars of his cell, to rise into the light from the dark hole in which he is entombed. A crucial "play" in *Féerie I* will take place between within and without, between the present of his imprisonment and the past during which he was free, as well as the future upon which he will speculate. His real journey having come to an end, his journey in language will range over various times and spaces. Indeed, Ferdinand defines *Féerie* as a confusion (in both the literal and figurative senses of the word) of times and spaces, of fact and fiction. This *féerie* is "for another time" because it touches past, present, and future:

> Je vous l'écris de partout par le fait! de Montmartre chez moi! du fond de ma prison baltave! et en même temps du bord de la mer de notre cahute! Confusion des lieux, des temps! Merde! C'est la féerie vous comprenez . . . Féerie c'est ça . . . l'avenir! Passé! Faux! Vrai! Fatigue! (p. 30)

> [In fact I'm writing it to you from everywhere! from my place in Montmartre! from the heart of my Baltic prison! and at the same time from our shack on the seashore! Confusion of places, of times! Shit! That's the fairyland you understand . . . A fairyland is just that . . . the future! The Past! The False! The True! Fatigue!]

Although Ferdinand is alone in his cell, the jail's other prisoners fill the air with their cries. Among Ferdinand's fellow-inmates there is one whom he singles out—the occupant of the cell adjacent to his, a man he refers to as the "putois" [polecat, skunk]. This neighbor continually beats his head against the walls of the cell. As the reader familiar with Céline's earlier works might anticipate, this activity recalls to Ferdinand his own head wound, a wound that we have already seen mythified as the source of Ferdinand's creativity and, consequently, of his difficulties. " 'Plus de médaille!' " Ferdinand remarks, "ils m'auraient soufflé pareil sur les blessures de ma tête je déconnerais plus à l'heure actuelle" [No more war medal! If they had snatched my head wounds the same way I wouldn't be running off at the mouth now] (p. 121). Ferdinand's recollection of his own head wound indicates that the *putois* serves, in this context, as a double of the narrator: they are similar in that they share a common disability, but they are radically different as to its nature and function. Ferdinand will use the *putois* as a foil for the (re)elaboration of the head wound myth.

One aspect of Ferdinand's injury is, of course, that it was received in battle. Despite his avowed antiwar sentiments, Ferdinand is, as we have already seen, unhappy at having lost his war medal, the medal he was accorded following the glorious exploit in which he was wounded. Further, as he never wearies of reminding us, the authorities are unjust in treating a war hero as if he were a common criminal. The validity of his injury is emphasized by the sham of the *putois,* whose only purpose in banging his head against the walls of his cell is to injure himself just enough so that he can be discharged from prison. If this is the case, then Ferdinand should, it would appear, be liberated too: "... je branlerais pas les briques par deux fois! Un coup! et pflouf! je sais ce qu'est de se fendre le crâne! Salut compère! Y a des héros! y a des faux! " [I wouldn't shake the bricks twice! One shot! and splat! I know what it is to split open your skull: Greetings comrade! There are heroes! there are phonies!] (p. 155).

The second aspect of the head wound, and more significant than its literal meaning, is its role in Ferdinand's creativity. His "running off at the mouth," attributed to his injury, is coextensive with his narration. As I noted in my examination of *Mort à crédit,* the head wound is depicted by the narrator as his source of inspiration, giving rise to the verbal delirium that is Céline's particular mode of poetic frenzy. Ferdinand plays on the notion of inspiration as breath or wind, *souffle* in French, to emphasize the relationship between the storms within and those without: "Tout au bout de mes bourdonnements et après encore des 'Tamtams' j'ai un grand choix de souvenirs, de souffles! après l'ouragan de mon oreille, bien d'autres" [At the end of my buzzings, and after still more tomtoms, I have a great choice of memories, of inspirations, after the hurricane in my ear, many others] (p. 188). Hence although Ferdinand complains that the "skunk's" head banging interferes with his own thoughts, he is, in effect, using the character of the *putois* as a rhetorical device to underline the heroism of his own artistic endeavors—the transformation of inner torment into art and, subsequently, the martyrdom that his artistic activity has brought him: "Il m'empêche de me recueillir, il me sabote mes inspirations! ... moi qu'ai une révolution en tête! Lui sa tête qu'est qu'à écraser! Il se l'écrase pas!

Moi, c'est de la réflexion ardente et du rire et de la plaisanterie" [He pre-
vents me from reflecting, he sabotages my inspirations! . . . I who have a
revolution in my head. His head is good only for smashing. He's not
smashing it! For me it's burning meditation and laughter and jokes]
(p. 165). Unlike the skunk's unsuccessful efforts to get out of prison,
Ferdinand's smashed head—his narrative activity—permits him, as we have
noted, to penetrate, if only metaphorically, the walls of his cell and create
his féerie.

Before we examine the two principal landscapes of Ferdinand's
féerie, we need to consider a third landscape, this one idealized, that he
"visits" from his cell—St. Malo, a city on the shore of Brittany, most famous, perhaps, as the birthplace of the nineteenth-century romantic novelist
Chateaubriand. Céline who, as we have seen, liked to consider himself a
Celt (the original inhabitants of Britanny were Celtic, and Breton, still
spoken by some of the inhabitants, is a Celtic language) spent several weeks
each year in St. Malo during the period 1935-38.

But the city that Ferdinand describes in *Féerie* is not the St. Malo of
the 1930s but that of the *belle époque,* typified by its casino. Ferdinand
transforms the latter into a baroque fantasy rising from the sea: ". . . le
monument d'étonnement même!. . . armorique-métro malgamés, granits,
cabochons, petites chimères, menhirs, briques ardoises! . . . et mille
lucarnes, redans, pertuis. . ." [this astonishing monument, armoric-metro
malgamated, blocks of granite, cabochons, little chimera, menhirs, slate
bricks! . . . and a thousand skylights, stepped-gables, openings] (p. 104).
Whereas St. Malo was ninety percent destroyed during the war, Ferdinand's casino, with its flowers and elegant patrons, remains untouched,
outside of time, outside of History, immune to those forces that have victimized the narrator: 'Enchanté, vibrant de mousses, sorti du temps" [En-
chanted, quivering with foam, escaped from time] (p. 107). Ferdinand's
vision of the casino is coextensive with his "return" to St. Malo through his
narration, leaving his prison to return to happier days. It is coextensive as
well with Ferdinand's project for the future—the sales of *Féerie* (in which
he will have exculpated himself) will permit him to return, literally, to St.
Malo and, in so doing, erase all the travail that he has experienced, as if he
too, like the casino, had escaped from time: ". . . on me sort de ma fosse,
on m'adule . . . je m'achète un vélo, un cottage, une bonne pour ouvrir la
porte . . . je pars plus en Sibérie du tout! . . . je me rétablis practicien sur la
Côte d'Emeraude" [I get out of my cell, I'm worshipped . . . I get myself a

bike, a cottage, a maid to open the door . . . I'm no longer on my way to Siberia! . . . I set up my practice again, on the Emerald Coast] (pp. 102-03). Ferdinand's cottage will become bigger and bigger as he continues to speculate on his future. The reader will doubtlessly interpret Ferdinand's visions as but another *féerie,* as an exercise in the incantatory power of language. However, one may indeed wonder, given Ferdinand's persistent denial of guilt, if a new life in St. Malo is more than idle rêverie.

The problem of Ferdinand's guilt—or innocence—leads him to create a narratee—an accusatory *vous* or *ils.*[4] If Ferdinand can journey outside his cell, he can also invite others to join him, notably his accusers. He transforms his cell into a courtroom, where he can put himself on trial as a collaborator. His accuser—sometimes singular, sometimes plural—is a special sort of narratee, a "lecteur-vengeur" [reader-avenger] (p. 59), intent upon punishing Ferdinand as a traitor. Two sorts of accusations are brought to bear against Ferdinand. The first of these is that he collaborated with the Germans during the Occupation by contributing pro-German or anti-Semitic articles to the collaborationist press: ". . . vous avez rien vendu. . . même pas signé un petit placet? un peu *'zeitungué'* quelque part? personne vous sauvera!" [You didn't sell anything . . . not even signed a little petition? wrote a bit for a German newspaper somewhere?] (p. 127). As if to suggest that his interrogator has already decided upon the prisoner's guilt, Ferdinand has the *vous* use the neologism "zeitungué," based upon the German word for newspaper *Zeitung.*

The question of whether Céline sold out generates a later series of accusations attributed to Jean-Paul Sartre, who in his book *Réflexions sur la question juive* (translated as *Jew and Antisemite*) published in 1954, stated that if Céline had sustained "the socialist [i.e., fascistic, anti-Semitic] theories of the Nazis, it was because he was paid. At the bottom of his heart, he did not believe them: for him the only solution [to the problems of mankind] lies in collective suicide, non-procreation, death."[5] Ferdinand's reply to Sartre in *Féerie* is to make fun of his name, calling him "le môme Bartre" or "Nartre" [the Bartre/Nartre kid] (p. 175) and to portray him in the clothes of a child peeing on Ferdinand.[6]

The second accusation, which gives Ferdinand the status of a "notoire vendu traître felon" [notorious bought traitor miscreant] (p. 12), was that he had also sold out to the Germans by writing his anti-Semitic pamphlets. In reality, only one of the pamphlets had been published during the war, *Les Beaux Draps,* in 1942; the preceding two, *Bagatelles pour un massacre* and *L'Ecole des cadavres* having appeared in 1937 and 1938 respectively (*L'Ecole des cadavres* was banned in 1939 as a result of a suit brought against the author but was reedited in 1943). Curiously, although Ferdinand will defend, with his usual vigor, his activities as a pamphleteer, the pamphlets are nowhere mentioned by name, nor is there any mention of the circumstances of their publication—or even of their anti-Semitic content.[7] When one "invents" one's accusers, such specifics are perhaps best left unspoken. Not only were the pamphlets written to keep France from engaging in another catastrophic world war, Ferdinand argues, but those who were to condemn their author are guilty of both misreading and, as events would subsequently demonstrate, ingratitude. Prophets, Ferdinand suggests, are without honor in their own country: "J'ai voulu leur sauver la glotte, compatriotes! leurs gueules infectes, leurs cœurs de merde, leur faire esquiver l'Abattoir . . . mes livres pour ça" [I wanted to save their necks, my compatriots! their stinking faces, their shitty hearts, to have them avoid the Slaughterhouse . . . my books for that] (p. 25).

Ferdinand speaks of "books," not pamphlets, which would lead the reader to surmise that he is referring to the entirety of his production. By lumping together pamphlets and novels Ferdinand can fall back upon the traditional antagonism between the writer and society—in which the writer is a heroic martyr—in order to exculpate himself. Myth once again is manipulated so as to replace History. Ferdinand's mistake was, therefore, to have become a writer in the first place: "Mon ambition n'est pas aux Arts! ma vocation c'est la médecine! . . . mais je réussissais pas beaucoup . . . et la médecine sans clients! . . . Le roman est venu . . . J'ai continué, alas! alas! tout petits bénéfices d'abord et puis menottes! cachots! haines! n'écrivez jamais!" [My ambition is not in the Arts! my vocation is medicine! . . . but I wasn't succeeding very well . . . and medicine without patients! . . . The novel came along . . . I continued, alas! alas! at first tiny profits and then handcuffs! prison cells! hatreds! never write!] (p. 40).

The consequences of Ferdinand's choice are not only the persecution he has suffered but, in a larger sense, self-exposure, self-fragmentation, self-dismemberment. In *Féerie* Céline focuses on the last of these, juxtaposing crime and punishment, literal and metaphorical meaning. In his cell Ferdinand depicts himself as literally coming apart as a result of the pellagra he has contracted: ". . . je perds des peaux . . . je perds des viandes des fesses . . . je perds des dents . . ." [I'm losing pieces of skin . . . I'm losing flesh from my buttocks . . . I'm losing teeth] (p. 163). These physical losses have their metaphorical equivalent, within the context of Ferdinand's writing, in the theme of the scapegoat/*pharmakos.*

"Ceux qui se donnent pas, qui foutent rien, ils gardent leurs mains. ils gardent leurs doigts ils gardent tout" [Those who give nothing of themselves, who don't do a damn thing, they keep their hands, they keep their fingers, they keep everything] (p. 97), Ferdinand remarks, comparing himself to workmen in factories, who, over the years, lose their limbs in the machinery they operate. Ferdinand's "work" has been his writing, in which he has given of himself but for which he has, supposedly, been unjustly persecuted. His persecutors will be depicted as adjusting their punishment to his "crime."

The struggle between persecuted and persecutors is often placed within a medieval setting, with an emphasis on cruelty and torture. Ferdinand becomes the hunted animal, or arch criminal, threatened with being flayed alive, drowned, drawn and quartered, decapitated: "Toute l'Europe pour moi est forêt et meute et veneurs" [All of Europe for me is forest and hunting packs and veneurs] (p. 127). Yet the torture to which he gives the most attention takes place when a group of his persecutors, among whom are to be found the writers François Mauriac, Jean-Paul Sartre, and Louis Aragon—all accused by Ferdinand of having done nothing during the Occupation but enhance their reputations and fortunes—piece his torn body together, as if to negate the sacrifices he has made, so that he can be properly disposed of:

> Ils font qu'un tas de tout mon corps! . . . ma personne poète! . . . ils
> me la tassent dans leur brouette! . . . rapetassent! . . . Ils ont leurs
> instruments de travail, pelles! pioches! balais! . . . Ils grattent ils
> récurent sous le bat-flanc, sous la tinette, dans les recoins . . .
> Ils me recollent ils raglutinent tout! . . . Ils me reretassent . . . et
> brouette! . . . En route! . . . Ils m'emportent . . . eux ils sortent de la
> prison! . . . Les géantes portes s'ouvrent! . . . Une magie! . . . (p. 169)

> [They make but one pile of my whole body! . . . my poet person! . . .
> they stack it for me in their wheelbarrow! . . . patch me up! . . . They
> have their tools, shovels! picks! brooms! . . . They scratch, they scrub
> under the bunk, under the toilet, in the corners . . . They glue me back
> together they stick everything back together! . . . They restack me

again . . . and the wheelbarrow! . . . Off we go! . . . They carry
me off . . . them they can get out of the prison! . . . The giant doors
open! . . . A feat of magic! . . .]

Having put Ferdinand back together again, his persecutors have a
particular fate in store for him. They intend to use him as fertilizer, as a
means of implementing their "folie maraichère" [craze for truck garden-
ing] (p. 171). Considered to be excrement—complete "merderie" [shit]
(p. 171)—he is brought in the wheelbarrow to the manure pond and
dumped in, shit to be drowned in shit. We need not dwell upon the significance of Ferdinand's being treated as *merde* insofar as it is a simple deval-
orization of his person in all its aspects. More interesting is the manner in
which his particular form of punishment fits his "crime" in this imaginary
inferno. Defecation—linked to excrement by metonymy—is, according to
Freud, a form of disintegration, witness the fear of the child of losing a part
of himself. Moreover, excretion has already been compared to an analogous act—that of writing. Hence we see that Ferdinand having been dis-
membered in the course of his writing has been put back together again,
only to undergo a negatively valorized dismemberment by being treated as
excrement, as a defecation, and subsequently drowned in it. This same
image of drowning in a manure pond will reappear in *D'un château l'autre,*
where a cripple, suggesting a projection of the narrator, undergoes the death
Ferdinand imagines for himself here in *Féerie.*

We have already noted how Ferdinand, hypothesizing enormous
sales for *Féerie,* saw himself once again returning to a mythical Britanny
landscape with reputation and finances restored, a landscape exempt, like its
future inhabitant, from time and the vicissitudes of History. This return to
St. Malo would, of course, be Ferdinand's ultimate refutation of the accusations brought against him by his persecutors. Ferdinand has yet another
line of defense in which time is not denied but rather affirmed. If Ferdinand
is to be a victim of time's passage, so too his persecutors. Time's destructive passage will level all. Here the doctor will abet the novelist.

At the very beginning of *Féerie,* Ferdinand relates the visit of
Clémence Arlon and her son to his Montmartre apartment. Although Ferdinand has known the family for more than thirty years, he suspects that this
visit is motivated by less than friendly intentions. He believes they are
inspecting his apartment so as to be able to seize the most valuable items
once Ferdinand has been killed by the Resistance as a German sympathizer.

The doctor knows, and this knowledge is the means by which he will take his revenge, that his enemies must inevitably submit to the disease and decay that await us all. Clémence will be his first "victim": "Les femmes ça décline à la cire, ça se gâte, fond, coule, boudine, suinte sous soi! . . . C'est horrible la fin des cierges, des dames aussi." [Women, they pass away like wax, it spoils, melts, flows, twists, drips under you. It's horrible the end of candles, with women too] (p. 16). Disease is, of course, the specialty of the doctor, and in a number of grotesquely funny passages he depicts one of his *vous* contorting himself in order to examine his rear end, fearing that some dreaded disease, such as cancer, has lodged itself in that part of the body. Ferdinand takes great pleasure in orchestrating this self-examination: "A quoi que votre trou du cul ressemble? . . . Re-quatre pattes! Hardi! . . . genétiste! anatomiste! gymnastiste! pathologiste comparatiste! Une page arrachée, d'une main! du Larousse! et à l'envers de tout votre corps votre visage dans l'entrefesse. . . ." [What does your asshole resemble? . . . On all fours again! Be bold! . . . geneticist! anatomist! gymnast! comparative pathologist! In one hand a page torn from the Larousse Medical Encyclopedia! and upside down from your body your face in the crack of your behind] (p. 217).

Ferdinand has yet another adversary, one immune from speculations about future disease and infirmity—his artist "friend" Jules, a legless amputee who moves about in a little cart, which he maneuvers by means of two short canes. However antagonistic their relationship may be, Jules haunts Ferdinand's memory as a kind of alter ego. They are both artists and wounded veterans of World War I; they are also both tenants of the same Montmartre apartment house: "Jules mon frère, mon cœur, mon faible" [Jules, my brother, my heart, my obsession] (p. 234).[8] These shared attributes will be the locus of a complex portrait of this ugly gnome, who will function as a projection of the evil, infernal self of Ferdinand, a mixture perhaps of how society has come to see him and his own latent possibilities, a self to which Ferdinand can give expression through the agency of his narration. In his famous study of the double, Otto Rank describes the creation of a diabolic alter ego as the "detached personification of instincts and desires which were once felt to be unacceptable but which can be satisfied without responsibility in the indirect way. . . ."[9] Jules's function as an evil double of Ferdinand will be further reinforced by the symbolism of the dwarf—to whose stature Jules has been reduced by virtue of the amputation of his legs. Dwarfs are traditionally associated with the nether regions of the earth, where, typically—like Vulcan—they labor as smiths. The chthonian aspect of dwarfs further associates them with the obscure, irresponsible, and sometimes demonic forces of the subconscious.[10]

Ferdinand's dark prison "hole" in Denmark provides an immediate spatial link with Jules. Having lost his lofty upper-story apartment, he has "descended" into a dwelling place similar to Jules's studio, a dank "sous-bassement obscur" [dark sub-basement] (p. 260). And concomitant with his change of spatial circumstances, he has been transformed, in society's eyes at least, into a crippled, disgusting creature occupying the lair befitting him. His behind stuck to the chair places him in a position analogous to that of Jules, who is "stuck" in his cart. The narrator explicitly compares his life in prison to that of Jules in his studio—"en fosse dix fois noire comme chez Jules! . . . pas de gaz . . . ni de becs! . . . ni de filles! . . . Si mes murs, moi, dégoulinent! dix fois comme chez Jules! Je voudrais le voir au gniouf lui . . ." [in a dungeon ten times darker than Jules's place! . . . no gas . . . nor lights! . . . no girls! . . . Do my walls drip! ten times worse than Jules's! I'd like to see him in the slammer] (pp. 266-67).

Jules's environment is inseparable from his nature as an artist. He is a sculptor-ceramicist as well as a painter. With regard to the former medium, his search for raw materials supposedly takes him under the Butte Montmartre—we can recall the chthonian symbolism of the dwarf—where he knows of a "tunnel spécial, le seul gypse 'statuette' de la butte" [a special tunnel, the Butte's only gypsum suitable for making statues] (p. 237). Jules's kiln—which we can associate with the forge of the dwarf—is the last one operating in Montmartre. As for fire, the fire that drives the forges of the dwarfs or torments the occupants of hell, Jules, as we might expect, is master of that element. Although his apartment is strewn with cans of gasoline, which he uses as a solvent, he smokes pipes and cigars with impunity—"Jules jouait l'incendie" [Jules plays tricks with fire] (p. 239). Thus Jules's studio becomes a symbolic hell or inferno-like region, with Jules presiding over it as a diminutive devil.

Jules's demonic energy is manifested by another aspect of the landscape he inhabits. Like Courtial in *Mort à crédit* and Van Claben in *Guignol's Band II: Le Pont de Londres,* he is able to create a world about him that is a perfect reflection of his own desires and which isolates him from the intrusions of external reality. Jules's studio is a "carphanaüm" [junkroom] (p. 240), a jumbled clutter of paint tubes, clay, cans of solvent, brushes, among which only its owner seems to be able to discern any order.

And after a day spent lurching about from one end of the studio to another, Jules himself becomes covered with paint, the artist becoming one with his materials, "je suis boîte à couleurs" [I'm a paint box] (p. 240), a grotesque living canvas.

The image of the paint box raises the question of the artist's transformation by means of his creation. Although we are not informed precisely as to what Jules paints, we are told that one of his favorite subjects is Infantas. The subject suggests that Jules is principally interested in creating works that appeal to a wide and undiscriminating public. We also know that he creates to procure himself alcohol and women—those who serve as his models. His perverted use of art would be antithetical to Ferdinand's self-imposed obligation to create. However, Jules's "utilitarian" view of art may be an expression of Ferdinand's otherwise repressed desires or at least a manifestation of the evil possibilities inherent in the artist. Despite these nefarious aspects of his art, Jules is nonetheless aware that creativity offers more to the artist than just the material goods to which the artist can gain access. Jules is apparently not satisfied with creating countless paintings of Infantas. His discontent is related to the nature of the subject, for Infantas, being of small stature, are too much like Jules himself. They constitute a mirror that yields an all-too-true reflection of Jules's amputated body. He turns to sculpture as a means, given its representational capacity, of transcending his physical limitations. His desire to do so through the use of clay becomes, in Bachelard's words, a "dream of the will."[11] Jules speaks of the "glaise du Créateur" [the clay of the Creator] (p. 245), arrogating to himself—using the romantic image of the artist as demiurge—the powers of God the creator, who, as Genesis relates made man from the clay [glaise] of the earth. And just as god created man in his own image, so too Jules wishes to make himself into a creature of his desire. "Je me mire, je me vois, toi [Ferdinand] tu ne vois rien! Je me vois immense! . . . puis miniscule! . . . la preuve que le vrai artiste se crée! Toi t'es blatte, la blatte qui ne se voit que blatte!" [I look at myself in the mirror, I see myself, you, you don't see anything! I see myself immense! . . . then miniscule! . . . proof that the true artist creates himself. You, you're a cockroach, the cockroach that can only see himself as a cockroach] (p. 245). Plainly, Jules's deprecating reference to Ferdinand indicates that he perceives nothing in Ferdinand but a crippled, impotent, innocuous buffoon, a self-image that he has rejected.

Jules's remarks reflect back upon Ferdinand as creator. Although

the man may be imprisoned, mistreated, infirm—questions of justice notwithstanding—the artist has a different stature. And it is precisely in his
elaboration of a *féerie* that we have seen him transcend the limits of time and
space and country, to create a world using the "clay" of language.

But the evil element inherent in the powers of the artist remains
forever present. No sooner does Jules speak of self-creation in a spiritual
sense than he returns to his worldly preoccupations. Once again using the
language of Genesis to compare himself to God, Jules perverts the function
of the artist. Artistic creation becomes a means of seducing women: "A
genoux! Adam, je me moulerai une Eve" [On your knees! Adam, I will
mould myself an Eve] (pp. 245-46). The Eve that Jules will eventually
attempt to "make" for himself will be Ferdinand's wife, the dancer Lili.

Jules is usually less than selective when it concerns luring girls
into his studio for sexual purposes. Ferdinand is simply disgusted by the
poor specimens that fall into Jules's clutches: ". . . une blèche, une
crachante! . . . une juste sortant de l'hôpital, pas guérie . . . Ah là, alors il
me révoltait! moi médecin, anatomiste, hygiéniste! fétichiste du muscle" [a
rotten one, one spitting up blood! one just out of the hospital not cured . . .
Ah there he disgusted me! me a doctor, student of anatomy, hygienist!
muscle fetichist] (p. 265). Ferdinand has a different reaction when Jules
tries to entice into his studio the young girls that attend Lili's dancing
classes. Here Ferdinand and Jules share the same tastes for young, nubile
bodies, impeccable complexions, and proper manners. "J'appréciais n'est-
ce pas en médecin," Ferdinand remarks [I appreciated them, did I not, as a
doctor] (p. 253), indicating by his "did I not" that his admiration for these
young dancers has a sexual aspect that he, as opposed to his satyrlike neighbor, is unwilling to admit. The ambiguity of Ferdinand's feelings about
these girls is reinforced by his aesthetic judgment. Unlike Jules, Ferdinand
perceives the dancers and, more significantly, dance itself, as "formes hors
de chair" [forms divorced from flesh] (p. 273).

It is with the seduction of Lili that Jules becomes the full-blown
"esprit du mal" [spirit of evil] (p. 256) that Ferdinand has deemed him.
"Seduction" is perhaps too strong a word to describe Lili's consenting to
pose in the nude for Jules. Although Jules has been pursuing her, it is Lili,
fascinated no doubt by Jules's demonic energy, who asks Ferdinand if she
can pose for him; and Ferdinand encourages her to do so, though he is
plainly aware of Lili's sexual attraction—"elle était sexuelle" [she was
sexual] and, of course, of Jules's proclivities: "Pose Arlette! Pose pour

lui! Va! Nue! Je l'ai incitée . . . Je m'entends encore" [Pose Arlette! Pose for him! Go! Nude! I incited her . . . I can still hear myself] (p. 305). Ferdinand is ready to violate moral principles as well as aesthetic concerns, for Lili is the quintessential dancer. "La nature toute harmonie, la danseuse en l'âme et au corps, noblesse toute" [Completely harmonious nature, the dancer in soul and in body, all nobility] (p. 158). Why should Ferdinand so easily acquiesce to Jules's demands? As if to tease the reader, the narrator in remembering this curious incident wonders whether rereading the pages he has written would reveal the "pensées secrètes" [secret thoughts] (p. 305) that had motivated his decision. The answer lies perhaps in Ferdinand's obvious fascination with the perverse character of Jules, the evil artist, as an exteriorization of his own repressed desires.

Jules has Lili lie on the bed nude, her legs spread apart, her flesh turning different colors in the murky, uneven light of his basement studio. He will caress Lili, though no sexual intercourse will occur. Jules causes a transformation to take place: the beautiful aesthetic object—Lili— is metamorphosed, reduced to a mass of multicolored flesh.[12] As for Ferdinand, having encouraged Lili to accede to Jules's wishes, he is left to become a spectator of this sordid scene. First he is chased form the studio and forced to watch Jules and Lili through a window (there is no indication here that Ferdinand is sexually aroused by what he sees, as a true voyeur would be); then he is invited back into the apartment, only to be shut out once again. This time Jules gives him a painting and a a small statue to placate him. As if to signal Ferdinand's defeat, the air raid sirens begin to wail.

The "loss" of Lili is not a simple sexual escapade. As I have noted, its social and aesthetic aspects reflect back upon the role of Ferdinand, both as character and narrator. The seduction of Lili, coupled with Ferdinand's engulfment by the war, are enlarged and given mythical scope. Patrick McCarthy has compared Jules's seduction of Lili to "original sin."[13] Although the comparison is perhaps exaggerated, it is certainly true that Ferdinand's banishment from Jules's studio can be compared to expulsion from the Garden of Eden. It marks the end of an "innocent" mode of existence and the beginning of the journey through war-torn Europe that will eventually bring him to prison in Denmark. "C'est de ce moment," Ferdinand remarks, "que les horreurs ont commencé . . . qu'on a été de ces traqués, je peux dire traqués si malheureux pires que bêtes!" [It is from that moment that the horrors began . . . that we became hunted animals, I can say such miserable hunted animals that we were worse than beasts!] (p. 290).

Having been expelled from Jules's studio, Ferdinand hears air raid sirens, but he cannot be sure of their objective status—to what extent are they real or just noises in his own head!: "... j'en avais des bruits moi! à moi! des miauleries hautes! ... plein les deux oreilles des moments" [me, I also had noises! my own! loud meowings! ... my two ears filled with them at times] (p. 294). Internal and external landscapes are explicitly and self-consciously confused—specifically through the device of the head wound and the hallucinations it provokes, by means of which the artist's power to transpose events, to create a semantically autonomous work, is repeatedly stressed. This confusion is not just a simple textual strategy by which the narrative designates itself as fiction. The war is a manifestation of the evil potential lurking within man, according to Céline's view of the human condition; for Ferdinand it will be the correlative on a world-wide scale of the disintegration of his existence. Standing outside the door of Jules's studio, Ferdinand vomits and begins to have hallucinations, both activities associated, as we have seen elsewhere, with the creative transformation of reality.

The principal element of these hallucinations is a transformation of the Paris landscape. A huge sewer opens up which threatens to swallow all of Paris, including, of course, Ferdinand. This menace is self-created, with its creator becoming an observer of the potential catastrophe. It is in the second volume of *Féerie pour une autre fois* that such a posture will be further explored. Ferdinand will become Pliny the Elder, to whom *Normance* is dedicated, staring into an erupting Vesuvius that he himself has created.

Féerie pour une autre fois II: Normance

Féerie pour une autre fois I was, as we have seen, a fragmented, discontinuous narration articulated about two widely separated points in space and time—Ferdinand's experiences in Montmartre, notably his relationship with Jules, and his incarceration in a Danish prison cell, where he debates the question of his innocence in order to finally assert that he had been unjustly treated by the authorities. *Féerie pour une autre fois II: Normance* is the sequel to the previous volume in that its point of departure will be the air raid that begins when Ferdinand stands outside Jules's studio vomiting, a victim of and accomplice to Jules's seduction of his wife Lili.

In *Féerie II* there is, however, no mention made of Ferdinand's flight from Paris and his eventual imprisonment. Thus the events of the second volume can be fitted with respect to their chronology within the framework of *Féerie I*.[1] In addition to the presence of Ferdinand and Lili, both volumes share the same Montmartre locale and Jules as a major character—the double of Ferdinand. Although there are many instances of delirium in *Féerie I, Normance* is related by a Ferdinand who exploits far more systematically and self-consciously than in the preceding volume the "play" between the real and the hallucinatory.

This tension between the transformation of the real by means of delirium and the ostensible realism of a narrator as chronicler is initiated by the use of a particular pattern of opening signals already employed in *Mort à crédit,* and which will later reappear in the opening volume of the wartime trilogy, *D'un château l'autre.* Before examining this pattern in *Normance,* it would be useful to review its essential elements, such as they emerged in *Mort à crédit:* 1) An introductory prologue in the form of a simultaneous narrative, in which the author, narrator, and protagonist—all three share the same name—tend to converge. Within this first stage of the narrative, as "narrative instance"—the term is Genette's—the social, temporal, and spatial circumstances of the narrator are established. 2) The appearance—or reappearance—of the narrator's head wound, as a physical wound or its metonymic substitution. This reactivated injury is accompanied by fits of vomiting, and subsequently gives rise to delirium—visions characterized by perceptual distortions. 3) These visions are tested by one or more of the characters, whose perceptions are assumed to be normal. 4) The narrator's visions become charged with images from the past, thus instituting the transition to an ulterior narrative, the story of that past, and terminating the visions as such. 5) This second, or meta-narrative, is then pursued as the principal narrative. Although the meta-narrative maintains certain spatio-temporal and causal links with the first narrative, it transcends the limits of simple retrospection, for it calls into question the relationship between autobiography and fiction, between Céline and Ferdinand. The transition to a meta-narrative as effected by delirium marks a change in narrative voice, a narrative metalepsis.

Normance will add a new element to the pattern just described. The novel begins with a short prologue in which the narrator establishes his present situation. Several years have elapsed, he informs us, since the period of the events he is about to relate. He is now lying in bed, though we are not told where that bed is located nor why he is in it. The narrator—perhaps ill—then addresses the reader as if to renew a dialogue previously interrupted, presumably the one established between narrator and narratee in the first volume of *Féerie:* ". . . mais je vous perds pas! . . . je vous rattraperai de ci, de là" [but I'm not losing you! . . . I'll catch up with you from here, from there] (p. 11). An initial transition to the past takes place through the mediation of a sound linking past and present—that of an explosion. That noise echoing in the mind of the narrator engenders a series of metonymic associations through which the narrator returns to the past. This return both denies the destructive passage of time, for it is a past to which the narrator has access, and affirms it—the interval between past and present has been concretized by death, destruction, and suffering: ". . . le temps n'est rien mais les souvenirs! . . . et les déflagrations du monde! . . . les personnes qu'on a perdues . . . les chagrins . . . les potes disséminés" [time is nothing, but memories! . . . and the deflagations of the world! . . . the people you've lost . . . the sorrows . . . buddies scattered] (p. 11).

"Ce n'est pas d'hier que je fais des braoum" [It's not yesterday that I began making booms] (p. 11), the narrator adds. He then specifies that the sounds he hears began with a head wound suffered during World War I. This reference to Céline's mythical head injury links the first World War with the period the narrator is about to recall. He also incurs a head wound during World War II, although Ferdinand is not, of course, a combatant properly speaking. This repetition suggests a view of history—not as progression but as renewal of folly, as an inevitable manifestation of man's penchant for destruction. As a rhetorical device the head wound will serve again to designate the narration as invention, transposition, poetic delirium. Indeed, not only will Ferdinand be the recipient of that wound, but the latter will be reinforced by two subsequent falls in the same elevator shaft in which the initial accident took place. As a result of these incidents Ferdinand's head is described as "fêlée" [cracked] (p. 12) and "sonnée" [groggy] (p. 179). It is not the literal meaning of these adjectives that concerns us here so much as their use in colloquial French to mean 'crazy'; and within the context of the novel, as we shall see, crazy—applied to Ferdinand—connotes the creative delirium that is synonymous with fictionmaking.

Those three falls call our attention as well to the departure in *Normance* from the pattern of opening signals used in *Mort à crédit*. Delirium is not merely a transitional device but becomes the primary mode of the metanarrative. This variation can perhaps be attributed to Céline's desire to emphasize the contrast between the particular events of which the narrator has become a victim and the timeless moment of experience seized through the mode of hallucination. The blurring of the frontier between the (mimetic) real and the hallucinatory will emphasize the narrator-protagonist's transformation of history.

A second transition to the past is achieved by the situation of the narrator in bed, for he will relate in the meta-narrative that Ferdinand had been transported to his bed after falling in the elevator shaft and sustaining a head injury. While recuperating from his injury, he begins to vomit. The reader familiar with *Féerie I* will recall that Jules had expelled Ferdinand from his studio after seducing his wife. Ferdinand was standing outside Jules's studio, vomiting, when the air raid sirens began to sound. Here in *Normance* Ferdinand's loss of innocence and the collapse of his structured existence will be magnified and projected onto the landscape, as the bombs begin to fall. The chaos wrought upon the external landscape will correspond to the disorder of Ferdinand's internal landscape, and this link will be reinforced by the role of Jules. The novel will end with Ferdinand once again standing in front of Jules's studio, vomiting. This circularity—which is, in fact, not limited to *Normance* but encompasses both volumes of *Féerie*— will, of course, underline the autonomy of the work by functioning as an ironic counterpoint to Ferdinand's self-defined role as chronicler. A chronicle implies a simple relating of events in their linear succession by a detached observer, one who would not impart so obvious a configuration upon those events. Linked to hallucination, circularity also implies an absence of historical progression, a self-enclosed fantasy, a *féerie*.[2] But are chronicle and *féerie* so radically opposed? As we shall see, they are not, for Ferdinand will demonstrate, in playing one off against the other, that his fantasy, however personal, is no less revealing a portrait of a particular moment of history than an objective chronicle would be. We shall return to this apparent opposition between chronicle and delirium later, but first we need to examine what sort of landscape emerges from the "vision" of the narrator.

Jules will occupy the center of that landscape. The legless cripple has succeeded in hoisting himself and his cart to the top of the nearby Moulin de la Galette. The latter, once a real mill when Montmartre was part of the countryside surrounding Paris, became a famous nightclub whose spectacles and clientele were immortalized by Toulouse-Lautrec, another crippled, dwarflike artist. The association between Jules and Toulouse-

Lautrec, established by the (referential) space in which the narrator places his deformed neighbor, adumbrates the artistic activity with which Jules will be involved as the bombs begin to fall.   Having been the agent of Ferdinand's expulsion from "paradise" in *Féerie I,* Jules extends his role in *Normance,* where he will be portrayed as directing a bombardment of Paris. "C'est sa faute tout! cataclysme et tonnerre de Dieu" [It's all his fault! cataclysm and God's thunder] (p. 40).   Jules's paintbrush merges with the canes with which he guides the bombers. He will "paint" Paris with multicolored explosions, summoning the destructive forces at his command with every gesture of his body, with every movement of his cart as he defies the laws of gravity by sliding back and forth atop the Moulin. Not only does he defy the laws of space but he defies those of time as well. The blades of the Moulin, which has not functioned as a mill for many years, suddenly begin to revolve. Amid the exploding bombs the mill is transformed into a gigantic pinwheel as the material covering its blades catches fire and produces a fantasmagoria of color: ". . . les panaches partent en paillettes . . . plein le ciel . . . vertes . . . jaunes . . . bleues! . . . en poudre crépitante! Je vous parlais de feu d'artifice! . . . féerie d'artifice" [the tufts fly off in spangles. . . filling the sky . . . green . . . yellow . . . blue! . . . as crackling gunpowder! I was speaking to you of fireworks! . . . a fairyland of fireworks] (p. 64).   The word *féerie,* recalling the title of the two volumes that we are considering, emphasizes the imaginary, fantastic nature of what the narrator perceives.

What he observes is a radical transformation of the Paris landscape, a visionary landscape no less colorful than the pinwheel Jules has set in motion, no less "illogical" than Jules's miraculous feats of acrobatics and magic atop his Moulin.   Crucial to the metamorphosis of the Parisian landscape is the role of certain of the city's well-known monuments. Their depiction constitutes a reorganization—spatial and material—of that landscape, corresponding to the reordering of a mode of existence hitherto considered permanent:

> Vingt quartiers crépitent! le Luxembourg est plus qu'une rose! une rose-
> raie ardente! . . . l'Académie fond . . . en beige . . . en vert . . . dégou-
> line au Quai . . . puis la Seine . . . la Coupole flotte un moment . . .
> se retourne! coule! . . . Ah, et la Madeleine et la Chambre! . . . elles
> ont l'air de s'envoler . . . gonflées montgolfières . . . elles s'élèvent un
> petit peu . . . balancent . . . passent bleu! rouge! blanc! éclatent!
> (p. 111)

[Twenty neighborhoods crackle! The Luxemburg Garden is nothing
more than a rose! a rose garden aflame! . . . the French Academy
melts . . . in beige . . . in green . . . drips onto the Quai and then
into the Seine . . . the Cupola floats for a moment . . . turns over!
sinks . . . Ah, and the Madeleine and the Chamber of Deputies! . . .
they seem to fly off . . . swollen hot air balloons . . . they rise slight-
ly . . . swing . . . turn blue! red! white! burst!]

Paris, as the above-quoted passage indicates, is transformed into a
féerie that once again emphasizes both the imaginary nature of those explosions and the role of the head wound in initiating and designating the
fictional process. Madame Toiselle, the concierge, admits to seeing Jules
swaying back and forth atop the Moulin, but as for such phenomena as
buildings flying into the air and monuments melting, she categorically
informs Ferdinand "vous inventez" [you're making it up] (p. 108). And, as
if to confirm what Madame Toiselle has claimed while, at the same time,
denying it, Ferdinand observes a conflagration of epic proportions: "Et le
gazomètre de Clichy? je l'invente? . . . Un Vésuve ce gazomètre! des
coulées de lave jusqu'à Saint-Denis! . . . je suis saoul? la berlue?" [And the
gas reservoir at Clichy? I'm inventing it? . . . A Vesuvius that reservoir!
lava flows up to Saint Denis! . . . am I drunk? delusions?] (p. 109).

The narrator's manipulation of the narratee functions in a manner
analogous to his use of characters in the novel as eyewitnesses. Instead of
letting the reader yield to his own scepticism with respect to the manifest
violation of physical laws or historical truth—the reader knows, for
example, that the French Academy never melted under the heat of a bombardment—the narrator incorporates the reader's disbelief into his narration,
affording the latter a voice with which to criticize what has been written:
". . . salaud! il hallucine, l'hargneux cocu! . . . rien du tout tel est arrivé!"
[the bastard! he's hallucinating, the disgruntled cuckold . . . nothing at all
like that happened] (p. 142). Once again, the object in resorting to other
voices to deny the veracity of the observer's vision is to emphasize the
heightened reality of the description, to reject a criticism based upon the
desire for factual representation. On the one hand, one might dispute
Céline's choice of such a narratee, since the reader of a novel such as
Normance would surely be sophisticated enough to appreciate the work on
its own terms. On the other hand, perhaps Céline is demanding in this
hyperbolic manner the same creative participation by his readers that any
novelist demands, implicitly or explicitly.

The exploding city is often described by the narrator as a volcanic eruption, consonant with his identification with Pliny the Elder—"fureurs volcanique féeriques" [fairyland volcanic rages] (p. 27). But unlike the real Pliny, so fascinated by his observation of the eruption of Vesuvius that he was overcome by toxic fumes and died, the narrator as Pliny, as Allen Thiher notes, is both the observer and the phenomenon observed, for he has invented the surrealistic scene that he sees before his eyes.[3] The reader is reminded of the unreality of these scenes by the narrator's frequent remarks on his relationship to the events portrayed and the shaping of the landscape. The narrator refers to himself as a neutral observer, detached from the events he portrays. "Je suis le simple témoin visuel" [I'm a mere eye-witness] (p. 24); "Je ne suis que chroniqueur" [I'm but a chronicler] (p. 55). These and similar commentaries, reiterated throughout the novel, would appear to emphasize the objectivity of the narrator, his detachment from the landscape he is describing. But such is not the purpose of these interventions; indeed, quite to the contrary, their function is to emphasize the "reality" of the landscape as a vision, a heightened perception that, although imaginary, is more revealing than any objective portrayal could be. And that perception is a manifestation of the subjectivity of the narrator whose sense of an existence transformed into chaos takes the real event—the R.A.F. bombing of factories on the outskirts of Paris in June 1945—only as a point of departure[4]:

> "Mais c'est un monde!" vous écrierez! Certainement! je suis bien d'accord! vérité de vrai! Je vous ai dit: je mentirai rien . . . les phéno-mènes surnaturels vous outrepassent, et c'est tout! les chroniqueurs sans conscience rapetissent, expliquent, mesquinent les faits. (p. 40)

> ["But that's a different world!" you'll exclaim! Certainly! I agree completely! completely true! I told you: I will tell no lies . . . supernatural phenomena are beyond your grasp, and that's all there is to it! Chroniclers without conscience shrink, explain, trivialize the facts]

To this notion of a deeper, imaginative reality Céline adds the element of writing for posterity—his vision is necessary so that others, not having lived through the same period, will have a more accurate record of what took place, so that the subjectivity informing the vision will be granted immortality. Once again Pliny the naturalist serves as a foil for the narrator:

... il achèteront plus tard mes livres, beaucoup plus tard, quand je serai
mort, pour étudier ce que furent les premiers séismes de la fin, et de la
vacherie du tronc des hommes, et les explosions des fonds de l'âme ...
un Déluge mal observé c'est toute une Ere entière pour rien! ... toute
une humanité souffrante qu'a juste servi les asticots! ... Voilà le
blasphème et le pire! Gloire à Pline. (p. 25)

[they'll buy my books later, much later, when I'm dead, in order to
study what the first eruptions were of the end, and of the dirty tricks
that come from men's heads, and the explosions from the depths of the
soul ... a Deluge poorly observed means an entire Era wasted! ... a
whole suffering humanity served up to the maggots! ... There's the
blasphemy and the worst kind! Glory to Pliny.]

Other narrative devices also serve to verify, in similar fashion, the
heightened reality of Ferdinand's observations. One of these is the use of
characters from within the novel as eyewitnesses, the other is the manipulation of a narratee—the reader as accomplice. In the first category we find
Lili and Madame Toiselle. Whatever the real models of these characters
may be, notably in the case of Lili, their fictional status puts into question
their objectivity. That they are suspect as witnesses once again permits the
narrator to emphasize the creative autonomy of his visions. When
Ferdinand tells Lili that he is hearing explosions, she replies, "c'est ta tête"
[it's all in your head] (p. 17). If the reader is unwilling to accept the
description of the bombing, what Paul Ricoeur refers to as an "enlarging of
[his] horizon of experience," in terms of an imaginary reality that has been
shaped by many factors, among them works of literature, then no communi-
cation between text and reader is possible.[5] "Vous imitez rien" [you imitate
nothing] the narrator laments of his narratee (p. 148). The reader does not
simply suspend disbelief; he becomes a partner in the writing of the novel
by means of a creative reading of its text. The narrator's commentary on his
visions, his dialogues with the reader, his use of the head wound as a
rhetorical device constitute one mode of self-dramatization. The interrela-
tionships between Ferdinand and the three principal characters of the novel,
Normance, Jules, and Norbert, constitute another.

The building in which Ferdinand resides is also threatened by the
bombardment. He and Lili take shelter, along with other tenants, in the
concierge's loggia. One of these neighbors is named André Normance. An
enormously obese man, he is accompanied by his wife Delphine and his

sister-in-law Hortense. Normance works as a transporter of paper, and his profession is reinforced in the reader's mind by a rectification in the text: "Je vous ai dit aux Halles! . . . Pardon! . . . plus aux Halles! le chroniqueur conscientieux se reprend! . . . dans les 'papiers' qu'il est Normance!" [I told you he worked in Les Halles! . . . Excuse me! . . . He no longer works there! The conscientious chronicler corrects himself! . . . He's 'in paper,' Normance!] (p. 95). As an author, Ferdinand is also 'in paper,' and this preliminary link between Normance and Ferdinand is subsequently reinforced when Ferdinand berates Normance for not having provided enough paper to his publisher during the Occupation so that his books could be printed in sufficient quantities: ". . . il me doit du papier je suis certain! . . . mais moi mes tirages un petit peu! . . . que Denoël [Céline's first publisher] a plus de papier! . . . faut qu'il le sache ce Popotam! . . ." [he owes me paper, I'm sure of that . . . my printings have been affected! . . . This Hippo should know that Denoël has no more paper!] (pp. 222-23). Two of the books published by Céline during the war were the anti-Semitic pamphlets *Les Beaux draps* (1941) and *L'Ecole des cadavres* (reprinted in 1943).

When the bombing first begins, Normance, unlike the wildly careening Jules atop his Moulin, is inert. He slumbers under a table and snores, an indifference that Ferdinand envies. But Normance quickly awakens when he discovers that his wife, who is suffering from a heart condition, has fainted. He forces Ferdinand to immediately come to Delphine's side and examine her by choking him and dragging him across the floor. When Ferdinand determines that Delphine needs some vulnerary alcohol but cannot provide any, Normance attacks him once again by attempting to crush him under his great weight.

Ferdinand envies Normance's ability to ignore the bombing but cannot remain indifferent to events around him. Normance desires Ferdinand's medical skill but possesses only the brute force of a common laborer. This rivalry between the two also serves to initiate a struggle at a different level, for Normance is one of the tenants, a microcosm of society in that they collectively view Ferdinand as a collaborator. The tenants have heard the broadcasts over the BBC denouncing him as a traitor for having used his "paper" to endorse Nazi ideology. Normance's attack against Ferdinand the doctor can be interpreted as an attack against Ferdinand the writer, as a representation of society's persecution of the anti-Semitic, pro-Nazi pamphleteer. Substituting by metonymy the material of writing for what has been written upon it, the "weight" of the pamphlets has been turned against their author through the agency of this ponderous transporter of paper.

Lili comes to her husband's aid: she strikes Normance over the head with a chandelier, stunning him, and thus permitting her husband to extricate himself. Normance's resultant head wound is an injury analogous to the one Ferdinand sustained as a result of his falls. Recalling his comparison with the Putois in *Féerie I*, Ferdinand notes the similarity between himself and his antagonist: "Le sang lui dégouline plein le nez . . . comme moi tout à l'heure" [The blood pours from his nose . . . like me a little while ago] (p. 189). Ferdinand has succeeded in passing his head wound to Normance and, by so doing, has transformed Normance into a potential double. The transfer of head wounds takes place through the agency of an artist—the dancer Lili. The text informs us that it was, in effect, by means of Lili's artistic ability that she was able to rescue her husband—"d'un bond! prestesse! on voit la danseuse!" [with a leap! quickness! one can see the dancer!] p. 187). Given that the dance is a privileged art form in Céline's novels, we can interpret Lili's action as another means used by the writer to emphasize the self-consciousness of the drama of persecution that the novel presents. "The artist has the power," Frederick Crews has remarked, elaborating on the famous essay by Freud, *The Relationship of the Poet to Day-Dreaming,* "to sublimate and neutralize conflict, to give it logical and social coherence through conscious elaboration."[6]

The tenants temporarily rally around the need to help Delphine and find some vulnerary alcohol for her. They believe a fellow-tenant has a supply in her apartment, but since she is not there and the apartment is locked, they decide to break in. They seize Ferdinand and push him up against the door so that he will be obliged to force it open. But his efforts are futile and, fearing to provoke the group which is already antagonistic toward him, he directs their attention to Normance, who is lying to one side, half-asleep and half-stunned from the blow to the head he had sustained. They commence to use Normance as a battering ram, with Ferdinand urging them on: ". . . ça serait plaisir que son crâne éclate! pas que la porte! . . . comment qu'il m'avait strangulé" [it would be a pleasure for his skull to crack open, not only the door, look how he strangled me] (p. 202). By virtue of the head wound he had received, Normance has now replaced Ferdinand as the victim, with Ferdinand now identified with the collectivity. His double can absorb the punishment that Ferdinand might have received, a punishment directed to the source of guilt—the head/mind that produced the pamphlets and articles as well as the "subversive" novels. The relationship between Ferdinand and Normance thus parallels the dual role (doubles) of persecutor-scapegoat that was assumed by the imprisoned narrator in his visions of being society's quarry. The tenants succeed in breaking down the door, but they leave Normance with a gaping wound in his skull that will eventually prove fatal.

Ferdinand manages to find a bottle of the vulnerary but is unable to reach Delphine with it, who lies on the other side of a fissure opened by the bombardment. Normance launches a final attack against Ferdinand. This time he seeks to transfer back to Ferdinand the head wound he sustained in battering down the door, an enlargement of the injury he had received earlier from Ferdinand through the intermediary of Lili. He will fail in the attempt and die: ". . . ma tête qu'il vise! . . . il voudrait me la fendre!" [He's aiming for my head, he'd like to split it open for me] (p. 271), the narrator remarks, and ironically notes that he had already cracked his skull, when he fell into the elevator shaft. As the teller of the tale, whose origin is the creative head wound, Ferdinand cannot be mortally wounded the way Normance has been.

But Normance's death poses a problem for Ferdinand: with his double now dead he must once again assume the role of victim. He is once again differentiated from the tenants, not only for all the former reasons but now, in addition, because some hold him responsible for Normance's death—transferring their guilt to Ferdinand—as well as for Delphine's worsening condition. In order to avoid the rekindled hatred of the group, Ferdinand tries to hide in the puddle of blood and gore that has poured from Normance's head: ". . . je me ratatine . . . que je rentre vraiment dans la flaque, sous la flaque . . . sous la croûte" [I shrink . . . I've got to sink right into the puddle, under the puddle, under the crust] (p. 277). This attempt to make himself as small as possible within a puddle of Normance's blood is, of course, doomed to failure. Just so long as the tenants' attention was displaced from Ferdinand to Normance, the latter could serve to make Ferdinand invisible, undifferentiated, because Ferdinand had become victimizer rather than victim. But having lost his double, having resumed his previous role as scapegoat, the narrator has become as large, symbolically, as Normance. His presence is quickly discovered, and two of the women tenants—two "Furies" as Ferdinand calls them (p. 286)—commence to beat him over the head with their umbrellas, to inflict upon him the sort of head wound from which Normance had suffered. Ferdinand finds he cannot avoid their blows because he has become stuck in the puddle, which has coagulated around him.

But, as I have already indicated, Ferdinand must, necessarily, be saved. The agent of his rescue will be Ferdinand's friend Ottave, who miraculously arrives just in time to save him from the wrath of the Furies. Described as a man of Herculean strength, Ottave orders the tenants to extract Ferdinand from the puddle in which he is stuck and then to dump Normance's body into the elevator shaft, which appears to have become enormously deep as a result of the bombardment. Ottave's actions recall Hercules's rescue of Theseus from the Underworld as well as Theseus's destruction of the monstrous Minotaur.[7] Ottave has been able to assume Ferdinand's differentiation from the collectivity and has thus neutralized its violence, since the tenants fear his great strength. He has also eliminated, through the removal of Normance's body, one of the elements upon which that violence was grounded. Ottave completes the rescue by taking Ferdinand in his arms and carrying him away to safety. Recalling the projected title for *Normance, La Bataille du Styx,* Ferdinand has emerged from a kind of underworld whose "monsters"—Normance, the "Furies," the tenants— had threatened him with death for his alleged crimes. But it is Normance, his alter ego, who is cast into Tartarus. Ferdinand is, of course, not Céline, despite their numerous similarities. Nonetheless, given those resemblances, one can speculate, echoing Frederick Crews's remark about art as a means of neutralizing conflict, that the situation in which Ferdinand has been implicated has permitted his creator to exorcize, at least provisionally, certain personal demons regarding his own guilt and punishment.

Ferdinand's escape also suggests a rebirth. He is torn from his bloody womb and cradled like a baby in his father's protecting arms. But what sort of rebirth is it? Given the reference to the Furies, we can assume that Ferdinand is comparing himself to Orestes as a scapegoat figure and therefore rebirth can lead only to renewed victimage.[8] The appearance of Ottave, the *deux ex machina,* points to the repeated use of scapegoating as an occasion for writing but also to repeated writing as an occasion for scapegoating. According to the narrator, the original cause for persecution arose with his first novel and was sustained by his continuing refusal to acquiesce to silence. "Mon ambition n'est pas aux Arts" [my ambition is not in the Arts], Ferdinand had remarked in *Féerie I,* "ma vocation c'est la médecine! . . . mais je réussissais pas beaucoup . . . Le roman est venu . . . puis menottes! Cachots! haines! n'écrivez jamais" [my vocation is medicine . . . but I did not succeed very well . . . The novel came along . . . then handcuffs! prison cells! hatreds! never be a writer] (p. 40).

Another aspect of Ferdinand's drama is played out through the character of Jules, who seduces Lili in the first volume of *Féerie*. In this second volume Jules continues to be for Ferdinand the incarnation of "le mal" [evil] (p. 27). Just as the external landscape of *Normance* is a projection of the narrator's interior landscape, so, too, Jules's role in the bombardment of Paris will constitute an exteriorization of the narrator's reaction to his having been a victim of the scheming, crippled artist. Once again, Jules with his demonic energy will contrast with the relatively passive Ferdinand. Like a god hurling lightning bolts from the sky, Jules directs the bombers from the roof of the Moulin de la Galette—a Zeus in the body of a Toulouse-Lautrec.

Contrasting spatial circumstances reveal opposing personal qualities. Ferdinand is forced to take shelter on the floor of the concierge's loggia, whereas Jules from the height of his Moulin seems endowed with magical, acrobatic powers as he slides back and forth across the roof in his cart. The dwarf, associated in *Féerie I* with chthonic forces, has now become a master acrobat: ". . . il avait des trucs secrets . . . il se serait lancé au vide, il serait peut-être resté en l'air? volant? voleur? oiseau? . . . toute la funambulerie céleste" [he had secret tricks . . . if he had launched himself into empty space, he would perhaps have remained in midair? flying? flier? bird? . . . all the celestial tightrope walking] (p. 34). Jules has become a tightrope-walking clown in the circus of the narrator's imagination; but, more than that, he is the artist as performer, an "acrobate-artist" (p. 37), a "vrai artiste" [true artist] (p. 43).

Whereas in the conflict between Normance and Ferdinand art served as an instrument of liberation, in the opposition between Ferdinand and Jules art becomes a means of transfiguration as well as elevation. This metamorphosis of the artist is reinforced by the confusion (literally and figuratively) between Jules as a painter and Jules as the director of the bombardment. His cane as magic wand has been assimilated to the artist's paintbrush. Unlike the Jules of *Féerie* with his mediocre, but very salable, paintings of Infantas, the Jules of *Normance* is depicted as a surrealist painter whose dreamlike landscapes shock the accepted canons of appreciation: "il bluffe les bourgeois! il leur peint des autobus sur la mer de Glace . . . et les Alpes elles-mêmes en neiges mauve, orange, carmin, et les vaches paissant des couteaux!" [he bluffs the bourgeois! he paints them buses on the glacier . . . and the Alps themselves covered with mauve, orange, carmine snow, and cows grazing on blades of knives] (pp 62-63). In similar fashion, Jules, elevated and endowed with prodigious capabilities, paints a surrealistic Parisian landscape with multicolored explosions from the bombs he calls down upon the city: "il y a du surnaturel dans Jules . . . la façon qu'il tenait la tempête, qu'il barbouillait le ciel, bleu, vert, jaune" [there's something supernatural in Jules . . . the way he grasped the tempest, daubed the sky blue, green, yellow] (p. 62). I too would like to be a "magicien" (p. 62), Ferdinand remarks, comparing his situation to that of Jules. We know of course that it is Ferdinand whose "vision" is creating the magical, multicolored fantasmagoria through the agency of Jules.

In a moment of self-deprecation Ferdinand comments upon his so-called mediocre talents: "Je suis insuffisant pour déluges! faudrait le genre pictoral . . . j'ai que du petit don du chroniqueur . . . oh, mais le Jules . . . l'artiste! plus qu'artiste" [I'm inadequate for catastrophes, you need the pictorial type . . . I've only got my little chronicler's gift . . . oh, but that Jules . . . the artist! more than an artist] (p. 57). Plainly, it is the narrator's art, and by implication that of Céline, that achieves both a metamorphosis of external reality as well as a transfiguration of the artist himself. Jules's "painting" transforms him into a figure that transcends the limiting confines of his ugliness and his handicapped body.

However, as in *Féerie I,* the relationship between Ferdinand and his artistic alter ego has its dark side as well. The incident between Jules and Lili, which served as a point of departure for the chaos of *Normance,* is both recalled and amplified. Jules continues to interest Lili. Given the heat generated by the bombardment, the tenants suffer constantly from thirst, and in particular Jules. He begs Lili to bring him something to drink. Lili pities Jules, but there is more to her reaction than just concern for a suffering man. His energy and his acrobatic skills, contrasted with Ferdinand's relative helplessness, attract Lili; and Ferdinand, in translating his wife's thoughts, evidences once again his own fascination with his fellow artist: "Et elle se réintéresse à Jules! . . . là tout de suite . . . la façon qu'il lutte, tangue . . . ah, superbe! la force! cette force! bien sûr qu'il est hercule du tronc" [And she's again interested in Jules! . . . that right away . . . the way he struggles, yaws . . . ah, superb! his strength! that strength! of course he's a Hercules from the waist up] (p. 47). Ferdinand's feeling of inferiority, as viewed through his own eyes as well as those of his wife, is transformed into a flash of hatred for Lili, the only time in Céline's novels when

Lili is not idealized: "Je vais l'envoyer par la fenêtre, chercher Jules" [I'm going to throw her out the window, so she can look for Jules] (p. 48). However, it is not Lili but an inferior substitute for her who gives Jules something to drink and brings him down form his elevated perch as well. The woman in question is one of the building's tenants, and her name is Mimi.

The woman's name recalls the heroine of Puccini's most famous opera, *La Bohème,* based upon Henri Murger's *Scènes de la vie de bohème* and first performed in 1896. Appropriately, she is dressed in a costume from the opera. She and her husband Rodolphe—Rodolfo is the poet who falls in love with Mimi in the opera—are engaged in presenting a music hall version of the Puccini work. The references to an opera that presents a fictitious Montmartre of the 1830s as the setting for a sentimental love story between an impoverished poet and a consumptive singer reflect back upon, as M.-C. Bellosta has shown, the situation of Ferdinand and Lili in Céline's mythologized Paris. On the one hand, Puccini's Paris and the love story he portrays are the material of popular romances and no longer obtain in the Paris of 1944. Mimi's conduct will reinforce the disparity between the opera and what transpires in *Normance.* On the other hand, as Bellosta indicates, the insertion of operatic characters in *Normance* emphasizes the element of invention in the Paris that Ferdinand is describing.[9] Céline's opera, with its shouts, explosions, sirens, and its multicolored decor, will both mythologize and demythologize the artist.

Mimi, like Lili, is attracted to Jules and decides to answer his cries for help and bring him something to drink. Unlike the Mimi of the opera and unlike Ferdinand's Lili this Mimi is neither a weak consumptive nor the sort who would rescue her husband. When Rodolphe tries to stop her from helping Jules, he is soundly thrashed. Mimi steals the bottle of vulnerary for which Normance had received his mortal head wound, and flees from the building into the rubble-strewn streets in front of the Moulin. There, illuminated by the flashes from exploding bombs, she does a vulgar cancan (Lili is an accomplished ballet dancer) and sings a song off key. Yet despite her vulgarity and her ineptitude, Mimi is still an artist. She does manifest a certain grace and agility as she climbs a ladder to the top of the mill. Ferdinand describes her as "encore agile" [still agile], "intrépide" and "preste" [lively] (p. 247)—this last term recalls Lili's "prestesse" when she rescued her husband from Normance. Moreover, Mimi's acrobatic feat permits her to ascend to a position of dominance, which she will share briefly with

Jules. Atop the Moulin, Mimi is able to accomplish what the others had
been unable to do—to subjugate Jules, who will return to being the perverted artist he had been. Mimi will appeal to Jules's physical appetites. As
he drinks the vulnerary, Jules loses his canes, the symbolic source of his
power, as well as his means of moving about. He is now powerless as
Mimi threatens him with being pushed off the roof. She adds insult to injury by stripping off her clothes and putting them on Jules. Although Jules
is attracted by Mimi's naked body, given his precarious position, he is
reduced to feebly biting and pinching his rescuer. Jules's demonic energy
had permitted him a moment of transfiguration, but now he returns to what
he had been before, a second-rate artist (like Mimi) whose productions were
subsumed by his desires for sex and alcohol. The once splendid surrealist
painting Jules created with the falling bombs dissolves as the sun emerges.
One of the remaining flickering fires colors Mimi with a greenish hue—
"verdâtre" (p. 258), the same color that was cast over Lili's body when she
was in Jules's studio. Mimi thus becomes what Jules had wanted Lili to be.
This last hypothesis is confirmed when we discover that Mimi, whatever
her feelings for Jules, may have made the climb as a kind of publicity
stunt—so she can sing and dance in the nude above the streets of Paris for
all the people to see. Her performance atop the Moulin is, however, no
better than it was on the ground. To further blur the distinctions in this
féerie between artifice and reality, Ferdinand speculates that what takes
place between Jules and Mimi may be a rehearsal for an act they are
putting together for a nightclub called, appropriately, The Angels' Relay
Station. Whatever the case, their performance ends with the submission of
Jules: they descend from atop the Moulin and head for the subway—the
underground to which they have been consigned—with Jules being towed
by the penis.

　　While breaking through a wall of Ferdinand's apartment in search of
water, Ferdinand and Lili in the company of Ottave enter an apartment of an
adjoining building that has remained intact. There they discover sitting in
silence at a well-laid table a man whose name is Norbert. Norbert, known
to Ferdinand and his companions, is, like Ferdinand and Jules, an artist—
not a writer or a painter but a famous silent movie actor. Silence remains
his primary attribute. He does not acknowledge the presence of his unin-
vited guests but stares straight ahead so as to offer them his profile—his
best camera angle. Indeed, the others think they have stumbled onto a
movie set. Although not true, this supposition is consonant with the

uncanny ambiance of Norbert's apartment, which suggests the atmosphere of a dream. The "play" between performance and reality once again underlines the ambiguous status of the events and people the narrator is describing to us. The strangeness of Norbert's "performance" is further emphasized by the presence in his apartment of two corpses, those of a woman and her maid. Norbert may be a murderer become insane, for when he finally speaks, he informs his visitors that the places at the table are set for Roosevelt, Churchhill, and the Pope, among others, who are supposed to arrive for a peace conference. Norbert himself is dressed as a diplomat, a mediator in the conference he has arranged.

Peace has indeed come to Norbert and the curious landscape he inhabits. He has—crazy or not—opted for withdrawal from the world and retreat into a self-created void. As artists, Norbert and Jules represent two extremes: the first elects ataraxia, the second chaos. But just as Jules's creative powers were perverted by sexual desires, namely by Lili—who returns to him in the degraded reflection constituted by Mimi—so too Norbert's withdrawal is shattered by his desire for the same woman. And just as Jules transformed the artistic dancer into something ugly, a mere sexual object, Norbert, it appears, is prepared to so the same. Although he claims that he wants Lili to stay in his apartment simply as a hostess for the peace conference he has organized, it is obvious that he wants her for sexual reasons. As the three leave the apartment and descend the staircase, Norbert watches them in the stairwell while he masturbates, having recourse to this form of delirium by which the world is reduced to silence and becomes a reflection of the masturbator's desires: ". . . il se tripote au-dessus de la rampe! voilà l'état du personnage! . . . en transe!" [he plays with himself above the bannister! That's the state of the personnage! . . . in a trance!] (p. 355).

All three characters in the novel, Normance, Jules, Norbert, play out their roles as dramatic projections of Ferdinand, each incarnating a facet of the narrator's personality: persecution as an author (and doctor); the evil, demonic powers inherent in the artist; the temptations of withdrawal into the silence of fantasy, realms in which the contingencies of existence can be ignored or transformed in such a way as to constitute a form of escape. Ferdinand as narrator is all of these characters, all of these attributes, but, at the same time, he transcends them. He is not only a spectator in this theatre of self but also writer, director, and actor as well. He is a pseudo-Pliny witnessing but also creating the eruption, an eruption that is not only thematic but verbal as well, in the staccato rhythms of the fragmented phrases that mark the "emotional métro" of Céline's later novels. The two volumes of *Féerie* emphasize the freedom of the novelist to construct mindscapes, fairylands which, in the case of Céline, reveal a self-conscious subjectivity that defies the chaos it attempts to encompass, the *history* it seeks to replace with *story,* the silence that lies at the heart of poetic delirium.

6
Flight to Safety,
The Wartime Trilogy:
D'un château l'autre, Nord, Rigodon

D' UN CHATEAU L' AUTRE IS THE FIRST VOLUME of a trilogy of
novels that will trace Ferdinand's flight from France, across war-ravaged
Germany, to the expected security—political and financial—of Denmark.
This initiatory novel begins with a now familiar pattern of opening signals:
the narrator situates himself in the present (contemporaneous, or nearly so,
with the writing of the novel); he undergoes an attack of fever accompanied
by hallucinations and delirium; the fever brings forth a flood of memories,
the elaboration of which is a self-reflexive fictionmaking process; the
narrator relates his earlier experiences as protagonist.

The text thus begins with the narrator living in the Parisian suburb
of Meudon, having settled there after his return from Denmark to resume his
medical practice and, of course, continue his writing. Although he has
supposedly kept himself up to date as a doctor, his reputation as an accused
collaborator and anti-Semite, as well as his impoverishment, has severely
limited the number of his patients. His wife Lili must give dance lessons to
supplement their income. The house in which Ferdinand and Lili reside is a
dilapidated structure surrounded by a large garden. Situated on the heights
of Meudon, the house affords a panoramic view of the Seine, the city of
Paris, and the surrounding countryside. On the very first page, the narrator
states without equivocation that it is in this house that he will finish his
days. A circle of sorts has thus been drawn. Having been born in the
suburbs of Paris—Courbevoie—he will end his life there. At the age of 63
there are no more voyages left open to him, save literary ones, and he must
now, immobilized, endure as best he can until he is able to retire and live on

his government pension. His writing, he tells us, is a means of alleviating his financial destitution—if his novels are bought.

The location of Ferdinand's house on the heights of Meudon recalls by its placement the seventh-floor apartment in Montmartre, from which Ferdinand could survey Paris from a dominant position. However, whereas the Montmartre apartment gave Ferdinand a view of the city from the perspective of someone who as yet could control the events of his life, Ferdinand's perspective in *Château* is far more limited, now that he has but a short time to live, and his remaining years must be devoted to examining and justifying his past. He now surveys his life, notably the period he spent crossing Germany in order to take refuge in Denmark. Insofar as the present is concerned, the narrator rails against a variety of "abuses," one of which involves his publisher Achille (Gaston Gallimard). The latter, according to Ferdinand is a "sordid grocer" (p. 11) who thinks only of enriching himself at the expense of the writers he publishes. Although he attacks the predominant role automobiles have come to play in modern society, Ferdinand would like to earn enough money so that he can purchase a car and thus at least present the proper image of a doctor. He is reminded of his lack of an automobile by the daily sight of the Renault factories across the river at Billancourt.

Surveying his past, Ferdinand once again sees himself as a scapegoat. Other writers such as Claudel and Mauriac who were, according to Ferdinand, collaborators became richer and more famous as a result of the war, whereas Ferdinand suffered numerous indignities, including the accusation by Sartre—"l'agent Tartre" (p. 11)—of having become a Nazi sympathizer for money. Ferdinand is proud to have triumphed over adversity— loss of property, imprisonment, condemnation as a traitor. As always, he claims to have been innocent of any and all charges made against him.

The narrator's meditations are interrupted by a visit to one of his patients, a certain Madame Niçois, who is suffering from cancer. In order to protect himself from any unpleasant encounters he might have along the way (since he has no car) Ferdinand takes with him one of his ferocious German shepherds. Madame Niçois lives close to the docks, which can be seen from the window of her bedroom. Docks of all kinds constitute, as we know, privileged landscapes in Céline's writings. Ferdinand reminds his readers: "Si vous êtes maniaque des bateaux, de leurs façons, départs, retours, c'est pour la vie" [If you're a nut about boats, their ways, departures, returns, it's for life] (p. 65). The sight of an old-fashioned *bateau-*

mouche, La Publique on the quai-side becomes the point of departure for a voyage in time, initially a simple recollection of the past. The narrator remembers that when he was a child, he and other children raised in the asphyxiating atmosphere of Paris were taken for day-trips on ships like *La Publique* to places like Meudon in order to receive the salutary benefits of fresh air. Recalling that period of his life, Ferdinand evokes a simple world of Sunday excursions, during which a slap on the behind was a sufficient correction, before "illusions" (p. 69) about childhood instincts and complexes were to radically alter familial relationships.

This recollection of a distant past, which sharply contrasts with Ferdinand's present, prepares the return to a more recent past. When Ferdinand leaves Madame Niçois's apartment in the company of his dog in order to examine *La Publique* more closely, he perceives hooded figures moving about the boat. Among them he recognizes a certain Emile, a mechanic who during the Occupation had joined the pro-Nazi Legion of French Volunteers against Bolshevism. He also recognizes Robert Le Vigan, an actor and friend of Ferdinand's, who had accompanied him, along with Lili and Bébert, during part of their journey across Germany to Denmark. Although Emile has ostensibly risen from the grave, having died as a result of a beating he received, and has the smell of decay around him, Le Vigan is apparently "alive" but unreal, since Ferdinand's otherwise ferocious dog pays him no attention.

As to the purpose of the voyage which these otherworldly figures are preparing, it remains shrouded in mystery. Caron, the captain of the boat, bears the same name as the rower of the barque that transported the dead to the underworld in Greek mythology. But unlike his legendary namesake, this Caron appears to be some sort of ferocious giant who, with his immense oar, strikes his passengers over the head so that he can seize their thoughts. Ferdinand sees that oar but never the one who wields it. Lili finally arrives looking for Ferdinand, but she does not notice anything unusual. When Ferdinand tells her that he has seen Le Vigan, she informs him that he must be mistaken, for Le Vigan is still in Argentina. Ferdinand decides not to pursue the matter any further.

The inability on the part of objective witnesses—Lili and the dog— to corroborate the scene Ferdinand has witnessed leads both Ferdinand and the reader to assume that what has been described is a hallucinatory experience. Le Vigan tells his friend Ferdinand that he is "fait pour nous voir" [made for seeing us] (p. 74), confirming that what Ferdinand sees is in his mind's eye. Playing on the notions of sight and light, Ferdinand terms himself the "extra-voyant lucide" [lucid super-seer] (p. 66). The presence of a ship in these visions, one that brings back material from the past, recalls the appearance of ships in the hallucinatory experiences that initiate the fictionmaking process in *Mort à crédit*. There, the combination of Ferdinand's head wound and a recurrent bout of malaria produced the physical delirium that led to the poetic delirium of the text.

Here in *Château*, Ferdinand thinks that he must be having another attack of malaria to have perceived Caron's ship. The head wound, however, has been displaced. It has been shifted to Caron who, wielding his oar, skims the ideas of his victims by removing part of their skulls in a manner somewhat analogous to the notion of an outpouring of fictions from the (re)opening of Ferdinand's head wound. Caron and Ferdinand are further linked by Ferdinand's perception of Caron as an instrument by which to torment his (Ferdinand's) enemies. Those same enemies will be "punished" by Ferdinand's recollections—"je me rattrape par la mémoire" [I catch up by means of my memory] (p. 11). Moreover, if Caron symbolizes death, then, given Ferdinand's present situation, he is the goad that forces the telling of the tale, before it becomes too late. Whatever may have prompted Ferdinand's hallucinations, he explicitly links them with the creation of fiction: ". . . de telles hallucinations? auditives, encore . . . peut-être? . . . mais visuelles? littérature! . . ." [such hallucinations? auditory, yet . . . perhaps? . . . but visual? literature! . . .] (p. 82). The novel will not continue in the hallucinatory mode, as was the case in *Féerie*. But the narrator has made it abundantly clear to the reader that whatever facts may serve as the point of departure for his writing, the substance of *Château* is to be understood as a fictional re-creation.

Hence the *bateau-mouche* serves to jog the narrator's memory of happier days as well as of the catastrophic events of the recent past, and points to the textual voyage that has been initiated. Once again that voyage is in itself a dangerous journey, for if it will treat, as we shall shortly see, Ferdinand's activities during the occupation and thus justify in the minds of certain readers the persecution Ferdinand has endured, then the very elaboration of such a text, the narrator's self-defense notwithstanding, can only engender further persecution. Thus the very impulse to write, whose first public manifestation was *Voyage*—"c'est le Voyage qui m'a fait tout le tort" [it's *Voyage* that did me all the harm] (p. 59)—is fraught with peril. Once again, the narrator will attempt to obviate some of that danger by maintaining a dual perspective, commenting upon present and past while relating his experiences as "naive" protagonist.

This time, however, the narrator informs us that we are reading the novel as he is writing it. Ferdinand is "appliqué à écrire . . . tant bien que mal" [applied to his writing . . . for better or for worse] (p. 145) while lying on his bed, wracked with malarial fever. There are no references to the problematics of writing as such—hesitation over the right word, rectifications, etc.: "Je ne suis pas l'homme à discuter les conditions du travail" [I'm not a man who discusses working conditions] (p. 145). One may wonder if the narrator is attempting to distinguish himself from the practice of the new novelists writing in France at this time, for whom the material act of writing is often the very subject of their novels. Ferdinand reminds us, nonetheless, of the illusory spontaneity of his novel. It takes many thousand manuscript pages, he states, to produce a novel of several hundred pages.

The narrator's memories of the past have as their locus the castle of Sigmaringen, in the Bavarian village of the same name. In September of 1944 the Germans had transferred to this castle, which once belonged to Hohenzollern royalty, many of the officials who had held posts in the collaborationist Vichy government. Uniting all these individuals, from Pétain and Laval[1] down to the minor bureaucrats, was their common condemnation under article 75 of the French penal code as traitors and collaborators. The maximum penalty provided by the Code is death. Standing trial for treason would at least afford them some legal protection. The fear hanging over the heads of the castle's inhabitants is that they will face summary execution by the Resistance, should they return to France. Ferdinand, also condemned under article 75, arrives at Sigmaringen—spelled *Sieg*maringen in the text as an ironic play on the German *Sieg*, 'victory'—to minister to the health needs of the colony of 1,142 officials, dependants, and various refugees. The latter group, consisting largely of collaborators from various parts of Europe, grows daily as the New Order crumbles.

The town is swollen to capacity, with space in the castle reserved for French and German officials. All others, like Ferdinand and Lili, are forced to find space in one of the town's hotels. Apart from the residents of the castle, the colony is left to fend for itself, with most of its activity devoted to finding sufficient food and medical supplies. Although many members of the colony are resigned to being eventually caught and prosecuted for their crimes, others dream of escape or, better yet, a resurgence of Germany that would grant them anew the privileges they once enjoyed.

Three localities occupy Ferdinand's attention: the castle itself, the inn where he resides (the Löwen), and the railroad station. Other localities are mentioned in passing: the town of Sigmaringen, the other inn (the Bären), the Fidelis hospital, the agricultural school where the pregnant women are housed, the three barracks occupied by members of the French Milice (a pro-Nazi internal security force).

The lives of many of the castle's inhabitants are shaped by some form of delirium; that is to say, various kinds of self-delusion by which they render their existence temporarily bearable:

> . . . une certaine façon d'exister, ni absolument fictive, ni absolu-
> ment réelle, qui sans engager l'avenir, tenait tout de même compte du
> passé . . . statut fictif, mi-Quarantaine—mi-Operette. . . . (p. 224)

> [. . . a certain way of existence, neither absolutely fictional, nor
> absolutely real, which, without commitment to the future, nevertheless
> took into account the past . . . fictive status, half quarantine, half
> operetta. . . .]

Consonant with their status, the French officials inhabit a castle whose architecture and decor are portrayed as a mixture of fantasy and historical reality:

> . . . stuc, bricolage, déginganderie tous les styles, tourelles, cheminées,
> gargouilles . . . pas à croire! . . . super-Hollywood! . . . toutes les
> époques, depuis la fonte des neiges, l'étranglement du Danube, la mort
> du dragon, la victoire de Saint-Fidelis, jusqu'à Guillaume II et Goering.
> (p. 103)

> [. . . stucco, tinkerings, odds and ends in every which style, tourettes,
> chimneys, gargoyles . . . unbelievable! super-Hollywood! . . . every
> period, from the year one, the narrowing of the Danube, the death of the
> dragon, the victory of Saint Fidelis, up to William II and Goering.]

Joining the many rooms of the castle is a complex network of winding corridors and secret passageways. This kind of architecture tends to place the inhabitants in apartments isolated from one another by spaces that are labyrinthine and difficult to negotiate. Their isolation favors a tendency toward self-delusion. Although Ferdinand admits to having problems orienting himself within the castle, he is nonetheless able to find his way from one apartment to another. This ability combined with his profession as a doctor—while still sharing the general condemnation under article 75—gives him a privileged perspective on the lives of the castle's inhabitants. Thus he is able to penetrate the illusions many of the castle's inhabitants entertain about their past actions and about their possibilities for the future. Ferdinand thus continues to be a "super-seer," discovering disorder and danger where others perceive order and security.

At the foot of the castle flows the river Danube. The alliteration and dislocated syntax of the passage that describes its progress amplify the destructive power of the river: ". . . si fougueux colère frémissant fleuve d'emporter le château et ses cloches" [such a furious anger boiling river to carry away the castle and its bells] (p. 112). The river's erosion of the castle's foundation is not merely a topographical detail, it symbolizes the corrosive forces of disorder in the world that will eventually topple all structures, architectural, political, social, no matter how permanent they may seem. Even so imposing a monument as the castle is "not eternal" (p 112), the narrator remarks. As for the residents of the castle, those who believed in a Reich that would last for a thousand years, how quickly their New Order has crumbled! And all around them swirl the forces of history that will soon sweep them away.

The presence of many layers of history in the castle sustains this theme of impermanence. The current inhabitants of the castle, the narrator suggests, might learn a lesson from the past, which is so manifest all around them. Although wars accelerate the decay of institutions, in so doing they more clearly reveal the evils inherent in the human character, which does not change. The rogue's gallery of portraits of Hohenzollern ancestors that line the walls of the castle, "dix siècles de démons-gangsters" [ten centuries of demon-gangsters] (p. 113) could readily be replaced by pictures of the officials now living there. Like the others, they too, will indulge their hatred and greed for a brief moment and then pass away. This view of history as an eternal repetition of same once again tends to absolve individuals of their specific crimes. Nowhere does the narrator make any mention of the most salient crime of the Vichy officials, notably, the deportation and extermination of Jews. To do so would perhaps remind the reader of Ferdinand's complicity—though by word not by deed—in those same acts of genocide.

As we have seen, the space of the castle is discontinuous in the sense that its inhabitants are isolated from one another by a formidable system of labyrinthine corridors and secret passageways. That spatial configuration is associated not only with the psychological atmosphere that prevails in the castle but also reflects the nature of the narrative. As J. H. Matthews has noted, there is little in the way of traditional plot structure in *Château*. The narrator offers the reader a series of scenes, vignettes of sorts, that have few developmental links between them. the narrator is himself aware of this discontinuity and attributes it to his intermittent bouts of fever—supposedly occurring while he is in the process of writing the novel. The reader familiar with such disclaimers will discern a concerted narrative strategy here. In Matthews's words: "The haphazard quality of the reminiscences brought together in *D'un château l'autre* is in perfect accord . . . with the novelist's disinterest in sustained plot and with his disinclination to impose an overt interpretive pattern on experience."[2] We can add one more element to the reasons for the (relatively) discontinuous nature of the novel's structure, as opposed to other novels by Céline, a simple commercial reason. As Céline indicated in an interview with Albert Zbinden, he was very much concerned with writing a novel that, as his first published work since returning to France, would be certain to make his name known once again to the reading public and generate good sales. He felt that a sure means of attaining those related goals was to provide creative portraits of controversial public figures such as the officials of the Vichy government.[3]

I have already noted the psychological analogue to the spatial organization of the castle. Bettina Knapp has remarked that individual rooms or apartments constitute a "closed-off area that can be viewed, psychologically, as a complex or phobia."[4] We can readily see how such notions apply to the most grandiose personnage inhabiting the castle, Maréchal Pétain, hero of the battle of Verdun in World War I and later chief of State under the collaborationist Vichy government, and how the narrator destroys such self-delusions. As the "incarneur total" [total incarnator] (p. 126) of the spirit of the French nation, Pétain lives in isolated splendor within the castle. Although the narrator in his capacity as doctor to the inhabitants of the castle never has an occasion to treat Pétain, and thus never sees him inside the castle, he describes Pétain in the context of the daily walks the Maréchal takes outside the residence. These promenades are organized with a formality and protocol befitting a king. Pétain walks at the head of the procession, separated from his fellow-officials by a distance commensurate with the rank of each. The solemnity of the walk described in the text is mockingly undercut, as the narrator describes it, when the procession is forced to take shelter in an archway after an English plane is sighted. Pétain and several members of his entourage are thus jammed together in a small space, distances between them having been obliterated by the fear of a bombardment or strafing. They share another common trait which adds a note of comedy to their stroll—prostate troubles. Having prolonged their time outdoors, they take advantage of their shelter to urinate, one after the other.

At one point the narrator is invited to dine in the castle by Otto Abetz, former German ambassador to Paris. Although Abetz should have no illusions about how badly the war is going for the Germans, he attempts to overcome Ferdinand's realistic appraisal of the state of the German army by telling him, in all sincerity, that the Germans have a secret army hidden in the Black Forest. He then perorates on the "affection" (p. 228) binding the German and French people, a feeling that will supposedly institute, even if military means are insufficient, a New Order in Europe. Abetz's self-delusionary optimism leads to his vision of a colossal statue of Charlemagne that will be erected in the middle of Paris in order to both symbolize and celebrate a new Franco-Germanic Empire.

Abetz's glorious visions are extended by those of another visitor to the ambassador's apartment—that of the collaborationist writer Alphonse de Chateaubriant. As if to announce the unrealistic nature of Chateaubriant's ideas, their purveyor arrives dressed in the same Tyrolean costume worn by one of the heroes of his novels. Somehow, he relates, a "moral bomb" (p. 231) will fall upon Europe, whose effect will be the reinstatement of peoples' belief in the leadership of Germany. The visions of both men are comical, given their exaggerated nature as well as the state of the German war effort (the reader knows, of course, that Germany lost the war). A humorous dispute that develops between the two men further emphasizes the delirium of which they are victims. When Chateaubriant learns of Abetz's plan to construct a statue of Charlemagne in Paris, he recommends that the unveiling of the statue be accompanied by music from Wagner's *Ride of the Valkyries*. But when Chateaubriant imitates the trumpet part in the piece, Abetz violently disagrees with his interpretation. Chateaubriant replies by throwing a plate at his host, and the dinner party degenerates into a melee of flying crockery.

Pierre Laval, prime minister under the Vichy government, occupies an entire floor of the castle, which is decorated in a "ferocious" (p. 236) Empire style. He invites Ferdinand to his apartment so as to have an audience before which he can discourse on Franco-German cooperation—although he accuses Ferdinand of having portrayed him as both a traitor and a Jew. When one of Laval's aides arrives, Bichelonne, minister of industrial production in the Vichy government, the already unreal conversation takes another turn. Amid the disaster all around him, Bichelonne is upset by a broken window pane in his apartment, not knowing whether it was caused by a stone, a bomb, or a shock wave from a passing airplane. The only way Laval can calm him is to ask him factual questions that draw upon Bichelonne's considerable erudition—the capital of Honduras for example, or the atomic weight of tungsten. Ferdinand, until now a listener, adds to the fantasy that fills the apartment and undercuts it at the same time by having himself named governor of Saint-Pierre and Miquelon, two islands owned by France that lie off the coast of Canada, in exchange for providing Laval and Bichelonne with doses of cyanide so that they can commit suicide should they fall into the hands of the Free French Forces.

A very different atmosphere reigns at the Löwen Hotel, where Ferdinand and Lili reside. There they occupy one small room which serves as both bedroom and doctor's office. The most conspicuous feature of the hotel is no doubt its toilets, located close to Ferdinand's room. It is here that some of the realities of the situation in Sigmaringen take tangible form. If the castle represents the head or mind of Sigmaringen, filled with dreams and nostalgia, then the Löwen is certainly the bowels of the village—the place where overcrowding, poor diet, disease, and disorder are focused. Although the magnitude of the task of keeping the toilets unclogged is comically epic in proportion, there is nothing humorous about the physical and social dissolution that is taking place, while the castle's inhabitants remain sheltered in their elegant apartments.

There is also a sinister presence at the Löwen Hotel. A certain von Raumnitz, an SS colonel in charge of security, keeps an office in the hotel. He uses another room as well, number 36, into which ostensible security risks are called for interrogation and are usually never seen again. But the narrator's attention is focused more on von Raumnitz's wife, Aïcha, than on the colonel himself. With her riding crop, her dogs, her boots, her exotic appearance (she is of Lebanese origin), she is another variation of the devouring woman that we have seen in other novels. Bettina Knapp refers to her as a "death goddess," "an embodiment of the castrating feminine principle."[5] The distant Aïcha, one whom Ferdinand can appraise only from afar, has a more intimate counterpart in the wife of the hotelkeeper, Frau Frucht. Frucht in German means 'fruit,' and the bearer of the name is indeed an overripe fruit, with her enormous vagina, large mouth, and burning eyes. She is passing through what Ferdinand, her doctor, terms an "ardent menopause" (p. 253), which apparently results in her engaging in orgies with some of the guards stationed at the castle. In addition to those revelries, she also delights in whipping her serving girls for the least infraction of her rules. When Ferdinand examines her, he fears that she might try to rape him—perhaps while Herr Frucht spies upon them. But Frau Frucht desires Lili more than she wants Ferdinand, attracted by the suppleness of the dancer which she seeks to appropriate to herself. She even offers Ferdinand extra food if he will bring Lili to her. Thus we can add sexual perversion to the hunger, disease, and excrement that are characteristic of residence in the Löwen as distinct from the fairy tale world of the castle.

The railroad station at Sigmaringen is another place where the realities of the war—such as the narrator perceives them—are in evidence. This depiction will also be a foreshadowing of the role railroad stations will play in the last volume of the wartime trilogy, *Rigodon*. The Sigmaringen station is a locus of confusion, with troop trains arriving and departing, with trains full of refugees vainly seeking refuge in Sigmaringen. The hierarchies that regulate life in the castle and, to a lesser extent, in the hotels are barely apparent here. Yet in this apparently ceaseless movement of trains, in the crowds of refugees, Ferdinand perceives a curious beauty, as if the station were similar to one of the busy docks he so admired in London. Like the activity of those docks, with their ships arriving from and departing for every corner of the globe, with their immense piles of exotic products, the railroad station evokes reveries of distant countries to which one may depart and whose products, in the form of people speaking diverse languages, pile up in the station. The atmosphere of the station becomes a "fête" (p. 159) and its movement a "farandole des aiguillages" [farandole of switching points] (p. 158).

Part of the "poésie" (p. 159) of the station lies in its sexually charged atmosphere. "La vie sur terre a dû commencer dans une gare" [life on earth must have begun in a railroad station] (p. 159), the narrator remarks, contemplating the hordes of sexually starved soldiers who disembark temporarily at Sigmaringen, and the young girls who come to greet them—among them the daughter of von Raumnitz. The railroad station becomes a point of exchange not only for sexual favors but for food, information, and disease as well. But despite his obvious admiration for the extraordinary vitality of this landscape of confusion, Ferdinand does not forget its ultimate significance for him—the possibility of escaping from Sigmaringen and attaining the safety of Denmark.

An unexpected event permitting Ferdinand to take the train north adumbrates the later voyages that will ultimately permit him to cross into Denmark. Bichelonne has died while being operated upon by a certain SS doctor named Gebhardt. Since the operation took place in Hohenlynchen, a city 1,200 kilometers to the northeast of Sigmaringen, Ferdinand has the opportunity to travel north with the funeral delegation from Sigmaringen. The true purpose of his voyage is to ask Doctor Gebhardt if he will grant him permission as a doctor to travel to Denmark. Gebhardt will not be there, however, when Ferdinand arrives.

Unlike Ferdinand's future departures, this one bypasses the confusion of the railroad station—the train is hidden on a siding in the forest, and the time of departure is known only to the members of the delegation. The order of the departure turns quickly into the disorder of the voyage. The train was originally built for the Shah of Iran and is opulently appointed, a decor that recalls the elegance of the castle. However, unlike their sheltered existence in the castle, the delegates are compelled to face some of the hardships that the end of the war is bringing to others. Short of food and lacking warm clothing, the delegates are forced to go hungry and tear fabric from the walls of the railroad car in order to make blanket-like coverings for themselves. Swaddled in layers of muslin, they become what the collapse of Germany must eventually make them—shapeless creatures, bereft of identity and dignity.

These figures are no doubt supposed to evoke from the reader a mixed reaction of laughter and pity. These were powerful men who believed that the order in which they participated would last a thousand years. Recalling the image of the Danube eating away at the foundations of the castle, they did not perceive the disorder lying at the heart of existence. Yet, here, as with all the later train voyages that will be described, it is difficult, if not impossible, to sympathize with the plight of the delegates or with that of Ferdinand himself when we remember that these delegates by their actions and Ferdinand/Céline by his writings contributed to the condemnation of millions of Jews to deportation by train to the death camps.

When the delegates disembark to render the final honors to Biche-lonne and receive in return a large French flag, they encounter a landscape that is more Russian than German—cold and snow and a strong wind blowing from the Urals across the plains of Prussia. Such a landscape evokes the obvious associations for the narrator and the delegates: Napoleon's failure to conquer Russia during the winter and, more recently, the disastrous defeat of the German army at Stalingrad. The vacuous, meaningless ceremony honoring Bichelonne is consonant with the desolate surroundings in which it takes place: the delegates view a coffin, which may or may not contain the body of Bichelonne; the band plays the Marseillaise; the flag is handed to the delegates who barely manage to keep themselves from being carried off by the wind; the cries from the delegates for provisions for the return trip are ignored by the officer in charge of the ceremony.

Consonant with their fallen status, the delegates find that the return trip is far more confusing than was the voyage to Hohenlynchen. At the Berlin station, a group of children under the supervision of the Red Cross boards the train, bound for Constanz (south of Sigmaringen). Although the children have been supplied with an abundance of canned goods, thus relieving the food shortage on the train, they also bring with them a singular lack of respect for the dignitaries with whom they are traveling. The children swarm all over them, stripping them of their muslin wrappings as well as their coats and jackets. Shivering in the cold, dressed in some cases only in their underwear, the hapless delegates arrive at Sigmaringen at midnight and are thus able to sneak off the train without being seen.

D'un château l'autre ends with the revelation of Ferdinand's reason for going to Hohenlynchen, thus pointing to further volumes of the wartime trilogy. Insofar as the Sigmaringen adventure is concerned, the narrator abruptly ends his story, having reached, he informs us, his maximum manuscript length of 700-800 pages. The series of disconnected episodes has come to an end. The linearity of the protagonist's adventures is offset, however, by the circularity of the narrator's commentary. The narrator, at the end of his story, situates himself once again in his dilapidated house in Meudon, from which he can view, particularly with the aid of binoculars, the splendors of Paris across the Seine, a Paris full of memories from which the narrator by virtue of his past has been exiled. His attention focuses on a locality in the western suburbs of Paris, Mont Valérien, a military fort used by the Germans during the Occupation for the execution of French prisoners. The narrator notes that it was in this same fort that Commandant

Henry, one of the guilty parties in the Dreyfus affair, committed suicide in 1898. The narrator muses on the tranquility he would have were he to be named governor of the fort. And if he were governor, he would make the silent cells of the fort speak through his writings.

These apparently idle reveries on a minor locale in the greater Paris landscape are by no means gratuitous, given the framework of the novel in which they appear and given the context of their observer's existence. The reference to the Dreyfus affair cannot help but recall the anti-Semitism connected with the persecution of Dreyfus. Céline's anti-Semitism is thought by some to have been engendered by family discussions of the Dreyfus case when Céline was a small boy—the petit bourgeois milieu in which Céline was raised was largely anti-Dreyfusard and anti-Semitic.[6] As to the more recent use of the fort, the atrocities of the German occupiers were sufficiently fresh in the minds of the readers of *Château,* a novel that deals with French collaborators, so that the narrator's reverie of becoming its governor could be understood either as a desire for vindication or simply a mocking challenge to his detractors. Could Ferdinand be the governor of a prison where innocent Frenchmen were shot, whereas he, the author of three anti-Semitic pamphlets, went free?

Although the narrator tells us that he writes for money, we also know that his writing is a compulsive activity, a project by which the narrator addresses himself to the inexhaustibility of the depiction of the human condition, with the character of Ferdinand as the exemplar of that condition. Since *Normance* that project has been shaped to a great extent by the narrator's need to justify his actions prior to and during the war. The prospect of death, the narrator informs us, intensifies his desire to demonstrate that he had been transformed into a "bouc providentiel" [providential scapegoat] (p. 214) because he was one of the few who "voyait juste" [saw things as they really were] (p. 265). the term "voyait juste" recalls the narrator's earlier description of himself as the "extra-voyant lucide" [lucid super-seer] (p. 66). It would appear that the narrator is asking us here to merge two perspectives: the first is political, the second is aesthetic. Does the creative insight concomitant with the transposition of the real justify the supposed political insight of the author of the pamphlets, who remains convinced that it was the Jews who drew France into a disastrous war with Germany?

The novel concludes with an image of survival. The narrator finds himself once again with Madame Niçois—an obvious element of circularity. Since he last saw her she has had a stay in the hospital, at the end of which she acquired a roommate, now living with her, a certain Madame Armadine. The latter is seventy-two years old, has undergone a mastectomy, and is perhaps a trifle crazy. She has a linguistic verve, recalling that of Madame Henrouille in *Voyage au bout de la nuit,* and she is given to vigorous back-slapping. As she walks away from the doctor, to whom she has been introduced, she does a backbend which, with one leg in the air, gives her a silhouette that causes the narrator to think of the Eiffel Tower. Like that monument, she too endures. This lively old lady serves as a counterpoint to her roommate but in a relationship of similarity to the narrator. Although he is unable to execute backbends and is physically decrepit, he too endures with a similar verve through his novels. He too, though perhaps a little "cracked," evinces in his novels, if not in his continuing practice of medicine, that certain something in the human spirit that remains undaunted despite the ravages of temporal and social disorder. The tenacity of that voice will be demonstrated in the continuing journey that is the wartime trilogy.

The Wartime Trilogy: *Nord*

The breech in Ferdinand's memory created by the hallucinatory experience described at the beginning of *D'un château l'autre* remains open to other memories of the war, such as he will recount in *Nord.* After a very brief preface in which the narrator notes his age (65), his problems selling his books, and condemns such modern-day opiates as theatre, television, and the cinema, he resumes the story of his wartime experiences. Although the writing and publication of *Nord* took place after *Château* appeared, the former treats events that occurred prior to Ferdinand's sojourn at Sigmaringen. Although he continues to describe himself as a "chronicler" (p. 304) in *Nord,* Ferdinand, as always, presents a subjective recreation of the events in which Céline was involved. Although the "disorder" of the trilogy occurred because of particular circumstances, notably, as we have seen, the author's desire for commercial success through the exploitation of his readers' interest in the officials of the Vichy government, Ferdinand notes that the chronological disorder of these two novels, and indeed of all three volumes, is in keeping with the disorder of the period the novels describe—which itself is a magnification of the disorder built into the very fabric of existence.

In *Nord,* Ferdinand juxtaposes the confusion created by the failure of the officers' plot against Hitler (July 20, 1944) with the disorder of his novel. "Donc trouvez aussi naturel que je vous raconte l'hotel Brenner, Baden-Baden, après le 'Löwen', Sigmaringen . . . où nous ne fûmes que bien après! . . ." [Therefore consider it just as natural that I am telling you about the Hotel Brenner, Baden-Baden, after the 'Lion,' Sigmaringen . . . where we were only long afterward] (p. 319). Moreover, as an artist, Ferdinand maintains that he is justified in taking liberties with the events he relates—"peintres, musiciens, font ce qu'ils veulent" [painters, musicians, do as they please] (p. 319). Ferdinand's statement needs, of course, to be qualified in that the artist-writer in this case choses to convey an illusion of disorder within an overall stylistic and thematic coherence.

The famous resort city of Baden-Baden is the first of the cities in which Ferdinand and his companions will reside as they attempt to cross Germany north to Denmark. The mode of life we would expect to find in a place like Baden-Baden persists despite the war. Luxuries and privileges, deriving from wealth or from rank, permit the city's "tourists" to protect themselves from the realities of the war, to live out an "opéra comique" (p. 310). Their delirium is shattered only occasionally by the passage of an English warplane on its way to some distant target. Ferdinand is out of place in such a setting because his poverty and powerlessness as well as his lucidity do not permit him to indulge in the self-delusion of those around him: "Je nous trouvais pas du tout dans le rêve . . . dans la vérité bien tocarde" [I found we were not at all in a dream world . . . but in the shabby truth] (p. 305). Terror suddenly intrudes upon the city with the announcement that Hitler survived the attempt on his life and the preliminary roundup of numerous anti-Hitler sympathizers.

The troubles in Baden-Baden cause Ferdinand and his companions to depart for Berlin. The capital radically contrasts with the resort city Ferdinand has just left. The New Order that was supposed to last for a thousand years has been reduced to the numbering of bricks from buildings devastated by allied bombing. Curiously, as if his body were disintegrating in a manner analogous to the country across which he is traveling, no sooner does Ferdinand arrive at the Berlin station than he begins to limp and must purchase a pair of canes in order to walk through the bombed-out streets of the city. He also discovers that his appearance has changed to the point where the photo on his passport has ceased to serve as proper identification: "Traîner par les rues? . . . pas bien recommandable! . . .

j'étais pas encore habitué à être identique et moi-même et cependant méconnaissable" [Drag myself through the streets? . . . not at all recommended! . . . I still wasn't used to being identical and myself and, however, unrecognizable] (p. 349).

Unwilling to risk the danger of appearing on the street with identification papers that are now of dubious validity, Ferdinand decides to seek help from an acquaintance, Doctor Harras, an officer in the SS and the head of the Reich Medical Society. Although he is an important Nazi official, Harras is an independent thinker and a francophile, all too happy to be able to speak French with Ferdinand and his companions. He is keenly disappointed by World War II, for it has not resulted in the kinds of epidemics that used to decimate military and civilian populations during wartime. As a student of such epidemics, he feels deprived of a worthwhile subject of research; as a neo-Malthusian he laments that epidemics are no longer present to regulate the size of armies and the extent of their fighting. Throughout *Nord,* Harras will serve as a guardian angel for Ferdinand and his companions, providing them with food, lodging, papers, and protection from a hostile population. He invites Ferdinand and his companions to share his luxurious bunker headquarters with him. Ferdinand thus realizes a reverie expressed in *Féerie pour une autre fois*—finding shelter in the bowels of the earth.

Ferdinand's idyllic existence in Harras's bunker is, however, short-lived, for the presence of these three foreigners begins to pose a danger to Harras. He decides to settle them on a farming estate 100 kilometers north of Berlin called Zornhof—the name means "anger estate" in German—where they can reside in relative safety. The estate is located in East Prussia, on the edge of a vast plain that stretches into Russia (Poland having ceased to exist). That empty, windswept expanse conveys a sense of the isolation and desolation of the place, but also evokes the conflict between Germany and Russia. The novel will conclude with a description of the German retreat from the Eastern Front related by a self-proclaimed historian on Napoleon's retreat from Russia—a certain high-ranking official in the health ministry whose name is Göring. Although not related to the strutting Air Marshall, the mention of the name evokes the disastrous destruction of the German air force. The half-mad Frau Kretzer, wife of the estate's chief accountant, will frequently display the blood-stained uniforms of two sons who were killed on the Eastern Front.

Other landscapes near Zornhof will be similarly invested with symbolic significance. Not far from the property there is a large marshy area from which reeds for weaving baskets and repairing wicker furniture are periodically gathered. More important, it is an area that is inherently deceptive, filled with concealed ravines and secret paths, and the implicit threat of being engulfed. Ferdinand compares this terrain to that of Flanders, where he had been wounded during World War I, a landscape of hidden dangers, where violence might erupt at any moment. Contrasting with this ambivalent landscape is an expanse of sequoia forest not far away, with a lake in the middle. Untouched by the war, the forest suggests a former, more tranquil mode of existence, when such areas were the hunting preserves of the nobility. For Ferdinand, this forest is more like a picture than a real wilderness. He characterizes the woods as "too beautiful" and the lake "too limpid, too blue" (p. 559). As we shall shortly see, both landscapes will actualize their suggested potential.

As for Zornhof itself, it is a domain belonging to the Von Leiden family (*Leid* means "sorrow" in German). There is a large, chateau-like manor house with various dependant and outlying buildings—kitchens, stables, servants' quarters, etc. The area is a center for the raising of geese, and Zornhof has a huge flock of them. But Zornhof is also a *Dienstelle,* a service area, in which are to be found numbers of Polish maids and cooks and German conscientious objectors. The latter spend their time constructing log buildings. There is also an encampment of gypsies on the outskirts of the domain. Their function, it appears, is to repair the estate's furniture with reeds gathered from the swamp. Two Frenchmen, forced laborers, are in charge of the farm. In the nearby town of Moorsburg, there is a refuge for diseased prostitutes.

Although the estate is outside the war zone, shocks from the bombing of Berlin can be felt in the vicinity. Zornhof, as its name suggests, will be presented by the narrator as a microcosm of the anger, spite, pettiness, and dementia that are the ingredients as well as the products of the war. Harras installs Ferdinand and his companions at Zornhof, introduces them to the Von Leidens and their staff, and then returns to his bunker in Berlin. Although not physically present, Harras continues to protect his French colleague. He gives Ferdinand the key to a huge cupboard that is stocked with ample supplies of liquor, cigarettes, and foodstuffs. Patrick McCarthy has compared this storehouse to Ali-Baba's treasure cave.[1] Ferdinand will dip into its treasures each time his and his companions' precarious existence at Zornhof is threatened.

Ferdinand, Lili, and Le Vigan are lodged in one of the stone manor houses on the estate. The couple occupies a room on the upper story, on which also live several of the secretaries assigned to Zornhof. Le Vigan, on the other hand, has been given a room in the sub-basement. Ferdinand describes Le Vigan's narrow room with its barred window (a room not very different from the one he occupies with Lili) as a sort of cell, a space appropriate to the status of the group as collaborators on the run: ". . . une cellule toute ronde, sombre, un lit-cage, une cuvette, un broc . . ." [a cell completely round, dark, a cot, a basin, a pitcher] (p. 406). Spiders and rats vie for space in the room, whereas Ferdinand at least has Bébert to keep away the vermin.

The location of Le Vigan's room also suggests that it can be compared to a kind of underworld—it is located at the lowest level of the house, it is dark, and outside in the corridor sleeps a huge, emaciated great dane named Iago, a beast that might be compared to Cerebus. The dog, owned by the elderly head of the household, is neither malevolent nor vicious (as his name might suggest) so long as he receives pacifying plates of food, for the dog is kept by his master on a starvation diet. But Le Vigan is in a very special sort of hell—not that of a Hercules or Theseus—but a self-generated underworld of psychological instability.

I have already examined the role of the double in several of Céline's novels: Robinson in *Voyage,* Jules, and Norbert in the two volumes of *Féerie.* The mental breakdown that Le Vigan will eventually suffer will constitute, given the protective nature of insanity, an alternative to the lucidity that Ferdinand will maintain as well as to the various forms of delirium that will be encountered at Zornhof.

The presence of rats in his room precipitates Le Vigan's decline. He begins to fear being devoured alive by the rodents. Although Ferdinand eventually lets Le Vigan sleep in his room, the former actor becomes a kind of "sleepwalker" (p. 525), lying in bed with his eyes open and muttering to himself. The narrator calls him an "homme de nulle part" [a man from nowhere] (p. 525), an epithet that evokes the title of one of Le Vigan's films released in 1937, based on a novel by Pirandello, in which the protagonist (not the role played by Le Vigan) lives as a "man from nowhere" because he has assumed a false identity after being reported dead. As Henri Godard has remarked, the notion of the "man from nowhere" stayed with Le Vigan

in such films as *Les Disparus de Saint-Agil* and *Quai des brumes,* in which
he played the parts of "mystical characters, wanderers, and visionaries."[2]
What had once been play-acting has become a form of delirium. A collaborator, a man without a country, his "mysticism" consists in no longer seeing
"les choses comme elles sont" [things as they really are] (p. 365) but in
escaping from the chaos and destruction of a Germany in its death throes.
He tells Ferdinand that he enjoys counting the bombs that he hears exploding on a not-too-distant Berlin. Subsequently, when the owner of the estate
is found drowned in a manure pond, Le Vigan confesses to the murder,
though it is obvious to everyone that he cannot be the criminal. Trial and
execution for murder would not only put an end to his troubled existence
but also place him within the order of the law, as opposed to the treatment
he would receive from the Resistance. Le Vigan's confession is also a
manifestation of a sacrificial self—his assuming, as a means of transcending
the contingencies of his existence, the sins of the world—that will emerge
more saliently in *Rigodon,* where he will pose in the position of Christ on
the cross.

Inhabiting a different part of the manor house is the sister of the
Rittmeister, Marie-Thérèse von Leiden, who has befriended Ferdinand and
his companions. Isolated in her tower room, aged but still spritely, she
incarnates another time, an older, more genteel order that has been forced to
yield to the chaos of the present. Although Marie-Thérèse has a library and
a piano in her room (Lili can practice her dancing there), she is no less of a
prisoner in her tower than Ferdinand and Lili are in theirs. She is a prisoner
of an outmoded existence that can extend no farther than the walls of her
room. Ferdinand and his friends are imprisoned by the choices they had
made to support a New Order that is no longer viable.

The manor house at Zornhof is no less of a prison than the château.
The Baron von Leiden is a misshapen cripple as a result of a neurological
disease and takes drugs constantly to relieve his pain. He is a bitter, spiteful
man as a result of his condition and although he physically resembles the
Jules of *Féerie pour une autre fois,* he lacks the latter's sensitivity and
energy, however perverted. The Baron cannot go anywhere without being
carried by a gigantic Russian prisoner of war. He "poisons" the environment in which he lives and is, in turn, imprisoned by his rage and hatred.
His wife Isis bears the name of the Egyptian goddess of medicine and of
marriage but she is, ironically, the antithesis of her namesake. She is a
voluptuous woman who vainly attempts to use her physical charms to

seduce Ferdinand into buying drugs that she can use to murder her husband. She is imprisoned by her hatred for her husband as much as he is imprisoned by his general scorn for humanity. Although Ferdinand refuses to becomes Isis's accomplice, she obtains a mind-altering drug which she administers to her husband's Russian bearer. Under its influence, the Russian dumps the Baron into a manure pond, where he drowns. The kind of hatred Isis bears toward her husband further infects the landscape of Zornhof. The Landrat (a "county officer") Simme's body is discovered in another manure pond. His head has been split open and he has been strangled. After the Baron's body has been buried, Isis, in the company of the hysterical Frau Kretzer, is caught trying to set fire to the château in which Ferdinand and his companions live as well as a number of secretaries attached to the office of the health ministry. No explanation is given for this attempted arson, but we can suppose that it is part of a spreading dementia that, once again, justifies the name Zornhof.

Yet another aspect of that dementia reveals itself in an incident that takes place in the swampy area bordering the Von Leiden property. As I have noted, Ferdinand compares the area to the Flanders countryside that he came to know all too well as a soldier in World War I. He evokes its deceptive appearance, its apparent innocence which may hide sinister dangers. This perception is consonant with the traditional image of the swamp as an ambiguous landscape owing to the shifting demarcation between water and land. Ferdinand's perception of the landscape as menacing is heightened by the possibility that it might contain some clue as to the fate of the Rittmeister von Leiden, the Baron's father and titular ruler of Zornhof. He wonders why the exploration of the swamp to which he has been invited, ostensibly for the purpose of looking for reeds so that the gypsies encamped on the property can repair the domain's furniture, necessitates the presence of several policemen. As for the Rittmeister, he is an imposing figure in the gallery of grotesques that inhabit Céline's novels. Well over ninety years of age, the Rittmeister served as a cavalry officer in both the Franco-Prussian war and World War I. He scandalizes his family by his predilection for having the daughters of the Polish serving women gently beat him and then urinate upon him. One morning, the Rittmeister in full uniform rides off on his horse toward the East, with the intent to singlehandedly engage the oncoming Russian troops. Disappearing on the horizon, he resembles a decrepit Don Quixote as he embarks on his mission.

The Rittmeister's action, though the product of an ostensibly senile mind, recalls a more heroic age. But his fate is not to be slain in honorable combat on the field of battle. The Rittmeister is found during the course of the reed gathering expedition to the swamp, bearing out the sinister implications of that landscape. He was defeated not by the advancing Russians but by a group of prostitutes from Moorsburg who had escaped from their confinement for venereal disease. They had seized him, stripped off his uniform, put him in women's clothing, and beaten him almost to death with a shovel. A second person, an official from Zornhof, lies alongside the Rittmeister, also badly battered. A group of prostitutes is found near the two men, occupied with the roasting of the Rittmeister's horse for food. The prostitutes, with their filthy, tattered clothing, their mud-covered faces, and their wild, unkempt hair, suggest a band of bacchantes frenzied by the brutality of what they have perpetrated. They embody in a particularly vivid manner the madness that has seized all of Europe, and which has manifested itself at Zornhof as well. The Rittmeister—who will subsequently die from the injuries he has received—and the Revizor are victims of a hatred that transforms human beings into animals or into deformed cripples.

Harras ultimately returns to Zornhof, accompanied by "doctor-general" Göring, in order to restore discipline after the murders and beatings. Harras informs Ferdinand that the latter's "idée fixe" (p. 694) of traveling north can be at least partially realized. Göring, apparently ignorant of the possibility that Ferdinand may wish to flee Germany, stamps a pass that enables him and his wife to make a tourist excursion to Wärnemünde on the north coast of Germany. It is only when Ferdinand returns to Zornhof, there being no possibility at the moment of his crossing to Denmark, that he will be informed of his assignment to the French government in exile at Sigmaringen, which lies to the south.

Nord, as we know, had to be revised in 1960 after two libel suits were lodged against Céline for defamation of character, by the family on whose farm Céline and his group were sheltered and by a doctor who saw himself as the model for Harras. The result of these suits was a change in the proper names used in the novel for the so-called definitive edition of 1974. Céline's strategy here as elsewhere was to use autobiographical materials as a point of departure for fictional recreation. As we have come to expect, the narrator always attempts to anticipate his critics. He notes of the characters he describes in *Nord:* "Tous ces êtres dont je parle seraient maintenant devenus fantômes par la force des choses . . . ils étaient déjà je dois dire" [All these beings of whom I speak would now have become ghosts by the very nature of things . . . they already were I must say] (p. 445). It is not the passage of time that has caused these individuals to pass away, nor the circumstances of the war, but rather, as the narrator himself indicates, they never existed other than as characters in a novel, whatever may have been the basis in reality for their creation. Zornhof itself is granted the same status. The narrator notes that twenty years later he doubts if the place ever existed at all and adds "il est temps qu'on refasse les cartes" [it's time to redo the maps] (p. 592). Ferdinand is toying with his readers, telling them that Zornhof, whatever its antecedents, can be located only on the map of the writer's (and reader's imagination).

The narrator has a particular reader in mind to whom he addresses the above-mentioned lesson on differentiating between fact and fiction. Once again the implied reader is a narratee who serves as an antagonist, who supposedly reads the novel because he despises its author. And once more the narrator manipulates his narratee so as better to defend what he has written. He notes ironically that the "small success" (p. 629) he has enjoyed is founded upon his having served as a focus for hatred, and therefore a force for unification, in an otherwise fragmented (French) society. The sacrificial victim thus ensures the "health" of the collectivity. Not only is its ethical or political "health" maintained, but its aesthetic "health" as well. The narratee hates Céline's style as much as he despises Céline's politics. He claims that Céline's use of ellipsis points, renders the novels after *Voyage* "unreadable" (p. 563). The narratee's reaction to the style of *Nord* permits Ferdinand to emphasize the uniqueness of his writing, as opposed to the acceptable, "classical" style of other novelists, to subvert the norms of the public. Ferdinand will have but one last struggle with his adversary readers—the writing of *Rigodon,* the third volume of the wartime trilogy and Céline's last work, completed two days before his death.

The Wartime Trilogy: *Rigodon*

On June 30, 1961, Céline wrote two letters to his publisher, the Editions Gallimard, indicating that the novel—entitled *Rigodon*—on which he had been working for the past eighteen months was completed. And he requested that the usual contracts be drawn up and the advertising prepared for its publication. The following day, Céline suffered a fatal stroke.

Although the novel was indeed finished, Céline was unable to give it the scrupulous editing that marked, despite appearances, the other novels whose publication he had been able to oversee. That we have this last novel at all attests to the tenacity of the author, who expresses in the text—through his narrative persona Ferdinand—his fear that poor health will cause him to die before he can complete the third volume of the wartime trilogy: "... je sais pas si je finirai ce livre ... je sens les Parques me gratter le fil" [I don't know if I'll ever finish this book ... I can feel the Fates scraping away at my thread] (p. 906). Despite these intimations of his impending death, the narrator is able to accomplish his goal—to "pick up" his readers at the point where he had left them in *Nord,* at the moment when Lili, Le Vigan, and Ferdinand depart from Zornhof, and deposit them in Denmark, when Lili and Ferdinand have reached the apparent safety of Copenhagen.

As many critics have noted, the novel's title is polyvalently significant as both an adumbration of the events of the novel and a reference to preceding novels. As for the lexical meanings of *rigodon* we can note the following: a dance performed by a couple in double time, in which the couple does not advance but takes one step forward followed by one step backward; a drum role used in the army to accompany the punishment of a soldier; a bulls-eye in target practice. All three meanings will be amplified in the novel: the voyage that Lili and Ferdinand take to Denmark (and let us not forget that Lili is a dancer) will constitute only a semblance of progress in the sense that they will be arrested and Ferdinand subsequently imprisoned; Ferdinand will once again serve as sacrificial victim, the target of persecution.[1]

The novel begins with a renewal of the narrative impulse that initiated the trilogy. Ferdinand is at home in Meudon, besieged by reporters and critics who, in addition to wanting his opinions on a variety of subjects, are motivated for the most part, he believes, by a desire to demonstrate to their audiences that Ferdinand is as "loathsome" (p. 715) as they imagine him to be. Ferdinand mocks them or simply chases them away. In the course of ridding himself of these bothersome interviewers, Ferdinand encounters a priest who has come to beg his pardon for having written about him in particularly villainous terms. In his attempt to send the man away, Ferdinand is caught in a downpour and subsequently catches a fever—that will later be aggravated by a recurrence of his malaria. Confined to his bed, Ferdinand has an attack of delirium. We can recognize here the pattern of opening signals to which I have already called attention.

An attack of delirium "stimulates" Ferdinand's memory, permitting a return to past experiences. The hallucinations associated with the attack announce, self-consciously, the onset of the fictionmaking process—the transformation of the (auto) biographical data into novelistic form. Such a transformation will be reinforced by hallucinatory episodes within the narration.

One constituent element of that pattern that I have not mentioned with regard to *Rigodon* is the metaphorical head wound, which, as we have seen so often, is linked to the outpouring of the narration. As was the case in *Château*, in *Rigodon* the head wound is displaced—this time onto the priest who causes the fever. When the man leaves, Ferdinand says to himself, "je voudrais qu'il culbute, qu'il s'ouvre le crâne! sous la pluie à déconner" [I'd like to see him stumble head over heels and split open his skull! talking nonsense in the rain] (p. 720). The novel that will emerge from Ferdinand's delirium will replace the "nonsense" of the priest. Subsequently, within the time frame of the narration, Ferdinand will sustain two head injuries: one from a fallen brick, the other from a collapsed shelf of groceries. Although both occurrences befall the dramatic protagonist rather than the narrator, both lead to hallucinations and thus reinforce the creative delirium with which the novel is initiated.

As the narrator lies in bed wracked by convulsions, the passage from past to present is immediately effected by an apparition. This time he perceives a certain Doctor Vaudremer, a colleague whom he had met during his flight from Paris to Germany. Vaudremer, greenish and phosphorescent like Mille-Pattes in *Guignol's Band*, has apparently risen from the dead. Vaudremer's appearance is Ferdinand's signal for "departure" (p. 724). The narrator extends his hand to the readers whom he had left behind at Zornhof: "Je vous reprenais à Zornhof . . . je ne vous perdais plus" [I was picking you up again at Zornhof . . . I wasn't losing you any more] (p. 726).

Unlike the first two volumes of the trilogy, which are organized around two principal stops on the voyage to Denmark, Sigmaringen in *Château* and Zornhof in *Nord, Rigodon,* as its title might suggest, is a novel that deals with almost constant movement, a movement which, of course, will ultimately prove illusory. As we saw in *Château*, movement meant travel by train. The train and notably the train station had become for the narrator an image of a Europe plunged into chaos and confusion, a Europe in which flight from one point to another, without any real notion of destination, had become a mode of existence. In *Rigodon* the "play" between the confused desperation of the station, where being stranded can be fatal, and the comparative order and safety of the train in motion shapes Ferdinand's journey. Thus, relatively speaking, the train ride itself will be uneventful. The majority of the novel will be devoted to the halts before a train can be boarded or reboarded. Each stop brings Ferdinand and Lili face to face with the war-ravaged wasteland into which allied bombing had transformed Germany. Ferdinand refers to himself as a "chroniqueur des grand guignols" [chronicler of punch and judy shows] (p. 732), and there is some truth to Alan Thiher's remark that the delirium of the narrator is appropriate to the delirium of the circumstances he is describing.[2] However, the only real danger Ferdinand faces is being stranded and thus eventually turned over to the French authorities as a collaborator—a situation of his own making. And once again, for this critic at least, Ferdinand's train rides cannot help but recall those other trains that crisscrossed Europe, bearing their passengers to very specific destinations with names like Auschwitz and Treblinka.

The first train Ferdinand and Lili take will bring them as far North as they will go before actually crossing into Denmark. The train they board at Moorsburg, outside of Zornhof, will convey them to Rostock and Wärnemünde, on the northern coast of Germany, just across from Denmark. Unable to cross over they will then swing south, going as far as Sigmaringen, before moving north again. Thus the two voyages north, the first to the coast, the second crossing over to Denmark, will frame the journey recounted in *Rigodon* as well as accentuate its difficulty—having to take the long way around to Denmark, to which they had been so close. At the Moorsburg station Le Vigan will be left behind with Bébert so that Ferdinand and Lili can ascertain the possibilities of finding a boat for Denmark. At the station we see what will become a familiar image of the war—a crowd of desperate people waiting to board the train, any train, that will perhaps bring them to a more hospitable locale, as far from the destruction of the war as possible. They must storm the train when it arrives, in order to overpower the soldiers guarding it, the others wanting to get on the train, and those who are already on board. The train is filled to capacity with fleeing soldiers and civilians, some healthy, some wounded, some already dead. The narrator compares the train to a "bristly caterpillar" (p 735), with its protruding legs, arms, and heads. The sight of such a train is not without its comical aspects, as the narrator notes. However, this confusion of body parts is equally an image of the fragmentation effected by the war, whereby soldiers and civilians alike have become so many scattered pieces of humanity jumbled together by the events in which they have been trapped. The regular cars of the train are so stuffed with bodies, alive and dead, that Ferdinand and Lili are compelled to find a place on the flatbed cars, amid the piles of war materiel.

So long as the train is in motion the passengers are relatively safe, despite the dangers of air attack or sabotaged tracks. Thus when the train comes to an abrupt stop in the middle of an open plain on the outskirts of Rostock, it can only mean danger for the passengers. In this case, as Ferdinand discovers, the train has been halted so that the dying and wounded can be sorted out according to a "nietzschean technique of natural selection" (p. 743), by means of which the Nazis decide who shall receive treatment: those who are alive after several days of exposure to the cold and snow are taken to hospitals; those who perish are buried in mass graves. For Ferdinand, intent upon reaching the coast so that the train may be exchanged for a ship that will take him to Denmark, the spectacle of the wounded being left to the elements is not one to divert him from his goal. As for this Nazi version of triage, it was not "dumb" (p. 743), he remarks.

Ferdinand perceives the ship he is seeking in the port area of Rostock, adjacent to a beach resort. The bright colors of the shuttered houses and the abandoned state of the resort put into sharper focus the bleakness of the war. As for his ship, Ferdinand can only watch it depart for its home port, knowing that there is no way to him to gain access to it. He compares the calm sea across which the ship is gliding to the flat plain surrounding Zornhof. Seascape and landscape merge to create an endless grey expanse that seems to mock the ineffective efforts of the voyager to ever reach the refuge of Copenhagen, lying somewhere beyond the limitless gray of land and sea and sky: ". . . une platitude grise . . . le ciel, les petits galets, l'eau . . . à Zornhof c'était la plaine qui faisait l'effet de ne pas finir . . . " [a grey flatness . . . the sky, the small shingles, the water . . . at Zornhof it was the plain that seemed never to end] (p. 748).[3]

Having come as far north as they could, Ferdinand and Lili are obliged to return south, to rejoin Le Vigan at the Moorsburg station. There they are informed by two soldiers sent by Ferdinand's friend Harras, the same medical officer who had arranged for their stay in Zornhof, that they are being sent to the town of Sigmaringen, where the remnants of the Vichy government have taken refuge. Although Céline and his party had indeed been sent to Sigmaringen after they stay at Kränzlin, the manor to which the

name Zornhof was given, their sojourn at Sigmaringen will not be related in
Rigodon, since it had already been described in *D'un château l'autre.* The
narrator postulates in *Rigodon* a second trip to Sigmaringen, which, as we
shall see, consists of a simple stopover. Their journey toward Sigmaringen
is uneventful until they reach a station in the suburbs of Berlin, where they
must change trains. The train in question has been appropriated by the
army, but the Wehrmacht officers and soldiers occupying it are helpless
against the crowd of men, women, and children who assault the train in
order to force their way aboard. German order quickly gives way to German anarchy. The narrator measures the contrast between the two as an
image of the war and remarks that of all the things he has seen he will never
forget "l'Allemagne en furie nihiliste" [Germany in nihilistic fury] (p. 759).
This time Ferdinand and his companions are forced to become part of the
tangle of limbs and torsoes, which they had formerly observed with ironic
detachment.

Ferdinand and his group disembark from the train when it stops at
Ulm, north of Sigmaringen. Whereas Ferdinand is pleased by the sight
before him of deserted streets and empty houses, grateful for the absence of
officials and for some air and sunshine, Le Vigan is in a very different
mood. Perhaps still only partly sane, Le Vigan has sunk into deep gloom,
and Ferdinand attempts to "warm him up" (p. 775) by perceiving the landscape through Le Vigan's eyes as a void, an ideal landscape because death
serving as a "vacuum-cleaner" (p. 775) has eliminated human beings, those
pernicious and evil creatures, from the scene. Although Ferdinand himself
has frequently expressed views that are no different from Le Vigan's with
regard to his faith—or lack thereof—in humankind, Le Vigan feels he has
transcended social criticism and longs for a nothingness that would provide
the ultimate relief from the tensions of contingent existence.

Insofar as the inhabitants of the now deserted town are concerned,
death, or possible death, has taken the form of a contingent of Storm
Troopers. Rommel's funeral is about to take place, and the residents of the
city have been driven into the surrounding forest for security reasons—and
there is some doubt as to whether or not all of them will return alive. One
of the few citizens left behind is the demented chief of the local fire brigade,
Captain Schmidt, who fills the empty space with his delusions. In order to
placate the mad captain and avoid any possible confrontation with Nazi
bureaucracy, Ferdinand and his companions accede to the captain's request
that they patrol the town's main street with fire extinguishers so that they

can put out incendiary devices dropped by allied aircraft. Le Vigan holds the fire extinguisher, with Lili walking behind him, and Ferdinand on his canes, feigning to be blind, bringing up the rear. There is, of course, nothing to see, since the incendiary devices exist only in the Captain's imagination. This comical parade constitutes an ambivalent image of the war and of the situation in which Ferdinand and his friends find themselves. They are caught up in the insanity of the war but, in this case at least, use that very madness as a means of protection. For Ferdinand the "super-seer" this moment of playing at being blind constitutes a respite from the effort to remain lucid that he has imposed upon himself, precisely so he will not become like Schmidt and Le Vigan.

Reality—or another variant of madness—suddenly intrudes upon Ferdinand's game in the form of a large procession of trucks and cars that constitute the entourage of Marshall von Rundstedt, who has entered the town to attend Rommel's funeral. Le Vigan in an attack of delirium, which takes the form of a hitherto unknown patriotic zeal (Le Vigan is on the run for having made pro-Nazi broadcasts), throws himself in front of the Marshall's car, forcing it and the whole procession to come to an abrupt halt: "Arrière Rundstedt! non, vous n'irez plus en France" [Back Rundstedt!, no you'll not go back to France] (p. 792). Paradoxically perhaps, but no doubt typical of the topsy-turvy world that Le Vigan and his friends have come to inhabit, his gesture, which might have brought about their death, saves the group from the crazy fire brigade captain. After being momentarily detained and interrogated, they are sent by Von Rundstedt to Sigmaringen in a special train, in which they are the only passengers.

I have already noted the place of this second journey to Sigmaringen within the chronology of the wartime trilogy. Here in *Rigodon*, Sigmaringen is simply a transit point. When they arrive at the station, the German Commandant von Raumnitz is waiting for them. They discover that, among other plans, arrangements have been made for Le Vigan to leave the group and travel south to Rome—a direction diametrically opposed to the one Ferdinand and Lili have resolved to take. The choice Le Vigan has made and his behavior at the railway station indicate that once again Le Vigan has opted for madness, for self-delusion, as opposed to Ferdinand's lucidity. Le Vigan assumes the pose of Christ crucified in order to emphasize to Von Raumnitz the martyrdom he has undergone. "Je voulais être seul" [I wanted to be alone] (p. 801), he tells Ferdinand—alone with his protective madness as he makes his pilgrimage to the holy city of Rome.

Ferdinand and Lili acquire new comrades as they leave Sigmaringen and begin to head north, to a city named Oddort—Horace de Restif and his band of pro-Vichy commandos. They are locked into boxcars which are to be opened only upon reaching their destination. The city to which they have been sent is not be found on a map of Germany, as Ferdinand and the others discover. The name of the city, a combination of the English "odd" and the German word for "place," *Ort,* alerts the reader that the destination in question will be of a very special nature.

When Ferdinand and his companions arrive at Oddort, they discover that the city is only a railroad station. Unlike most of the other stations that Ferdinand has encountered, this one is free from frenzied crowds willing to take any train. The waiting room is a kind of office, in which they are welcomed by General Swoboda, commandant of the district. However, Restif knows that Swoboda's welcome is no less deceptive than the station itself, for the latter is a station only in appearance. It will be the last stop for trainloads of refugees and functionaries, for whom there is no longer any room in the concentration camps. Ferdinand and the others are to be destroyed along with the station. But Restif is aware of the plans, and he and his men assassinate the General before they can be put into effect. Ferdinand and Lili flee toward Hanover just as a flat car comes rolling up equipped with artillery pieces to destroy everything in sight. The scene dissolves into a chaos of exploding bombs and shadowy forms as the station is obliterated. One can interpret the events at Oddort as a transition point in a symbolic journey. Ferdinand and Lili have passed through the gates of death at Oddort and will shortly find themselves in the inferno of the bombed city of Hanover, a necessary passage before they can "ascend" toward the hoped-for paradise of safety in Copenhagen.

Hanover is a city in flames from the effects of allied bombardments, a city guarded by dead soldiers incinerated at their posts. Ferdinand's perception of the devastation of the city is juxtaposed with an aesthetic appreciation of the horror—the fantasmagoria of multicolored flames gives the city, which Ferdinand had known before the war, a gayness and beauty it had not hitherto possessed.[4] Ferdinand is particularly struck by the rhythm of the flames that dance their way across this inferno-like landscape. One may recall a similar perception in *Normance,* when Ferdinand described the beauties of Paris as it burned. Whereas in the case of *Normance* the spectacle in question was plainly a hallucination, Ferdinand's perception of the beauties of Hanover on fire is a visionary recreation of the real:

... les flames vertes roses dansaient en rond ... vers le ciel! ... il
faut dire que ces rues en décombres faisaient autrement plus gaies, en
vraie fête, qu'en leur état ordinaire, briques revêches mornes ... ce
qu'elles arrivent jamais à être, gaies, si ce n'est pas le chaos, soulève-
ment, tremblement de la terre, une conflagaration que l'apocalypse en
sort. . . . (p. 817)

[. . . the green pink flames were dancing in a circle ... toward the sky!
. . . you've got to say that these streets in ruins were far gayer, really
merrymaking, than in their usual state, sullen gloomy bricks ... what
they never succeeded in being, gay, if not for the chaos, rising and
quaking of the earth, a conflagration that was brought forth by the
Apocalypse. . . .]

Ferdinand, Lili, and Felipe, an Italian brickworker whom they have
recently met, make their way through the smoldering city to the Hanover-
South station, only to discover that their next train will leave from the
Hanover-North station. While at the South station they manage to procure a
hand truck so as to more easily transport their baggage across the city.
Their act provokes the rage of several of the people waiting at the station,
who then begin to pursue the trio across the ruined city. The chase is not
without a certain slapstick quality since neither pursued nor pursuers are
able to move with any great speed or agility. The chase comes to an end
when bombs begin to fall and the participants are obliged to take shelter. At
this point Ferdinand is struck in the head by a brick, ostensibly dislodged
by one of the exploding bombs. The literal head wound serves to reinforce
the symbolic head wound recalled at the beginning of the novel and thus
reaffirms the creative autonomy of Ferdinand's perceptions.

At the North station, Ferdinand and Lili are able to board a train but
must ride in a flat car loaded with searchlights of the sort used in anti-
aircraft defense. Among their fellow passengers is a class of retarded children in the care of a tubercular Frenchwoman. When the train stops at an
improvised station on the outskirts of Hamburg, Ferdinand and his
companions disembark in order to look for food. However, given the
Frenchwoman's precarious health, they discover that they have been put in
charge of her group. The ruins of Hamburg will constitute an immense
playground for the children. Unable to speak except for an occasional
grunt, lacking sufficient intelligence to be even vaguely cognizant of the war
and the destruction it has produced, their handicap becomes a form of

protective delirium that shelters them form external reality. Ironically, the childrens' imbecility will serve as the means by which Ferdinand and Lili will be able to cross over into Denmark.

Ferdinand informs us that he knows Hamburg from his days as a medical representative for the League of Nations. But the city he now sees before him bears little resemblance to the bustling port he once knew. Once again, he describes a world turned upside down—sometimes literally—with trams lying upended, buildings reduced to massive piles of rubble, melted asphalt, bodies burned beyond recognition.

But Ferdinand thinks less of the Hamburg of the past than he does of Montmartre, to which he repeatedly compares the ruined city. He frequently uses the term "buttes," "knolls" or "mounds," as in the Butte Montmartre, to describe this German city, where upheavals of the earth have created hills similar to the one upon which Montmartre stands. Unlike the latter—and we may recall the significance of Ferdinand's seventh-story apartment as opposed to Jules's sub-basement—these mounds have huge fissures leading to parts of the city that are now underground. It is literally an underworld into which Ferdinand will enter before once again emerging into the light for the final passage to Denmark. This underground necropolis along with the inferno of Hanover and the void of Oddort suggests a variant of the symbolic death the initiate undergoes in the typical *rite de passage* before being "reborn" as an adult equipped with the spiritual knowledge essential to his culture. In the case of Ferdinand that knowledge is but a reaffirmation—of what he had discovered about the horrors of war when he was a soldier, and of the need to reach the shelter of Denmark.

When the group of children enters one of the above-mentioned mounds through a large fissure, Ferdinand follows them. While exploring a grocery store that has been buried almost intact, Ferdinand is struck on the head by a collapsing shelf of groceries, reinforcing once again the vision engendered by the creative head wound. Ferdinand's underground exploration will subsequently be linked by the narrator to the basement prison cell he will occupy in Denmark. We are reminded that Ferdinand has been a metaphorically underground man and that his journey to Denmark has been a underground adventure. The narrator comments: ". . . j'aime pas surtout les sous-sols, ni les crevasses . . . l'expérience de très vilaines choses, réclusions et le reste . . . si on vous invite en sous-sol c'est pour vous malmener horrible" [I dislike above all basements and crevasses . . . the experience of very ugly things, incarcerations and the rest . . . if they invite you to the basement, it's to mistreat you horribly] (p. 890). As I have already noted, the narrator's residence at Meudon may be shabby but at least it is on the heights of the town and that elevation is symbolic of the narrator's triumph over adversity, notably his transformation of experience into novelistic form.

Like the others, Ferdinand enters the mound through the fissure. He confesses to being fascinated by such openings. He extolls the Romans for their circuses, during the course of which men and women were torn open. He also recalls his experience in obstetrics, when he was able to witness during the birth of a child the "play" between interior and exterior: "J'ai été accoucheur, je peux dire passionné par les difficultés de passages, visions aux détroits, ces instants si rares où la nature se laisse observer en action" [I was an obstetrician, I can tell you I was excited by the difficulties of passages, visions at straits, those so rare instances when nature lets herself be observed in action] (p. 870).

Although the narrator speaks of these moments of insight, literally and figuratively, as rare, even a casual reader of Céline's fiction can readily discern the thematic implications of the sort of vision he is describing. Céline's view of the human condition has been predicated upon a revelation of "nature in action"; that is to say, human nature as it is laid bare by the narrator's verbal scalpel. And within this context of a "play" between appearances and reality giving way to the revelation of the diseased body of society exposed by the author-doctor, one can discern the "difficulties of passages" of all sorts that have been overcome by the protagonist so that he might attain those insights—the passage in which he was raised, the *rites de passage* of the war, the passages of journeys, and, lastly, the verbal passages by which the vision is textualized.

Ferdinand, Lili, and the children, for whom they continue to care, finally board the train that will take them to the border city of Flensburg and then into Denmark. The children provide the necessary cover story, for the group is taken aboard a Red Cross train whose officials are willing to accept the children as Swedish and Ferdinand and Lili as their guardians. Once again we can note the irony that it is a group of moronic children that permits the "super-seer" finally to reach his goal. But as Ferdinand contemplates the Danish landscape, his perceptions become distorted by his knowledge that what awaits him is not political and financial refuge but incarceration: "Ils m'ont eu deux ans en cellule, pour rien du tout, pour s'amuser" [They had me for two years in a cell, for nothing at all, to amuse themselves] (p. 906). Thus his perception of the Danish landscape reflects that future suffering—"terre ingrate," "hiver impitoyable," "Tivoli, prisons, monarchie et agriculture, toutes ces horreurs" [barren land, pitiless winter, Tivoli, prisons, monarchy, and agriculture, all those horrors] (p. 906).

Arriving in Copenhagen in the early morning, Ferdinand and Lili register at the Hotel d'Angleterre. But Ferdinand begins to suspect that they are somehow out of place. Copenhagen seems unreal, a stage decor for a play whose conclusion will be discovery and imprisonment: ". . . c'est un théâtre où nous sommes entrés . . . où nous n'avons aucun rôle, où tout va disparaître, bientôt, s'abattre: décors, les rues, l'hôtel, et nous dessous" [we've entered a theatre . . . where we have no role, where everything is going to disappear, soon, come crashing down, and us beneath it] (p. 917). And as if to confirm his suspicions, Ferdinand notices that at one end of the square upon which their hotel is situated stands the Royal Theatre. At the other end of the same square is located the French Embassy, from which the demand for Ferdinand's detention and extradition will emanate, a request that will transform the apparent safety of Denmark into a nightmare of imprisonment and exile.

There is another area of Copenhagen that draws Ferdinand's attention, and it too is charged with symbolic meaning. Ferdinand and Lili go to a park along the sea where they can examine at their leisure the hidden contents of the sack in which they have been keeping Bébert—passports, marriage certificate, cyanide capsules, and a small Mauser pistol. While in the park, Ferdinand observes the ruins of the Citadelle, a fortress-like prison, and describes to Lili, in an obvious adumbration of his own incarceration, the "cachots en sous-sol . . . les barreaux, les chaînes" [the subterranean cells . . . the bars, the chains] (p. 920). Ferdinand also perceives in this same park several tropical birds obviously not native to Denmark—an egret, a lyre-bird, a toucan. He speculates that these birds must have escaped from a bombarded German zoo. Ferdinand is no less of an exotic bird in Denmark; he too is temporarily "en rupture de volière" [broken out of the aviary] (p. 923).

"Je vous ferai visiter Körsor" [I'll take you on a visit to Korsor] (p. 904), the narrator had informed his readers as Ferdinand's train approached Copenhagen. Körsor is the village on the Baltic Sea near which was located the property of Céline's Danish lawyer Thorwald Mikkelsen. Céline was to spend almost three years there under house arrest while awaiting extradition to France. But that sojourn was never to become the subject of the next novel that Céline had apparently intended to write. He died just two days after completing *Rigodon*. Perhaps conscious of his impending death, the narrator sounds a note of exhaustion as he approaches the end of the novel: "A vrai dire c'en était assez . . . 791 pages" [In truth, that's enough of that . . . 791 pages] (p. 923). Having completed his commitment to his publisher, the narrator begins to ruminate on his present situation. He tells his persecutors that had Hitler won, they would have been happy to hang as many Jews as possible. He would have us believe that it was merely a quirk of history that caused Hitler to lose the war and thus make him come out on the losing side. The anti-Semitic pamphleteer once again, and for the last time, dissolves his guilt by making himself a scapegoat, sacrificed in order to restore health to an otherwise diseased community of equally guilty compatriots.

Rigodon ends with two views of the future. The first is that the narrator is sure of joining with François Mauriac and André Malraux as the only living authors to enjoy the prestige of being published in Gallimard's Pléiade edition. But the second vision negates the first one. The narrator foresees France invaded by Asiatic hordes, who will easily dominate a white race that is inherently inferior. The only defense against these barbarians, the narrator tells us, is a natural one—the cellars of champagne bottles at Reims and Epernay, or, as a last resort, the supplies of brandy in Cognac. If these barbarians can be tempted by these immense supplies of alcohol, they will be rendered helpless. In such a world a Pléiade edition will be of little importance, the narrator suggests, for no one will be able or care to read it.

Conclusion

A FRENCH CRITIC HAVING MET CÉLINE shortly before the latter's
death subsequently described him as an "inspired *clochard,*" a "visionary
tramp."[1] The terms used by the critic no doubt refer in part to Céline's
appearance toward the end of his life—the haggard, unkempt look of a man
who was relatively poor and in ill health but, above all, did not care to
maintain the appearance of middle-class respectability, even though he was
still a practising physician. However, the epithets in question obviously
transcend mere physical description and reflect—at least in my understanding of them—upon the long night's journey undertaken by Céline
himself as well as by his fictional persona Ferdinand. As a means of concluding this study, I would like to use the critic's portrait of Céline as a
point of departure for some final remarks on the character of that journey.

The word *clochard* evokes for a certain romantic imagination
something more than a repugnant vagrant, usually drunk and surly, always
filthy, reduced to sleeping under bridges or on the ventilation grates of the
métro. It suggests a rejection of social definitions and material comforts for
the freedom of existence on the margins of society. We can recall in this
context Bardamu's taking his leave of the beautiful Molly, putting aside the
temptations of the soft life so as to be available for a further exploration of
existence—"the true mistress of real men" (p. 232). The inexhaustibility of
such a pursuit is inseparable from the continuing generation of texts that will
relate the nature of what the protagonist discovers in his quest, a quest that I
have analyzed in this study from the perspective of theme and landscape.
Considering the chronology of the protagonist rather than the order in which
Céline's works were published, the above-mentioned passage points not
only to the future incarnations of Ferdinand but to his antecedents as well—
the youth in *Mort à crédit* and the demobilized soldier adrift in London in the
two volumes of *Guignol's Band.*

As an adolescent in Paris inculcated with bourgeois rectitude but out of place in the society in which he is supposed to function, as a veteran of the mindless carnage of World War I seeking refuge in the London underworld, as a doctor to the poor in the Parisian *zone,* Ferdinand's experiences reveal, as we have seen, a remarkable consistency. He is usually portrayed as an exemplary victim of individual and collective exploitation, oppression, hatred, madness, greed, egotism, bigotry, delusion. He often seems to be the prisoner of a tragicomic conspiracy—cosmic and human—that thwarts his every attempt to find success and happiness. His apprenticeship of life, his "deflowering" as it were, while exposing him to the horrors of existence, produces a tenacious will to survive, an open mind for compromise, and a refusal to adopt the illusions that others are so willing to entertain. Bardamu's acquisition of a medical diploma, after he abandons Molly and America and returns to Paris, serves less as a means of sincerely assisting the ill—unlike the Bardamu of *L'Eglise*—or of attaining respectability and comfort, than a guarantee of sorts that Bardamu-Ferdinand will relentlessly continue to examine his diseased society but with even greater acuity. He will be primarily interested in portraying its maladies, with relatively little concern for healing the patient, other than apocalyptic pronouncements about the eventual overwhelming of the white population by more numerous and sturdier races.

Voyage au bout de la nuit is, among other things, a powerful antiwar novel, and, indeed, most of Céline's works will be marked by fear and hatred of the war—World War I and, later, World War II. Although Bardamu learns to loathe the war and will forever bear the scars from the wounds he acquired on the battlefields of Flanders, his personal destiny does not become indissociable from the war. In the case of the Nazi conquest of Europe during World War II, as it is reflected in the later works (*Féerie* and the trilogy), the fate of the protagonist will merge with the fortunes of Europe. These later works are shaped by essentially the same vision of the human condition that informed the earlier writings, but now Ferdinand, bearing Céline's condemnation as a Nazi supporter and traitor to his country, will confuse his personal Story with the History of Europe under German oppression. His attempts at self-exculpation will support that confusion, while at the same time he attempts to replace history with ritual so that he can proclaim that he has become yet another example of a prophet without honor in his own country, persecuted by the very society he supposedly had sought to save from the horrors of yet another war.

Despite Ferdinand's laudable hatred of war, there can be no doubt whatsoever for anyone who has read the pamphlets or the newspaper articles, or is familiar with the Intellectual Right of the period, that his protests of innocence as a misunderstood pacifist are as absurd as they are unconvincing. However much we may be fascinated by the two volumes of *Féerie* or the wartime trilogy, it should not be forgotten that the anti-Semitic pamphlets (which sold well and were widely publicized) propagated the same racist lies used by those who murdered six million Jews, and—who knows?—may have by the persuasive power of their rhetoric provoked the death or imprisonment of French Jews. The Ferdinand of the trilogy is perhaps more hobo than *clochard,* searching for handouts of food and protection, staying just long enough in one place to bear witness to scenes of madness, delusion, and death, before moving on, unscathed. Riding the rails across Germany to Denmark, he profits from the chaos all around him to make good his escape from authority.

One can argue, and the argument is by no means a new one, that the later novels are less interesting because they are so concerned with Céline's political difficulties, difficulties that are transmitted with comparatively little displacement through the author's persona Ferdinand. One might differentiate these novels from the earlier works, particularly *Voyage* and *Mort à crédit,* but *Guignol's Band* as well, in terms of the structure of apprenticeship they present. Bardamu-Ferdinand passes from a state of ignorance of self to knowledge of self—inseparable from knowledge of the world—by means of a series of trials that are as much a matter of interpreting the nature of reality as of confronting its problems and dangers. As we saw in these earlier works, the protagonist's initial naivete and optimism will be rather quickly shattered. The wisdom he acquires is, however, problematical in that there is no clearly defined attitude or ethos—short of self-preservation at any price—that he can adopt as the result of what he has learned.

The later fictions modify this structure of apprenticeship, according to the models (simplified here) proposed by Susan Suleiman, and thus tend to more closely resemble the *roman à thèse.*[2] The problematic apprenticeship of the earlier novels does not entirely disappear but is overshadowed by a dichotomous opposition which seeks to transmit to the reader the value system embodied by both the protagonist and the narrator, serving as advocates for the author. The use of a hostile narratee as a foil for the narrator is one of the principal strategies employed to convince the reader of the "truth." The "truth," or value system, in question concerns Ferdinand's presupposed and self-proclaimed innocence—his reading of the anti-Semitic pamphlets as an act of unalloyed pacifism grounded upon the rejection of war. Those who would interpret the pamphlets differently and condemn their author as a pro-Nazi sympathizer and traitor to his country must, accordingly, be in possession of a negative, false value system.

One might also claim, from a different perspective, that Ferdinand is correct in stating that his apprenticeship of life would indeed be incomplete without persecution and imprisonment and the threat of sudden death, in that his having Law 75 "up the rear" permits him to experience more directly the condemnation to suffering and death that is inherent to the human condition. Given Ferdinand's circumstances, inseparable from their historical context, the later works are marked more saliently by the presence of death—on a short-term installment plan, as it were. There is, of course, the physical destruction of World War II, not confined only to the battlefield, as was the case with Bardamu's experiences in Flanders during World War I, but pervasive in the form of bombarded cities, civilian casualties, trains stuffed with dead and dying bodies, disease, and hunger. There is as well another sort of death, also pervasive, in the form of dementia, murderous rage, panic, and despair, and in the manifest decay and crumbling of structures of all kinds. The "play" between Ferdinand's case and the war transforms history (and autobiography) into myth. That transformation is, of course, consonant with the role of the narrator as seer and appropriate to a fiction that incorporates historical material. However, what is lost, once again, in this metamorphosis is the real—historical—circumstances upon which the accusations against the narrator were made.

As we have seen, the landscapes perceived, occupied, traversed by Céline's protagonists reflect the nature of that long night's voyage. These spaces tend to embody a tension between reality and appearance; they are frequently illusory, like the railroad station at Oddort, in *Rigodon*. Initially presenting possibilities of success, or happiness, or shelter, they become negatively valorized in their association with death, or danger, or imprisonment. Places that are usually negatively valorized, such as hospitals and asylums frequently take on a positive value as shelters from the insanities of existence in the outside world. Ferdinand, like the *clochard,* is essentially a homeless creature, someone out of place.

Foreign lands with their inherent promises of new beginnings, of a liberation of the self, do not fulfill their expectations—hence the successful voyage is that of the imagination. Africa becomes a monstrous hothouse in which decay and disease are accelerated, and a hostile nature runs rampant. America offers a forbidding verticality built to an inhuman scale, cold, hard surfaces, and locked doors to those who cannot afford the price of entry. London, despite the romance of its docks, becomes a place of persecution. As for the Germany of the trilogy, it is a landscape haunted by death and despair, escape from which is dependent upon the capriciousness of fate. Copenhagen, that long sought-after refuge, is a stage set concealing prison and exile.

Familiar landscapes turn out to be no less deceptive and, finally, no less oppressive. For the young Ferdinand of *Mort à crédit,* anxious to escape the confines of a cramped apartment whose space is filled with the odors of mouldering lace and the tirades of a perpetually enraged father, the Paris that lies beyond the apartment and the *passage* is a deception. His Paris is not the city of light with its broad tree-lined avenues and picturesque side streets, a horizontal landscape of multiple possibilities, but rather an extension of the family apartment—an essentially vertical landscape, where torturous staircases lead to minor, exploitative positions or to the hives of artisans whose goods, like Clémence's lace, are an anachronism in a society eager for inexpensive machine-made products. When Ferdinand appears to have conquered that Parisian landscape, dominated it from his apartment in Montmartre, the landscape abruptly changes into a fantasmagoria of exploding bombs and melting buildings. The concierge's loggia and Jules's sub-basement studio replace the apartment, measuring Ferdinand's decline and his entrance into a netherworld of war and persecution.

The countryside too is invested with different values by the presence of the protagonist. The narrator in *D'un château l'autre* can recall, as a child, happy trips to the countryside (the Parisian suburbs) made to escape the insalubrious air of the city. In *Mort à crédit,* Ferdinand opposes the rustic simplicity of the area where his uncle Edouard's house is located to the oppression of Parisian life in general and that of the family apartment and the *passage* in particular. However, the Ferdinand who retreats to the farm with Courtial has a radically different experience of country life. A hostile nature and inimical neighbors threaten the group with starvation and death. In the case of Bardamu, the natural life of the countryside has been replaced by the terrors of war—the hum of insects has been drowned out by the whine of bullets, and every crease in the landscape becomes a potential place of ambush. The swamp that borders the Von Leiden estate in *Nord* shelters enraged bands of diseased prostitutes. The desolate windswept plains of East Prussia become a fitting location for a funeral such as that of the collaborator Bichelonne in *Château,* for they evoke memories of Napoleon's retreat from Moscow and, more recently, the disintegration of Hitler's Russian campaign.

The temporal voyage that embraces the diverse landscapes encountered by Céline's protagonists return us full circle to the suburbs of Paris. From the heights of Meudon Ferdinand can look down upon Paris, not as a conqueror but as a semi-recluse largely excluded from the life he surveys below him. His landscape has become that house with its surrounding garden, more a prison than a paradise but, at least, an oasis of tranquility so long as it can be protected by gates and fierce dogs. He is left in relative isolation to cultivate his garden—the interior one in which memory is transformed into narrative.

"Inspired" and "visionary" were the terms the critic used to describe Céline as *clochard.* They obviously allude to the creative artist, to the kind of imagination that transforms Ferdinand-Céline into what is termed in *Château* as the "lucid super-seer" (p. 66). Throughout this study I have attempted to show the narrator's insistence upon the specific autonomy of his art, a self-conscious autonomy, by calling the reader's attention to the frequent references to the narrator's head wound. As I have noted, Céline himself did not actually sustain a head injury in the war, nor was he consequently trepanned for it. The injury with its recurrent complications is borne by Ferdinand, though in some instances it is displaced, as was the case with the "putois" in *Féerie.* It becomes inextricably associated with the onset and fictional nature of the narrative, as we saw in Céline's repeated use of a certain pattern of opening signals, a pattern that first appears in *Mort à crédit.*

If the protagonist is indeed the faithful lover of the mistress called life, sworn to follow her wherever she may lead him, that pursuit is predicated upon the transformation of those experiences into narratives, works of art. Living all and telling all are two sides of the same coin. The distance between protagonist and protagonist-narrator, temporal and spatial, becomes the space of fiction. So long as protagonist-turned-narrator and protagonist only approach one another (in time and space) but do not coincide, there are further stories to be told.

It is perhaps paradoxical that whereas the process of experiencing life and its subsequent transformation into the language of fiction require the maintaining of lucidity, the onset of the fictionmaking process is dependent upon the aleatory resurgence of the head wound, its symptoms aggravated or reinforced by accidents or by recurrent bouts of malaria. One might add to these tensions, yet another—the meticulous craftmanship of Céline, whose writing deceptively give the appearance of spontaneity, of a first draft. Céline castigates as "pauvres crétins" [poor jerks] those who would believe that his books were written with some sort of careless abandon.[3]

Since the "seer" is by definition someone who possesses powers of insight that transcend mere accuracy of observation, this gift is signaled by the role played by the head injury. One of the principal manifestations of that injury is the resurgence of the past, creating a break in the narrator's spatio-temporal continuity which leads to the crucial transition from the meta-narrative (the narrator's present situation) to the narrative of past experiences. The means used to effect his transition make explicit that the past will be both recollected and recreated, since one of the symptoms of the narrator's reactivated injury will be hallucinations, distortions that sanction, as it were, the transposition, to a lesser or greater degree, of autobiographical material into fiction. Seers, one might note, are frequently considered to be crazy—as are artists—a trait that sets them apart from ordinary individuals and is supposed to afford them a heightened perception of reality. One might recall the testing of Ferdinand's perceptions in *Normance* against those of Lili, where he (his skull) is described as "cracked," both literally and metaphorically. One might contend that it is sufficient to have but one example of the kind of opening signals I have been describing to render an entire corpus "suspect," to alert the reader to the special nature of Céline's fiction.

What I mean by "special nature" here might be summed up by the notion of Céline's writings as heteroclite—their intermingling of the real and the hallucinatory, the serious and the comic, the sublime and the grotesque, the beautiful and the ugly, their confusion (literally and figuratively) of values and categories. What we have is a poetic delirium that pours forth from the opening in the narrator's skull occasioned by his mythical head wound and his no less mythical trepanation. As Céline indicated in his *Entretiens avec le professeur Y,* all the elements of the surface, the so-called objective reality of the naturalists, are swept up by his "métro émotif," jumbled together, recombined, and re-energized so as to yield new insights into the human condition that are meant to explode upon the reader's consciousness.

I have devoted this study to the elucidation of Céline's extraordinary vision of that human condition. In so doing, I have not sought to conceal my own ambivalent feelings toward the body of literature I have analyzed— my fascination with the creative imagination of its author, my repugnance for his refusal to acknowledge his anti-Semitic and pro-Nazi writings. As I indicated in my preface, let the reader (and perforce the critic) board Céline's métro at his own risk, and be prepared for a ride that will leave no one complacent.

Notes

Preface

[1]The most complete bibliography of works by and about Céline can be found in Stanford L. Luce and William K. Buckley, *A Half-Century of Céline: An Annotated Bibliography, 1932-1982* (New York and London: Garland Publishing, 1983).

[2]Philippe Lejeune, *Je est un autre: L'autobiographie, de la littérature aux médias* (Paris: Seuil, 1980), pp. 217-21.

Bibliographical Introduction

[1]*Céline: 1894-1932, Le Temps des espérances,* Vol. I of *Céline* (Paris: Mercure de France, 1977), p. 57, *Céline: 1932-1944, Délires et persécutions,* Vol. II of *Céline* (Paris: Mercure de France, 1985), pp. 156, 159.

[2]The document is reprinted in Gibault, *Céline: 1944-1961, Cavalier de l'apocalypse,* Vol. III of *Céline* (Paris: Mercure de France, 1981), pp. 100-33.

[3]The two poems, "Gnomographie" and "Le Grand Chêne," and *Des Vagues* have been published in *Cahiers Céline, 4: Lettres et premiers écrits d'Afrique,* ed. Jean-Pierre Dauphin (Paris: Gallimard, 1978), pp. 79-82, 187-98.

[4]Louis-Ferdinand Céline, *Progrès* (Paris: Mercure de France, 1978). His five ballets have been collected in *Ballets, sans musique, sans personne, sans rien* (Paris: Gallimard, 1959).

[5]Throughout his life Céline desired to keep his medical career separate from his activities as a writer. That desire was to be frustrated with his condemnation as a Nazi sympathizer. His *nom de plume* pays homage to his maternal grandmother Céline Guillou, whom he adored and who had helped raise him. She died in 1904.

[6]Similar reflections on Céline's trip to the Soviet Union can be found in *Bagatelles pour un massacre,* pp. 113-23.

[7]See the "chronologie" by Henri Godard in the revised Pléiade edition of Céline, *Romans,* I (Paris: Gallimard, 1981), p. lxxiii. During this period, anti-Semitic literature of all kinds was readily available in bookstores and at corner newsstands. In his review of *Bagatelles pour un massacre,* Emmanuel Mounier discusses some of Céline's sources. See *Esprit,* 66 (March 1938), 951-61; reprinted in *CH,* 3 (1963), pp. 341-42. The best study to date of the pamphlets is that of Jacqueline Morand, *Les Idées politiques de Louis-Ferdinand Céline* (Paris: Librairie Générale de Droit et de Jurisprudence, 1972).

[8]See Herbert Lottman's study of the Intellectual Right in *The Left Bank:*

Writers, Artists, and Politics from the Popular Front to the Cold War (Boston: Houghton Mifflin, 1982).

[9]In a letter dated October 15, 1940, Céline wrote: "Vichy, c'est de l'inexistant, de la fumée, de l'ombre. Ce qu'il y a de vrai, c'est que les Fritz ont perdu la guerre" [Vichy, it's a non-entity, smoke, shadow. What truth there is, is that the Jerries have lost the war]. Lucien Rebatet, "D'un Céline l'autre," *CH,* 3 (1963), p. 46.

[10]Helga Pedersen, *Le Danemark a-t-il sauvé Céline?,* trans. François Marchetti (Paris: Plon, 1975). Helga Pedersen was a magistrate at the time of Céline's arrest and later became Danish Minister of Justice.

[11]Céline's "Reply" can be found in *CH,* 5 (1965), pp. 319-23.

[12]Céline died on a Saturday, around 6 p. m. In order to avoid publicity, only a few close friends were immediately informed of his death. It was not until his burial the following Tuesday that the media learned of his decease. See François Gibault's account of the circumstances surrounding Céline's death in *Céline,* III, pp. 346-50.

Some Comments on Céline's Style

[1]Roland Barthes, *Le Degré zéro de la littérature* (Utrecht: Editions Gonthier, 1965), p. 9.

[2]Barthes, p. 53.

[3]Barthes, p. 74.

[4]"Interview avec Madeleine Chapsal," *Cahiers Céline, 2. Céline et l'actualité littéraire, 1957-1961,* ed. Jean-Pierre Dauphin, Henri Godard (Paris: Gallimard, 1970), p. 19.

[5]See "Interview avec Louis Albert Zbinden," *Cahiers Céline,* 2, pp. 68-69.

[6]"Interview avec Madeleine Chapsal," p. 39.

[7]Letter to Louis Combelle, February 12, 1943, *CH,* 5, pp. 65-66.

[8]Letter to Milton Hindus, May 15, 1947, *CH,* 5, pp. 73-75.

[9]"L'Argot est né de la haine. Il n'existe plus," *CH,* 5, p. 31.

[10]See Jean-Pierre Richard, "Prendre le métro," in *Microlectures* (Paris: Seuil, 1979), pp. 205-19.

[11]See Henri Godard, "Le Français de Céline," in *Poétique de Céline* (Paris: Gallimard, 1985), pp. 19-124.

1. Setting the Stage: *L'Eglise*

[1]*CH,* 5, p. 76.

[2]*CH,* 3, p. 102.

[3]Gilles Sandier, *La Quinzaine littéraire,* No. 58, 16-28 février 1973, p. 37.

[4]There are two references to Jews in Act II. Max, a friend of Vera's, has sailed for France on the *Youpinium* (p. 69). *Youpin,* 'kike,' 'yid,' will become Céline's preferred term for the Jews in his pamphlets. The name given to the ship connotes that transatlantic crossings are frequented by (obviously wealthy) Jews and disparages the company Max can expect to have. The second reference concerns Bardamu's preoccupation with understanding. That desire, he states, is derived form fear rather than intelligence. Drawing upon the cliché that Jews are more intelligent than other "races," Bardamu denigrates their intelligence while identifying with them: "Les plus intelligents parmi les hommes, ce sont les plus froussards. Voyez les Juifs! Ce n'est pas l'intelligence qui est noble, c'est la peur. Faire dans sa culotte, voyez-vous, c'est le commencement du génie" [The most intelligent people are those that are the most yellow. Look at the Jews. It's not intelligence that's noble, it's fear. To make in your pants, you see, is the beginning of genius] (p. 85).

[5]For an opposing point of view see Rabi, "Un ennemi de l'homme," *CH,* 3, pp. 263-64.

[6]See Eugen Weber, *Action Française: Royalism and Reaction in Twentieth-Century France* (Stanford University Press, 1962), pp. 115-23, and Norman Cohn, *Warrant for Genocide: The Myth of the Jewish World Conspiracy and the Protocols of the Elders of Zion* (New York: Harper and Row, 1969).

[7]Roger Lambelin, *Le Règne d'Israël chez les Anglo-Saxons* (Paris: Grasset, 1921), p. 241.

[8]Yudenzweck is apparently modeled upon Céline's superior at the League of Nations, a Polish Jew named Rajchman. In *Bagatelles pour un massacre* Céline describes how he read a copy of *L'Eglise* to Rajchman, who, understandably, never forgave him for it. That Céline should mention both the play and the incident in this manifestly anti-Semitic pamphlet, as if to call attention to his long-standing hostility towards the Jews, is a further indication of the play's anti-Semitism. In *Bagatelles* Rajchman is called Yubelblat, German: *Yubel* = rejoicing and *Blatt* = leaf, sheet, newspaper. To a French ear (or eye) the name would suggest *jubiler* 'to rejoice' and *blatte* 'a cockroach.' Despite everything, Céline expresses admiration for Jubelblat and avows that he "liked" the man (p. 102).

[9]Erika Ostrovsky, *Céline and His Vision* (New York: New York University Press, 1967), p. 196.

[10]Julia Kristeva comments on the subject of the American dancers in *L'Eglise:* "[They] best incarnate [the] absolute phallus of inalterable beauty: a purely natural feminine body, free from any other (man or language)." *Pouvoirs de l'horreur* (Paris: Seuil, 1980), p. 195.

[11]For a different interpretation of the play's title see Bettina Knapp, *Céline, Man of Hate* (University, Alabama: University of Alabama Press, 1974), p. 53.

2. The Journey Begins: *Voyage au bout de la nuit*

[1]Jean-Pierre Richard, "La Nausée de Céline," *Nouvelle Revue Française*, no. 115 (July 1962), p. 34.

[2]Julia Kristeva, *Pouvoirs de l'horreur* (Paris: Seuil, 1980), p. 176.

[3]Patrick McCarthy comments that Bardamu provides his tormentors with a Pascalian *divertissement*, so that they are distracted from thinking about the true nature of human existence. See *Céline: A Critical Biography* (London: Allen Lane, 1975), p. 63.

[4]See the treatment of this concept in Michael J. Donley, "L'Identification cosmique," *CH*, 5, p. 193.

[5]Allen Thiher, *Céline: The Novel as Delirium* (New Brunswick, N.J.: Rutgers University Press, 1972), p. 22.

[6]Céline preferred to think of himself as a Northerner: "Moi-même Flamand par mon père et bien breughélien, par instinct, j'aurais mal à ne pas délirer entièrement du côté du Nord" [Me, Flemish on my father's side and very Breughelian, by instinct, it would be hard for me not to wholeheartedly rave on behalf of the North]. Letter to Eveline Pollet, March 1933, *CH*, 3, p. 97. Lucien Rebatet attributes to Céline a remark published in the collaborationist newspaper *Je suis partout* in which Céline opposed the abolition of the frontier separating Occupied France from Vichy France. He based his argument on the grounds that the removal of the frontier would permit an "invasion" of Southerners (all Frenchmen, of course) into the North. Céline calls the Southerners "narbonnoïdes négrifiés" [Negrified Narbonnoids (Narbonne is a city in southwest France)]. "D'un Céline l'autre," *CH*, 3, p. 47. For Céline's racist geography see also Marc Hanrez, "Céline, prophète à long cours," *Les Lettres nouvelles* (Sept.-Oct. 1969), p. 170 and Jean-Pierre Richard, *op. cit., Nouvelle Revue française,* No. 116 (August 1962), p. 248.

[7]David Hayman, *Louis-Ferdinand Céline* (New York and London: Columbia University Press, 1965), p. 22.

[8]Marc Hanrez has commented extensively on this passage in his *Céline* (Paris: Gallimard, 1961), pp. 70-75.

[9]I am grateful to Professor David Hayman of the University of Wisconsin for calling my attention to the significance of the street as "wound" as well as to several of the links between the various "temples" that Bardamu visits.

[10]See the chapters "The Excremental Vision" and "Filthy Lucre" in *Life Against Death* (New York: Vintage Books, 1959), pp. 179-201, 234-304.

[11]See Michel Beaujour's treatment of the theme of softness as regards the human body in "Temps et substances dans *Voyage au bout de la nuit,*" *CH*, 5, pp. 173-88.

[12]*Ibid.*, p. 179.

[13]Marie-Christine Bellosta, "De la foire au pitre," *Céline: Actes du colloque international de Paris, 1976* (Paris: Société d'études céliniennes, 1978), p. 368.

3. A Legendary Childhood: *Mort à crédit*

[1]"Le Récit comme provignement: *Mort à crédit*," *Australian Journal of French Studies*, 13 (Jan.-Aug. 1976), 69.

[2]*Céline: The Novel as Delirium* (New Brunswick: Rutgers University Press, 1972), p. 53. Critical opinion remains divided as to the relationship between *Krogold* and *Mort à crédit*. See Erika Ostrovsky, "Céline et le thème du roi Krogold," *CH*, 5 (1965), pp. 201-06.

[3]Nicholas Hewitt refers to the *galerie des machines* as the "brutal prediction of [the] social and economic decline" that would befall the Parisian artisan in the first decade of the twentieth century. "*Mort à crédit* et la crise de la petite-bourgeoisie," *Australian Journal of French Studies*, 13 (Jan.-Aug. 1976), 112.

[4]*La Nuit de Céline* (Paris: Grasset, 1973), p. 97.

[5]See Marie-Christine Bellosta, *Le Carphanaüm célinien, ou la place des objets dans "Mort à crédit"* (Paris: Minard, 1976), p. 28.

[6]Bellosta notes that in *Mort à crédit* the impoverishment of character and situation finds its correlative in the removal of objects. *Carphanaüm célinien*, p. 21.

[7]Nicholas Hewitt believes that the point of departure for these hallucinatory scenes in the Tuilerie Gardens was the attack of the Fascist Leagues against the Chamber of Deputies on February 6, 1936. See "*Mort à crédit* et la crise de la petite-bourgeoisie," p. 116.

[8]The model for Courtial was Raoul Marquis, who wrote under the pseudonym of Henri de Graffigny. As a young man Céline worked briefly for Graffigny, who directed a review similar to the *Génitron* called, appropriately, *l'Eureka*.

[9]According to Erika Ostrovsky, Irène "exemplifies sudden decay, a change from beauty to ogrelike hideousness, from health to illness, from life to its corruption." *Céline and His Vision* (New York: New York University Press, 1967), p. 149.

[10]As Michel Beaujour has noted, once the delirium that had become his "reason for living" can no longer sustain him, Courtial must commit suicide. "La Quête du délire," *CH*, 3 (1963), p. 283.

4. Down and Out in London: *Guignol's Band I*

[1]Stephen Philip Day has studied the diversity of emotions expressed in the prefaces. See "Ponts et creux dans les premiers chapitres de *Guignol's Band*," *Céline: Actes du colloque international de Oxford, 1981* (Paris: Société d'études céliniennes, 1981), pp. 243-51.

[2]Bettina Knapp calls Ferdinand a "kinetic hero." She notes, however, that "paradoxically, though he moves about with frenetic speed, his very mobility gives him a static quality. He is not actually budging an inch; his philosophical concepts remain

stationary. He does not become; he is." *Céline: Man of Hate* (University, Alabama: University of Alabama Press, 1974), p. 134.

[3]Jill Forbes remarks that Ferdinand "oscillates" between the working-class neighborhoods and docks of East London and the bourgeois areas that lie to the west of London, with Soho in between as the geographical center of *Guignol's Band.* "Symbolique de l'espace: le 'Londres' célinien," *Céline: Actes du colloque international de Paris, 1976.* (Paris: Société d'études céliniennes, 1978), p. 35. Nicolas Hewitt also examines the topography of *Guignol's Band* in "Londres, la capitale du vingtième siècle: Esquisse d'un topographie de *Guignol's Band,*" *Céline: Actes du colloque international de Paris, 1979* (Paris: Société d'études céliniennes, 1979), pp. 31-44.

[4]Titus is identified as Jewish, since he is described as being given to muttering to himself in Yiddish. Colin Nettlebeck interprets van Claben's death as a specifically anti-Semitic act whose consequences for Ferdinand will reflect Céline's rejection of the anti-Semitic pamphlets. See "the Antisemite and the Artist: Céline's Pamphlets and *Guignol's Band,*" *Australian Journal of French Studies,* 9 (1972), 180-89.

Guignol's Band II

[1]Alan Thiher refers to the "love" between Virginia and Ferdinand as a parody of the relationship between the *chevalier* and his beloved. *Céline: The Novel as Delirium* (New Brunswick: Rutgers University Press, 1972), p. 95.

[2]The novel will also serve as the point of departure for Céline's ballet *Voyou Paul. Brave Virginie,* published in 1959.

[3]Cf. David O'Connell's analysis of the rape scene—"one of the most comical descriptions of sexual intercourse to be found in modern literature." *Louis-Ferdinand Céline* (Boston: Twayne Publishers, 1976), p. 125.

[4]Cf. the statement by Merlin Thomas that the two volumes of *Guignol's Band* are characterized by "humour" and "tenderness." *Louis-Ferdinand Céline* (London and Boston: Faber and Faber, 1979), p. 191.

5. Scapegoats and Traitors

Féerie pour une autre fois, I

[1]See Christine Sautermeister, "Pitreries et dérobades dans *Féerie pour une autre fois,*" in *Lectures (2) de Féerie pour une autre fois,* ed. Jean-Pierre Dauphin and Henri Godard (Paris: Minard, 1979), p. 103.

[2]See Albert Chesneau's brief study of myth and history in Céline's fiction in "Esquisse d'une conception de l'Histoire chez Céline," *Australian Journal of French*

Studies, 13 (Jan.-Aug., 1976), 126-33.

[3]See the chapter "Delirium As System," in *To Double Business Bound: Essays on Literature, Mimesis, and Anthropology* (Baltimore: Johns Hopkins University Press, 1978), pp. 84-120.

[4]The term "narratee" was devised and defined by Gerald Prince. See "Introduction à l'étude du narrataire," *Poétique,* 14 (1973), 178-96. See also Seymour Chatman's comments on the function of the narratee in *Story and Discourse* (Ithaca and London: Cornell University Press, 1978), pp. 253-55.

[5](Paris: Gallimard, "Idées," 1954), pp. 47-48.

[6]In 1948, Céline, replying to Sartre's accusation that he was paid by the Germans to support their cause, published a violent diatribe against Sartre entitled *A l'agité du bocal,* which, literally translated, means "To the excited one in his jar." The jar is probably associated with Sartre's play *Les Mouches* (*The Flies*), Sartre himself becoming in Céline's imagination the angry fly buzzing within. The text of *l'Agité* was included in Albert Paraz's *Le Gala des Vaches* (Paris: Les Editions de l'Elan, 1948), pp. 282-86. Paraz was a friend and admirer of Céline, and his book, a kind of journal, contains several letters from Céline. *A l'agité du bocal* was also published as a pamphlet by P. Lanauve de Tartas (Paris, 1948).

[7]The rhetoric of anti-Semitism dies hard. Ferdinand remarks "ils me voyaient au bûcher en France, pas seulement les Palestins, les Français du sol" [They saw me burned at the stake in France, not only the Palestinians, but born Frenchmen] (p. 119). the use of "Palestins" for Jews indicates the irradicable foreignness of the French Jew as compared with the genuine Frenchman (non-Jewish of course). Céline should have been aware that such distinctions, legalized by the Nazis in Germany and in the occupied countries, facilitated the deporting of millions of Jews to the death camps.

[8]Jules was no doubt modeled upon the painter Gen Paul, a friend of Céline's, who had lost a leg in World War I. He had a studio in Montmartre not far from where Céline lived.

[9]*The Double,* translated and edited with an introduction by Henry Tucker, Jr. (Chapel Hill: University of North Carolina Press, 1971), p. 76. Jean Guénot remarks that Jules is "another face of the Célinian personality. He is to Ferdinand what Robinson is to Bardamu: the product of a deforming mirror." *Louis-Ferdinand Céline damné par l'écriture* (Paris: Diffusion M. P., 1973), p. 31.

[10]See Chevalier, Jean and Gheerbrandt, Alain, *Dictionnaire des symboles* (Paris: Laffont, 1969), p. 527.

[11]See the chapter "La Dialectique de l'énergétisme imaginaire" in Gaston Bachelard, *La Terre et les rêveries de la volonté* (Paris: Corti, 1948), pp. 17-35.

[12]Cf. Patrick McCarthy's examination of the role of Jules, *Céline: A Critical Biography* (London: Allen Lane, 1975), pp. 252-53.

[13]*Ibid.,* p. 254.

Féerie pour une autre fois, II

[1]Portions of *Normance,* notably scenes of the bombardment of Paris, were written before *Féerie I.* Céline began working on *Normance* as early as 1947, while he was still under arrest in Denmark. The volume was originally entitled *La Bataille du Styx.* Gallimard has published *Maudits Soupirs pour une autre fois,* edited by Henri Godard (Paris, 1985), which combines several manuscripts that Céline had drafted for a third volume of *Féerie.*

[2]Allen Thiher comments: "This circular movement completes the absurd narration in a manner perhaps designed to suggest mythical time, for the novel turns in upon itself, undermining its own reality." *Céline: The Novel as Delirium* (New Brunswick: Rutgers University Press, 1972), p. 155.

[3]*Ibid.,* p. 156.

[4]In a letter to Milton Hindus, dated June 1974, Céline wrote: "Il s'agit du bombardement de Montmartre en 1945 par la R.A.F. avec incidents divers—le tout dans le fantastique" [It's about the bombardment of Montmartre in 1945 by the R.A.F. with diverse incidents—all in the realm of fantasy] *CH,* 5, p. 79.

[5]Paul Ricoeur, *Interpretation Theory* (Fort Worth: Texas Christian University Press, 1976), p. 37.

[6]*Out of My System: Psychoanalysis, Ideology, and Critical Method* (New York: Oxford University Press, 1975), p. 11.

[7]See Philip S. Day, *Le Miroir allégorique de L.-F. Céline* (Paris: Klincksieck, 1974), p. 231.

[8]Cf. René Girard's concept of "mimetic desire" in *To Double Business Bound: Essays on Literature, Mimesis, and Anthropology* (Baltimore: Johns Hopkins University Press, 1978), pp. 84-120.

[9]"*Féerie pour une autre fois* I et II: un spectacle et son prologue," in *Lectures (1) de Féerie pour une autre fois,* ed. Jean-Pierre Dauphin (Paris: Minard, 1978), pp. 52-58.

6. Flight to Safety, the Wartime Trilogy

D'un château l'autre

[1]Maréchal Philippe Pétain (1856-1951), hero of the Battle of Verdun in World War I, served as "Chief of the French State" in the Vichy government. Condemned to death as a collaborator at the end of the war, his sentence was commuted to life imprisonment. The real head of the Vichy government was Pierre Laval (1883-1945), who, unlike Pétain, pursued a policy of active collaboration with the Germans. He was executed by firing squad for his crimes.

[2]*The Inner Dream: Céline as Novelist* (Ithaca: Syracuse University Press, 1978), p. 172.

[3]See Céline, *Romans II*, pp. 936-37.

[4]*Céline: Man of Hate* (University, Alabama: University of Alabama Press, 1974), p. 192.

[5]*Ibid.*, p. 193.

[6]See Albert Chesneau, *Essai de psychocritique de Louis-Ferdinand Céline* (Paris: Minard, 1971), p. 82.

Nord

[1]*Céline: A Critical Biography* (London: Allen Lane, 1975), p. 303.

[2]See Henri Godard's note on the actor Le Vigan in Céline, *Romans II*, p. 1081.

Rigodon

[1]See Alain Hardy's study of the word *rigodon* in Céline's works, "Rigodon," *CH*, 5 (1965), pp. 268-77.

[2]*Céline: the Novel as Delirium* (New Brunswick: Rutgers University Press, 1972), p. 182.

[3]Cf. Patrick McCarthy's interpretation of this passage in *Céline: A Critical Biography* (London: Allen Lane, 1975), p. 310.

[4]See the article by Yves de Le Quérière, "L'Ecriture et le contre-courant: *Rigodon* de Céline," *Australian Journal of French Studies,* 13 (Jan.-Aug. 1976), 27-28.

Conclusion

[1]Marcel Audinet, "Dernières rencontres avec Céline," *Les Nouvelles Littéraires* (July 6, 1961), p. 4. Quoted by Erika Ostrovsky, *Céline and His Vision* (New York: New York University Press, 1967), p. 188.

[2]See *Authoritarian Fictions: The Ideological Novel as Literary Genre* (New York: Columbia University Press, 1983), pp. 63-100.

[3]Robert Poulet, *Mon ami Bardamu: Entretiens familiers avec L.-F. Céline* (Paris: Plon, 1971), p. 25.

Bibliography

Principal works by Céline:

Voyage au bout de la nuit. Paris: Denoël and Steele, 1932.

L'Eglise, comédie en 5 actes. Paris: Denoël and Steele, 1933.

Mort à crédit. Paris: Denoël and Steele, 1936.

Mea Culpa suivi de *La Vie et l'œuvre de Semmelweis.* Paris: Denoël and Steele, 1936.

Bagatelles pour un massacre. Paris: Denoël, 1937. Rpt. 1943.

L'Ecole des cadavres. Paris: Denoël, 1938.

Les Beaux draps. Paris: Denoël, 1941. Rpt. Paris: Nouvelles Editions françaises, 1941.

Guignol's Band. Paris: Denoël, 1944.

Casse-pipe. Les Cahiers de la Pléiade, 5 (1948), 45-87. With *Les Carnets du cuirassier Destouches.* Paris: Gallimard, 1970.

Féerie pour une autre fois, I. Paris: Gallimard, 1952.

Féerie pour une autre fois, II: Normance. Paris: Gallimard, 1954.

Entretiens avec le Professeur Y. Paris: Gallimard, 1955.

D'un château l'autre. Paris: Gallimard, 1957.

Ballets sans musique, sans personne, sans rien. Paris: Gallimard, 1959.

Nord. Paris: Gallimard, 1960. Definitive edition, 1964.

Guignol's Band II: Le Pont de Londres. Paris: Gallimard, 1964.

Rigodon. Paris: Gallimard, 1969.

Maudits Soupirs pour une autre fois. Paris: Gallimard, 1985.

Miscellaneous Writings, Correspondence, Interviews, Songs:

Among the important sources for these materials are the following:

The two numbers of the *Cahiers de l'Herne,* No. 3 (1963), No. 5 (1965). Reprinted and augmented as *L'Herne: L.-F. Céline.* Ed. Dominique de Roux, Michel Beaujour, Michel Thélia. Paris: Minard, 1972.

The various numbers of the *Cahiers Céline.* Ed. Jean-Pierre Dauphin and Henri Godard. Paris: Gallimard, 1976 to present.

Céline, L.-F. *Chansons.* Ed. Frédéric Monnier. Paris: La Flûte de Pan, 1981.

Mahé, Henri. *La Brinquebale avec Céline.* Paris: Ed. de la Table Ronde, 1969.

Monnier, Pierre. *Ferdinand furieux.* Lausanne: Ed. l'Age d'Homme, 1979.

Paraz, Albert. *Le Gala des vaches.* Paris: Ed. de l'Elan, 1948.

Poulet, Robert. *Mon ami Bardamu: Entretiens familiers avec L.-F. Céline.* Paris: Plon, 1971.

Current English Translations of Major Works:

Journey to the End of the Night. Trans. Ralph Manheim. New York: New Directions, 1983.

Death on the Installment Plan. Trans. Ralph Manheim. New York: New Directions, 1966.

Mea Culpa and *The Life and Work of Semmelweis.* Trans. R. A. Parker. New York: H. Fertig, 1979.

Guignol's Band. Trans. Bernard Frechtman and Jack T. Nile. New York: New Directions, 1969.

Conversations with Professor Y. Bilingual Edition. Trans. Stanford Luce. Hanover: University Press of New England, 1986.

Castle to Castle. Trans. Ralph Manheim. New York: Delacorte, 1968. Rpt. London: Blond, 1969; New York: Penguin, 1976.

North. Trans. Ralph Manheim. New York: Delacorte, 1972. Rpt. with introduction by Kurt Vonnegut, Penguin, 1976.

Rigadoon. Trans. Ralph Manheim. New York: Delacorte, 1974. Rpt. with introduction by Kurt Vonnegut, Penguin, 1975.

Selected Bibliography:

Bachelard, Gaston. *La Terre et les rêveries de la volonté.* Paris: Corti, 1948.

Barthes, Roland. *Le Degré zéro de la littérature.* Utrecht: Gonthier, 1965.

Beaujour, Michel. "La Quête du délire." *CH,* 3, pp. 213-18.

———. "Temps et substances dans *Voyage au bout de la nuit.*" *CH,* 5, pp. 173-82.

Bellosta, Marie-Christine. *Le Carphanaüm célinien, ou la place des objets dans Mort à crédit.* Paris: Minard, 1976.

———. "*Féerie pour une autre fois* I et II: un spectacle et son prologue." *Lectures (1) de féerie pour une autre fois.* Ed. Jean-Pierre Dauphin. Paris: Minard, 1978, pp. 31-62.

———. "De la foire au pitre." *Céline: Actes du colloque international de Paris, 1976.* Paris: Société d'études céliniennes, 1978, pp. 353-70.

Brown, Norman. *Life Against Death.* New York: Vintage Books, 1959.

Chatman, Seymour. *Story and Discourse.* Ithaca: Cornell University Press, 1978.

Chesneau, Albert, *Essai de psychocritique de Louis-Ferdinand Céline*. Paris: Minard, 1971.

———. "Esquisse d'une conception de l'Histoire chez Céline." *Australian Journal of French Studies,* 13 (Jan.-Aug. 1976), 126-33.

Chevalier, Jean, and Alain Gheerbrandt. *Dictionnaire des symboles.* Paris: Laffont, 1969.

Cohn, Norman. *Warrant for Genocide: The Myth of the Jewish World Conspiracy and the Protocols of the Elders of Zion.* New York: Harper and Row, 1969.

Crews, Frederick. *Out of my System: Psychoanalysis, Ideology and Critical Method.* New York: Oxford University Press, 1975.

Day, Stephen Philip. "Ponts et creux dans les premiers chapitres de *Guignol's Band.*" *Céline: Actes du colloque international de Oxford, 1981.* Paris: Société d'études céliniennes, 1981, pp. 243-51.

———. *Le Miroir allégorique de L.-F. Céline.* Paris: Klincksieck, 1974.

Donley, Michael. "L'identification cosmique." *CH,* 5, pp. 189-200.

Forbes, Jill. "Symbolique de l'espace: le 'Londres' célinien.' *Céline: Actes du colloque international de Paris, 1976.* Paris: Société d'études céliniennes, 1978, pp. 27-40.

Förster, Eva. *Romanstruktur und Weltanschauung im Werk L.-F. Célines.* Heidelberg: Julius Groos Verlag, 1978.

Fortier, Paul A. *Le Métro émotif de L.-F. Céline: Voyage au bout de la nuit, étude du fonctionnement des structures thématiques.* Paris: Minard, 1981.

Gibault, François. *Céline: 1894-1932, Le Temps des espérances.* Vol. I of *Céline.* Paris: Mercure de France, 1977.

———. *Céline: 1944-1961, Cavalier de l'apocalypse.* Vol. III of *Céline.* Paris: Mercure de France, 1981.

———. *Céline: 1932-1944, Délires et persécutions.* Vol. II of Céline. Paris: Mercure de France, 1985.

Girard, René. *To Double Business Bound: Essays on Literature, Mimesis, and Anthropology.* Baltimore: Johns Hopkins University Press, 1978.

Godard, Henri. *Poétique de Céline.* Paris: Gallimard, 1985.

Guénot, Jean. *Louis-Ferdinand Céline damné par l'écriture.* Paris: Diffusion M. P., 1973.

Hanrez, Marc. *Céline.* Paris: Gallimard, 1961.

———. "Céline, prophète à long cours." *Les Nouvelles littéraires* (Sept.-Oct. 1969), pp. 165-72.

Hardy, Alain. "Rigodon." *CH,* 5, pp. 268-77.

Hayman, David. *Louis-Ferdinand Céline.* New York: Columbia University Press, 1965.

Hewitt, Nicolas. "*Mort à crédit* et la petite bourgeoisie." *Australian Journal of French Studies,* 13 (Jan.-Aug. 1976), 110-17.

Hindus, Milton. *The Crippled Giant: A Bizarre Adventure in Contemporary Letters.* New York: Boar's Head Books, 1950.

Kaminski, H. E. *Céline en chemise brune, ou le mal du présent.* Paris: Editions du champs libre, 1983.

Knapp, Bettina. *Céline, Man of Hate.* University, Alabama: University of Alabama Press, 1974.

Krance, Charles. "Le Récit comme provignement: *Mort à crédit.*" *Australian Journal of French Studies,* 13 (Jan.-Aug. 1976), pp. 64-79.

Kristeva, Julia. *Pouvoirs de l'horreur.* Paris: Seuil, 1980.

Lambelin, Roger. *Le Regne d'Israël chez les Anglo-Saxons.* Paris: Grasset, 1921.

La Quérière, Yves de. *Céline et les mots.* Lexington: University Presses of Kentucky, 1973.

———. "L'Ecriture et le contre-courant: *Rigodon* de Céline." *Australian Journal of French Studies,* 13 (Jan.-Aug. 1976), 25-35.

Lejeune, Philippe. *Je est un autre: L'autobiographie, et la littérature aux medias.* Paris: Seuil, 1980.

Lottman, Herbert. *The Left Bank: Writers, Artists, and Politics from the Popular Front to the Cold War.* Boston: Houghton Mifflin, 1982.

Luce, Stanford L., and William K. Buckley. *A Half-Century of Céline: An Annotated Bibliography 1932-1982.* New York: Garland Publishing, 1983.

Matthews, J. H. *The Inner Dream: Céline as Novelist.* Ithaca: Syracuse University Press, 1974.

McCarthy, Patrick. *Céline: A Critical Biography.* London: Allen Lane, 1975.

Montant, Annie. "La Poésie de la grammaire chez Céline." *Poétique.* No. 50 (April 1982), pp. 226-35.

Morand, Jacqueline. *Les Idées Politiques de Louis-Ferdinand Céline.* Paris: Librairie Générale de Droit et de Jurisprudence, 1972.

Mounier, Emmanuel. "Bagatelles pour un massacre." *CH,* 3, pp. 341-42.

Muray Philippe. *Céline.* Paris: Seuil, 1981.

Nettlebeck, Colin. "The Antisemite and the Artist: Céline's Pamphlets and *Guignol's Band.*" *Australian Journal of French Studies,* 9 (May-Aug. 1972), 180-89.

O'Connell, David. *Louis-Ferdinand Céline.* Boston: Twayne, 1976.

Ostrovsky, Erika. "Céline et le thème du roi Krogold." *CH,* 5, pp. 201-06.

———. *Céline and His Vision.* New York: New York University Press, 1967.

Pedersen, Helga. *Le Danemark a-t-il sauvé Céline?* Trans. François Marchetti. Paris: Plon, 1975.

Poulet, Robert. *Mon ami Bardamu: Entretiens familiers avec L.-F. Céline.* Paris: Plon, 1971.

Prince, Gerald. "Introduction à l'étude du narrataire. *Poétique,* 14 (1973), pp. 178-96.

Rabi. "Un ennemi de l'homme." *CH,* 3, pp. 262-67.

Rank, Otto. *The Double*. Trans. and ed. Henry Tucker, Jr. Chapel Hill: University of North Carolina Press, 1971.

Rebatet, Lucien. "D'un Céline l'autre." *CH*, 3, pp. 42-55.

Richard. Jean-Pierre. "La Nausée de Céline." *Nouvelle Revue française*. No. 115 (July 1962), pp. 33-37.

———. *Microlectures*. Paris: Seuil, 1979.

Ricocur, Paul. *Interpretation Theory*. Fort Worth: Texas Christian University Press, 1976.

Sandier, Gilles. *"L'Eglise."* *La Quinzaine littéraire*. No. 58, 16-28 février 1973, p. 37.

Sartre, Jean-Paul. *Réflexions sur la question juive*. Paris: Gallimard, 1954.

Sautermeister, Christine. "Pitreries et dérobades dans *Féerie pour une autre fois.*" *Lectures (2) de Féerie pour une autre fois*. Ed. Jean-Pierre Dauphin and Henri Godard. Paris: Minard, 1979, pp. 93-105.

Smith, Andre. *La Nuit de Céline*. Paris: Grasset, 1973.

Solomon, Philip H. "Céline's *Death on the Installment Plan:* The Intoxications of Delirium." *Yale French Studies*. No. 50 (1974), pp. 191-203.

———. "The View from a Rump: America as Journey and Landscape of Desire in Céline's *Voyage au bout de la nuit." Locus: Space, Landscape, and Decor in Modern French Fiction*. Ed. Philip Solomon. *Yale French Studies*. No. 57 (1979), pp. 5-22.

———. "Louis-Ferdinand Céline's *Normance:* The Weight of Guilt." *Fearful Symmetry: Doubles and Doubling in Literature and Film*. Ed. Eugene J. Crook. Tallahassee: University Presses of Florida, 1981, pp. 113-24.

Suleiman, Susan. *Authoritarian Fictions: The Ideological Novel as Literary Genre*. New York: Columbia University Press, 1983.

Thiher, Allen. *The Novel as Delirium*. New Brunswick: Rutgers University Press, 1972.

Thomas, Merlin. *Louis-Ferdinand Céline*. London: Faber and Faber, 1979.

Weber, Eugen. *Action Française: Royalism and Reaction in Twentieth-Century France*. Stanford: Stanford University Press, 1962.